Praise from the left, right, and center for *The Opposite of Hate*

"Sally Kohn has really done it this time. Brilliant."
—Sarah Silverman, comedian and host of *I Love You, America*

"A stunning debut by a truly gifted writer—an eye-opening read for both liberals and conservatives—and it could not come at a better time."
—Adam Grant, bestselling author of *Originals*

"Brilliantly illustrates the immense and disarming power of changing course and driving not toward division, but toward civility and mutual respect."
—*Ms.*

"A testament to the power of understanding others deeply."
—DeRay Mckesson, social activist and host of *Pod Save the People*

"An uplifting and inspiring plea to promote peace, kindness, and humanitarianism in the face of hate."
—*Kirkus Reviews*

"Sally and I agree on very little politically, but somehow in spite of that, we have navigated a friendship that transcends everything else."
—Sean Hannity, host of *Hannity* and bestselling author of *Let Freedom Ring*

"I came away from this book feeling a sense of curious happiness. [Kohn] has a talent for writing in a way that speaks directly to you and challenges your instinct to remain objectively distant when the topic turns to ideas you already know you disagree with."
—*The Federalist*

“[Kohn] never preaches but rather approaches each story with humility. This book offers unique, smart, and poignant guidance for the emotionally mired times we’re living in.” —Goop.com

“Kohn is funny and warm as she shares the best ways to shift the hate and dissolve the barriers between those of us with divergent views.” —*Esquire*

“An important book for the times.” —Sir Patrick Stewart

“Sally Kohn’s book is uplifting, funny, and full of inspiring solutions.” —Van Jones, host of *The Van Jones Show* and bestselling author of *Beyond the Messy Truth*

THE OPPOSITE OF HATE

THE Opposite OF Hate

A Field Guide to Repairing Our Humanity

Sally Kohn

ALGONQUIN BOOKS
OF CHAPEL HILL
2019

Published by
ALGONQUIN BOOKS OF CHAPEL HILL
Post Office Box 2225
Chapel Hill, North Carolina 27515-2225

a division of
WORKMAN PUBLISHING
225 Varick Street
New York, New York 10014

First paperback edition, Algonquin Books of Chapel Hill, March 2019.
Originally published in hardcover by Algonquin Books of Chapel Hill in April 2018.
Printed in the United States of America.
Published simultaneously in Canada by Thomas Allen & Son Limited.
Design by Steve Godwin.

Some names have been changed to protect the privacy of individuals.

Library of Congress Cataloging-in-Publication Data
Names: Kohn, Sally, author.
Title: The opposite of hate : a field guide to repairing our humanity / Sally Kohn.
Description: First edition. | Chapel Hill, North Carolina : Algonquin Books of Chapel Hill, 2018. | Includes bibliographical references.
Identifiers: LCCN 2017051398 (print) | LCCN 2017061463 (ebook) | ISBN 9781616208356 (ebook) | ISBN 9781616207281 (hardcover : alk. paper)
Subjects: LCSH: Hate—Psychological aspects. | Hate—Prevention.
Classification: LCC BF575.H3 (ebook) | LCC BF575.H3 K64 2018 (print) | DDC 152.4—dc23
LC record available at https://lccn.loc.gov/2017051398

ISBN 978-1-61620-939-1 (PB)

10 9 8 7 6 5 4 3 2 1
First Paperback Edition

To Sarah and Willa,
my reasons for everything

FOREWORD

The Opposite of Hate was a welcome contribution to political dialogue when it was first published in the spring of 2018. Now, with the divisive times we are living in, it's downright vital. As the United States and the world have seemingly devolved into even deeper levels of hate and otherizing and inequality and injustice, Sally Kohn's book offers us something increasingly rare and precious: a road map to discourse, understanding, and civility.

If you want evidence of just how bad things are today compared to how bad they've been before, and how much worse things could get in the future, you will find plenty in this book to support those positions. But then you'll be motivated to roll up your sleeves and do something about it. You'll find concrete steps to help you make a difference and inspiring stories to show you it's possible. This book isn't for people who want to self-righteously point fingers at the other side while patting themselves on the back for their latest social media post. This book is for people who want to do the hard work of clarifying their moral values and confronting hate, not just in others but in themselves. If you're sick of the vitriol and the inhumanity but, more than that, you're sick of feeling helpless and want to do something to turn the tide, you will find much that is incredibly useful in the following pages.

The Opposite of Hate is refreshing because Sally emphasizes the *process* of change, not the destination; the constant process of awakening and the very human condition of trying to be a better version of ourselves. Of opening our eyes to see the world and ourselves in new ways. Of learning to recognize hate and injustice and inequality, and recognize our role within them. Of recognizing ourselves as part of the problem so that we can become part of the solution. This is what's extraordinary about not only Sally's book but also her mission—to not give up on anyone, whether it's the people acting in the most hateful ways imaginable, or our loved ones who we think voted for the wrong candidate, or even ourselves. To confront hate not with more hate, but with grace and understanding. To invite change and to engage with one another in ways that can constructively lead to change for all of us on all sides. To go high when everyone around you is going low.

I'm not going to sugarcoat what follows. This is not an easy book. While it's beautifully written and surprisingly funny for a book about hate, it's a hard book because the topic is hard. Because change is hard. It would be easier to write a book about how awful and hateful and monstrous *they* are—those people on the right or those people on the left, or their political leaders, or you name it. But it wouldn't lead to change. Change takes work. Change takes struggle. Change takes complicated, big-picture thinking and patient understanding. And most important, change takes all of us. If you're wondering how to make a difference amid the enormity of hate, and want to stop shouting at your television or fighting with trolls on social media, this is your place to start. Hate is not inevitable. Change is possible. Let this book be your talisman and your tool.

Sunny Hostin is the Senior Legal Correspondent and Analyst for ABC News as well as a co-host on ABC's morning talk show *The View.*

CONTENTS

THE OPPOSITE OF HATE

INTRODUCTION

What Is Hate: The Bully

No one is born hating another person because of the color of his skin, or his background, or his religion. People must learn to hate. —NELSON MANDELA

I GUESS WHAT I did to Vicky Rarsch isn't really that bad. But still, it haunts me. People seem to think I'm a nice person. In fact, a lot of people "know me" as a nice person in my public life, for being able to get along with even the people I vehemently disagree with. As a liberal commentator on Fox News for two years and now on CNN, I developed a reputation as a fierce progressive who is able to talk respectfully with conservatives, including extreme ones. I even gave a TED talk about how people with the most diametrically opposed views can practice what I call "emotional correctness"—holding ourselves accountable for talking to each other with respect and finding empathy for one another, no matter how strongly we disagree.

Emotional correctness is about communicating compassion and mutual respect, not only with our words but with our intent and tone. I'm still an ardent fan, but I've been finding it increasingly difficult to practice, catching myself slipping into anger and swimming in hate. Especially in the last few years.

I was sort of trained to hate. Before I became a television commentator, I worked for fifteen years as a community organizer, fighting for policy reform on issues like lesbian, gay, bisexual, and transgender (LGBT) rights, health care, criminal justice, and immigration. Right-wingers were my enemies, and I hated them.

The father of community organizing, Saul Alinsky, called his political enemies "devils" and defined the goal of organizing as attacking one's enemies—not just institutionally but personally, because personal attacks hurt more. Good organizers must "rub raw the sores of discontent," Alinsky said. That's what I was taught it meant to be a good organizer, and I considered myself a good organizer. And the truth is, I still have friends, on the left as well as the right, who think that hate is one of the most useful tools in their civic-engagement tool belt. But when I became a commentator, I realized that I could have more influence if people would actually listen to me, which, practically speaking, they weren't going to do if they thought I hated them. Also, it turns out I prefer being liked, and if you want to be likable, it helps to like others.

But Donald Trump's election to the presidency of the United States of America made my blood boil. I couldn't believe the level of hate he so readily and proudly spewed—against Muslims and women and immigrants and African Americans.

I remember feeling dumbfounded when George W. Bush was reelected in 2004; there was a map that my friends and I all shared over email that showed the United States carved up into blue parts and red parts, with the red parts labeled "Dumbfuckistan." I may not have consciously categorized Bush voters as less than human, but I certainly thought they were less than American and certainly less than *me*—less smart, less understanding, and, ironically enough, less compassionate. I didn't think any of that was particularly hateful. I just thought I was correct.

But this was worse. I truly couldn't fathom that anywhere near a majority of my fellow Americans had voted for Donald Trump, and as much as I tried to pretend to be magnanimous and uniting, I hated them for it. Suddenly, all the partisan nastiness I'd tried to suppress or even solve as a talking head came rushing back to me with even more vengeance. Instead of being a prominent critic of incivility, I felt like I was auditioning to be the poster child for partisan hate. And though I knew this wasn't the first hateful moment in US history, or even the worst, it felt like the crisis that was bubbling up in me was also bubbling up throughout the United States and around the globe, in politics and pop culture, in sporting matches and mass shootings.

As I would catch myself in these little moments of hateful hypocrisy—whether I was just noticing them more or they were getting worse—the more I thought about Vicky (not her real name). I kept asking myself: If I could backslide into such anger so readily, was I really just a hateful person? Was all this stuff about niceness and emotional correctness an attempt to mask my true nature? Was it inevitable that the spreading crisis of hate would engulf not only me but all of us?

I should probably tell you what I did to Vicky. I'm ten years old, and in the middle of the school day I'm in the hallway outside the fifth-grade classrooms all by myself. The classroom doors are all closed, students burbling behind them. The bell is about to ring, and soon the hall will thunder with kids. But right now it's just me, standing in the quiet corridor with its ugly army-green-tiled walls and those floors that screech when you drag your sneakers just so, waiting with a pen in one hand and a clipboard in the other.

I don't remember how I managed to get out of class; maybe I asked to go to the bathroom. I must have seen Vicky go and followed her. Because I had a plan.

Using the Apple IIe my mom had at home, I had hunted and pecked out a "survey" about shampoo preferences. At the top, it asked, "What kind of shampoo do you use?" and then offered a list of possible responses, with a space next to each for a tick-mark tally. I had printed it out and carefully folded and torn off the edges of the dot matrix paper so that it would look as official as possible when I approached Vicky.

Everyone called her Sticky Vicky. Looking back, I know her life must have been difficult. She clearly didn't bathe very often. Maybe she had no one loving or capable enough at home to make sure she took care of herself. I didn't think about that then. I just knew that Sticky Vicky smelled. Which was only one of the ways that Sticky Vicky was different. She also gave herself nosebleeds all the time, and sometimes when teachers called on her, she would make a honking noise like a goose and crawl under her desk. She didn't have any friends except for the kids who one of the teachers assigned to be friends with her out of pity. All of this now makes me feel terribly heartbroken for Vicky—for whatever her life was like then, for whatever she was going through at home or in her mind.

But still, there I am, in the hallway with my pen and my clipboard, holding my pen like a precise and official-looking person. Like I was conducting some kind of study for science class. Sticky Vicky comes out of the bathroom, and I ask her what shampoo she uses.

White Rain. She says White Rain shampoo. I can't remember the name of any of my fifth-grade teachers, a single book I read that year or any year in elementary school, what I liked to eat back then, what movies I watched, or what street my best friend lived on. But I remember that Vicky Rarsch told me she used White Rain shampoo like she just said it ten seconds ago.

As I get Vicky's answer, the bell rings and the hallway fills up with students. I run down the hall shouting: "Sticky Vicky uses

White Rain shampoo! Sticky Vicky uses White Rain shampoo! Don't use White Rain shampoo or you'll smell like Sticky Vicky!" All the kids laugh, and some point at her. That's where my memory, thankfully, ends.

I had buried this memory and hadn't thought of Vicky for decades. But when I started getting this reputation for being nice, I kept finding the scene flitting back into my mind, as though my conscience were taunting me. I realized I needed to find Vicky. I needed to find out what had happened to her, to find out how her life had turned out. And I wanted to make amends. I'd moved to a different school the year after I pulled my stunt on her, but I still had a few friends from those days. I called them to ask what they knew about her, and they told me that Vicky had changed schools the same year I did. Nobody knew where she went. I tried searching for her through Google, but nothing at all came up.

After months of looking without any luck, I hired a private investigator. Even as I called him, I wondered if I wasn't maybe getting just a little oddly carried away with my determination to find Vicky. Then I realized I didn't just want to find out what happened to her; I also wanted find out what happened to me. Was I really a nice person after all? Because what kind of nice person would do something like that?

I wanted to understand not only my own hate but the hate that seemed to be engulfing the planet. So I set out to do just that.

The bad news is: we all hate. All of us. That includes me—and I'm afraid it also includes you. I promise that although this is a book about hate, it will end on an uplifting and positive note. But we first have to face the hard truth. In different ways and to different degrees, consciously or unconsciously, all of us, in one way or another, sometimes treat other individuals and entire groups of human beings as though they are fundamentally less deserving than we are.

We're only a few pages in, and you might already be bristling at this point. How dare I suggest that you hate? And I am, for the record, doing just that. But let's be clear that I am deliberately using a broad definition of "hate," one that's consistent with the definition used by many of the experts in the field. So while I don't mean the sort of tedious hate as in "I hate broccoli" or "I hate the music of Kenny G" or even "I hate my math teacher," I would include pretty much everything else—from partisan incivility to overt sexism to implicit racial bias to any other tendency to discriminate against, dehumanize, or demean someone because of some aspect of who they are or the group to which they belong.

Building on the theories of Harvard University psychologist Gordon Allport, who pioneered human personality research and wrote the influential book *The Nature of Prejudice*, the Anti-Defamation League argues that different kinds and severities of hate build on one another. The organization classifies five overall categories in its "pyramid of hate." At the base of the pyramid are things like stereotyping, the use of exclusionary language, and the belief in the inherent superiority of some groups and the inferiority of others. The next level includes individual acts of prejudice, like bullying, name-calling, and unspoken but harmful acts of social avoidance—like the way I and other kids in fifth grade moved to the other side of the hallway when Sticky Vicky walked by. Then there are institutional forms of discrimination, whether in employment or housing policy or the political system—the kind of hate baked into our institutions and our norms, and actually encouraged by them and taught to generation after generation. One step further is bias-motivated violence, such as terrorism or hate crimes, and at the top comes genocide.

I wanted to explore the whole pyramid—from online trolling against Jews and Muslims to hyperpartisan nastiness between

Democrats and Republicans; from rudeness in the public sphere to racially biased legislation; from slaughtering people because of their ethnicity to bullying. And if you're wondering what on earth my bullying of Vicky has to do with hate, it wasn't an accident that I was a rich kid picking on a poor kid—or that Vicky, it turns out, would eventually end up being gay. Poor kids and LGBT kids are statistically more likely to be bullied. There was plenty else going on in my little ten-year-old mind, and I'm not suggesting hate was the only reason I picked on Vicky or even that I was consciously hateful, but still, the same groups of people we discriminate against in our society as a whole are also the groups most likely to be picked on in school. That's not just a coincidence. That's hate.

In fact, it's not only inaccurate but dangerous to reserve the term "hate" only for conscious and extreme forms of cruelty. What I've learned is that different forms and degrees of hate all stem from the same societal and psychological phenomena, which divide communities against each other and dehumanize groups of "others," creating a climate in which further hate becomes more likely and even, potentially, deadly. "We are all potential dehumanizers, just as we are all potential objects of dehumanization," writes philosopher David Livingstone Smith. I wanted to understand not only how these different kinds and degrees of hate are related but how we can stop small hates from growing out of control.

THE UNITED STATES was founded on hate—the hatred that justified colonial annihilation of American Indians and that perpetuated the enslavement of Africans. Hate divided the country during the Civil War and, a century later, spawned protest movements and backlash movements, with activists vying over issues of justice and human rights. And Americans are not alone in this legacy. Obviously, our globe's history of colonial conquest and brutality, and the many current hot spots of extreme violence and displacement, reflect deep currents of hate. It would be naive to argue we're in the most hateful moment in history. But relativity on this topic is cold comfort. The hate that's brewing now is harmful, frightening, and increasingly acute. It doesn't have to be the worst moment in history for it to be bad enough to warrant a concerted effort at reckoning—and change.

In the twenty-five years the Pew Research Center has surveyed Republicans and Democrats about how they view the other party, the majority of respondents in both parties answered "very unfavorable" for the first time in 2016. "More than half of Democrats (55%) say the Republican Party makes them 'afraid,' while 49% of Republicans say the same about the Democratic Party," the poll found. And just under half of the members of both parties say that the other party makes them feel "angry."

We talk about politics and political engagement in aggressive, apocalyptic terms. Republicans are launching a "War on Women." Democrats are launching a "War on Christmas." Immigrants are "invading." During the 2016 election, Donald Trump and his supporters repeatedly chanted, "Lock her up!" regarding Hillary Clinton. And at one rally I attended, a Trump supporter shouted, "Hang her in the streets!"

Our problem with hate is not only a matter of speech or sentiment. Since the 2016 election, the United States has seen a rise in attacks on Muslims and immigrants and Jewish communities. Hate crimes in the US increased by 20 percent in 2016, fueled in part by the contentious election. In the first three months of 2017 alone, anti-Semitic incidents rose by 86 percent. In January 2017, swastikas were drawn on three synagogues in the town of Clearwater, Florida. In June 2017, a teenage Muslim girl wearing a hijab and an abaya was murdered with a baseball bat, then dumped in a pond. Later, a memorial to the girl was burned. In February 2017, four black teenagers were charged with hate crimes after they kidnapped a white teenager with a mental disability and broadcast a livestream on Facebook Live as they beat the man and yelled, "Fuck white people!" White supremacists, rebranded as the "alt-right," have become more visible and emboldened—not to mention empowered—including high-level alt-righters given posts in the Trump White House.

Hate is also coming from the other side of the political spectrum. As I was writing this book in June 2017, an avowed liberal who had volunteered for Bernie Sanders's presidential campaign opened fire on Republican members of Congress practicing for an annual bipartisan baseball game. He allegedly wanted to kill conservatives. When a wildfire destroyed one thousand homes in Gatlinburg, Tennessee, in November 2016, killing fourteen people and injuring two hundred others, one Trump opponent tweeted, "Laughing at all the Trump supporters in Gatlinburg as their homes burn to the ground tonight. Too bad it's not the whole state burning," and another tweeted, "Maybe it's 'god' punishing them for voting for Trump."

We've gotten to the point where hate is such an acceptable norm that we not only believe it's inevitable but we try to overtly market its benefits—and exploit hate for profit. There's now a dating app called Hater, which will match you with a potential love interest based on the things or people you mutually hate. Really. If you hate the saxophone stylings of Kenny G, we might be a match! Meanwhile, much of the media relies on making animosity not only palatable but virtually addictive. More and more of us get our news primarily, if not exclusively, from television channels and websites that cater to our hate and present information in ways that reinforce our biases. This not only exploits hate but exacerbates it.

Across all media, ratings aren't going up because viewers are getting more informed but because they're getting more inflamed. I know I get more clicks and claps every time I roll my eyes on air, whether I mean to or not, and whether you think that's the meanest thing in the world or not. I'm not going to argue about which side or group does it worse. We all hate. And we all do it too much. So what do we do now?

Is hate an inevitable part of human nature, so deeply rooted that none of us can ever really be immune? How can people be so mean to complete strangers? What kind of person calls someone they don't even know a "cunt" or a "nasty ass lesbo" on Twitter? Do they really mean it? And can people who've lived lives of deep hatred, like white-supremacist skinheads and terrorists, change?

And even if we can combat hate one hater at a time, incrementally in each of our own lives, can we ever overcome hate in our society as a whole? How does hate become systematized and institutionalized so that our governmental policies and communities and culture not only provide cover for hate but, worse, promulgate it? And what's the solution?

Sure, we can blame Donald Trump for bringing open hatred once again into the top ranks of visible political power, but hate has been coursing through the veins of our society since English colonizers set foot on North America's shores, and it has been aided and abetted by elected leaders and judges and bankers and textbooks and TV shows. I want to understand how hate infects our entire society. And I want to know how we can fight back.

A YEAR AGO, when my daughter, Willa, was seven years old, she told me about a joke she'd played on a kid at school. Willa and three of her little friends had agreed that the next day they would all wear pants to school. She told me they'd formed a club, the Pants Club, in which they were the members and all the other kids weren't. But then, behind one girl's back, Willa convinced the other two to pull a prank on her. Willa and those two girls actually showed up the next day in dresses, deliberately making the third girl feel left out.

Now, this wasn't the meanest prank in the world, just like there are kids who commit worse transgressions than mouthy shampoo surveys. But the similarities socked me in the gut. Willa had plotted to mock and marginalize another child. Was I setting a bad example without even realizing it—my supposedly reined-in hatred somehow seeping out?

Then I started to see it all around me. During the summer before the 2016 election, my street in the leafy, liberal neighborhood of Park Slope in Brooklyn, New York, held its annual block party. As always, there was a piñata. And this year, the guy who always organizes the block party got a piñata of Donald Trump's head. I was furious. I'd been spending months trying to teach my daughter not to hate Trump in spite of all the vitriol she was picking up in slips of the tongue at home, and at school and in the media. And now here was my neighbor literally stringing up Trump's head so little kids could whack at it. I conveyed my strong disappointment to the block party organizer in the form of a few choice curse words (yes, the irony!). Thankfully, other neighbors expressed their irritation, too. But no one wanted to forgo the ritual, and so up the head went.

I told my daughter she wouldn't be able to participate.

"But, Mom, it's just a piñata," Willa protested. "It's not his real head!"

"Yeah, but it's still not okay," I said.

Willa was listening, and I could see I was making her think, but I could also see a tantrum brewing. Duh, of course there was.

There was candy in that piñata! And my daughter loves any opportunity to hit anything with a stick. She pleaded. And wanting deeply to avoid a complete meltdown, I selfishly relented.

"Okay," I groaned. "But can you imagine that you're not actually hitting Trump and instead pretend you're hitting the views he stands for?"

Willa agreed, and I let her take her turn as other little kids stood around gleefully cheering. Then we all got a nice candy reward.

Too often, we begrudgingly accept hate, or even cheer it on. Too often, we don't see the hate around us. Too often, we don't see it in ourselves. Too often, people in our communities and around the world are beaten down by hate that we consciously or unconsciously spread. But it's hate we should be beating. The prize for doing so is a sweeter future for all of us.

ONE

Why We Hate: The Trolls

I would permit no man . . . to narrow and degrade my soul by making me hate him.
—Booker T. Washington

THE HATE THAT I most often personally encounter, on a daily basis, comes from the mean people on the internet known as trolls. So when I decided to explore the conditions and contortions that fuel hate, my trolls were a natural first place for me to start. I've always wondered how the hell complete strangers can berate and belittle me on a daily basis and, honestly, what the hell is wrong with these people. Also, the more hate mail and hate tweets I got, the more I started to worry that it was normal—that it's just human nature to be mean and to even enjoy it, especially if you can do it hiding behind an anonymous online avatar, and I was the weirdo for thinking everyone should be nice. Admittedly, it was a fair amount of perverse curiosity that got me calling my trolls on the phone in the first place. But by the time I hung up, I'd learned more about myself. It had never dawned on me that my trolls thought *I* was the mean one. It had also never dawned on me that *they* might be nice.

In my early days at Fox News, I experienced emotional whiplash. On the one hand, I was surprised, even shocked, to find that people I'd thought of as the very definition of hate, people like conservative talk show host Sean Hannity, in real life didn't have horns and fangs but were actually pretty nice—certainly way nicer than I'd expected. On the other hand, for the first time in my life I started getting hate mail—which shocked me in a whole other way. Admittedly, I had walked into Fox News with pretty low regard for conservatives in general, but even so, my trolls shocked me. I was amazed by the constant torrent of hostility directed at me by viewers, both over email and on Twitter. I tried to reassure myself that most people, indeed even most Fox News viewers, didn't send hate mail. But still, a staggering number of people did. And they were so incredibly mean, sometimes even threatening violence. I felt devastated and depressed.

I don't mean to suggest I took it personally; I know this stuff comes with the territory of being a public voice, and I was grateful to be getting well-known enough to be attacked. Plus I didn't actually think I was a "moronic libtard" or a "stupid bitch." But it was the fact that people were sending it that disturbed me. Who even does that? And what kind of sick society produces people who do that? I'm not a big drinker, but there were a few months there that I was drinking way more than usual, and definitely way more than I should have been.

During this time, I had a meeting with one of the network executives. He asked how I was doing and wanted to know how everyone was treating me. He was particularly curious to know if I was getting any pushback or attacks from the left for being on Fox. I told him no, not a one. In fact, as a side note, I was never attacked from the left for being on Fox News, at least not that I heard about.

But I was getting a lot of hate mail from the right, I told him. A lot. I confessed that it was shaking my faith in humanity.

"Oh, you're not reading that crap, are you?" he blurted out. "Don't! Those people are crazy lowlifes, and I oughta know, because they're our viewers." He smiled broadly at me, like calling his own audience "lowlifes" was a point of pride. I shouldn't be worried for humanity, he said, because the people who were sending me hate mail were barely human.

He suggested I skim for any messages containing genuine threats—like the time someone tweeted, "@sallykohn looks like a good place for a bullet to me." I was supposed to send those ones to network security so they could investigate and notify local authorities if necessary. (I still have to do this with disturbing regularity even now that I work at CNN.) The rest he said to stick in a folder and forget about. But I couldn't forget. And it didn't help to think of my trolls as crazy or less than human. I didn't want to give them too much power, but it also felt wrong to just stereotype them as fringe lunatics or deny their basic humanity.

I've toughened up a whole lot since then, but honestly, my trolls still get in my head. It's not only that their messages can be so horrifically hostile—like "@sallykohn stupid u should have been aborted u fuckin commie!!!!!!!!!!!!!!" and "Next to the radical Islamic extremist who murdered 49 human lives on Saturday, you are truly one of the most hate-filled individuals I know of in this country." How can someone who objects to me supposedly being so hate-filled write those words without, apparently, seeing the irony of how hate-filled that message is? Also: *Really? I'm as bad as ISIS?!?!* (Other trolls have tweeted that one at me, too—even before the hateful alt-right smear that "CNN is ISIS.")

The fact is, I can post the most benign, apolitical thing in the universe and I still get trolled. During the 2016 elections, I posted a picture of my dog in the park, and pro-Trump trolls filled my Instagram feed with #MAGA (as in "Make America Great Again"). Trolling my dog? To be fair, one person did post, "#MAGA but your dog is cute." And, yes, my golden mountain doodle, Sadie Pig, is about as adorable as she sounds. But that's not my point.

I don't want to brag, but someone from Twitter once told me that I have some of the worst trolls on the platform. Okay, I am bragging, and I know that's a weird thing to brag about, but in my less horrified moments I can see it as some indication that people who don't agree with me are at least paying attention, which I guess is constructive. Still, I've had people ask me to never retweet them again, because my trolls are just too intense. Trolling really is hateful, and it often hurts. Sometimes a lot.

Trolling also very clearly hurts our society. Trolling was once only a creepy fringe phenomenon affecting the corners of the interwebs, but in 2016 the United States elected a Twitter troll as president. Suddenly, we all had a trolling problem. Then, more and more people were feeling empowered to spew hate, and the subjects of that hate were firing back with their own. As if overnight, trolling not only entered the lexicon of mainstream society but our bloodstream, too, infecting every aspect of our lives, online and off, and threatening the entire prospect of a civil and democratic society.

In reaching out to see if I could convince some of my trolls to talk to me, I focused on Twitter, because, frankly, that's where most of them are. Twitter seems to be the most alluring modern platform for hateful expression. Sure, there's a fair amount of hate spilled on Facebook and Instagram, and there are entire sites like 4chan and parts of Reddit basically devoted to hate, but most of my daily interaction with trolls is on Twitter. And they're not all bots, not even most of them, from what I can tell. They're actually real human beings. So I wanted to know what possesses human beings to spew such vile attacks. And does online trolling spill over into real-life hate? Do trolls believe the things they write? Do they think about the consequences? Or do they selfishly just want attention? Who are these people hiding behind their hashtags? And perhaps most importantly, given that the internet was supposed to be a neutral platform to bring humanity closer together, does the fact that it's now infested with trolls reveal something profound not only about technology but about our essential human nature?

My plan was to contact my nastiest trolls. In the back of my head, I was optimistic that I'd have some transformative effect on them—like what happened when the author Lindy West wrote a blog post about how hurt she was by a troll who had impersonated her recently deceased father on Twitter in order to harass her. After reading her post, the troll emailed West in a confessional breakdown, admitting that he had been jealous of her self-esteem and thus was trying to destroy it. He vowed he would never troll again, and the two ended up talking on the phone for a heart-wrenching episode of the radio show *This American Life*.

Yes, I thought, as I heard her account. *That's how change will happen, when we all start confronting hate with compassion rather than more hate.*

But my encounters with my trolls didn't go quite like that. I did end up with one offer for a date, I think, but mostly what I got from my conversations with my trolls was a deeper understanding of why perfectly sane people can be so bizarrely venomous.

I HAVE SO many trolls that I had to find a way to narrow the field. So I had an analysis done of my top trolls on Twitter, courtesy of the very helpful and tech-savvy folks at a company called Spredfast. They looked at my Twitter data for the fifty weeks prior to August 16, 2016. During that period, I had 158,000 replies on Twitter from 46,694 users. Many were from fans, but a distinct subset were from trolls, including a number of "supertrolls," some of whom tweeted at me, on average, more than once a day. I followed all of them and either tweeted at them or sent them messages asking them to follow me back so we could communicate. In all, I tried to contact more than a dozen trolls, including all of my worst offenders, and I heard back from about half.

Some of them didn't want to talk. "My apologies to you/whoever handles your Twitter ma'am since I have tweeted some dick things in your direction," @bmenyhert messaged me. Where is this magical intern who supposedly reads my social media feeds for me and takes all the hurt? Oh, wait: I don't have one! Anyway, in the spirit of hiding behind their avatars, most of the trolls who said they didn't actually want to speak to me were nonetheless delighted to message back and forth. "People have forgotten how to sit down and look people in the eye," @bmenyhert wrote to me. "Myself included sometimes." This is the same person who once tweeted me, "Not sure thinking is your strong suit, Sally. Stick to munching the rug."

But thankfully, some of my trolls were willing to talk with me on the phone, and those exchanges were far more revealing. Imagine my surprise when they were not only civil to me but rather nice. I ended up realizing how much I had been thinking of them as either robots or monsters—anything but humans. Of course, one could fall down a rabbit hole pondering which version was their authentic self, whether they were being fake nice on the phone or fake mean on Twitter, or whether it's perfectly possible that both manifestations are authentic, because, as Walt Whitman wrote, we "contain multitudes." There's also the possibility that my trolls were nice to me because I was paying them attention, or because they were simply uncomfortable being so cruel when talking to me directly. But my conversations with them, and research that helps explain trolling, led me to conclude that deeper forces were shaping these contradictions—and that these are contradictions we all contain.

Let's start with @LindaLikesBacon, one of my more colorful trolls. She has tweeted, "Sally Kohn is a mental midget" and told me to "GO JUMP OFF A BRIDGE." She also tweeted, "Your dog is cute. But you are freaking hideous." (Clearly, my dog is very popular with the trolls.) It turns out that @LindaLikesBacon is the avatar of a fifty-four-year-old retired white woman named Linda, who lives in a town in Mississippi called Picayune. When I hear @Linda LikesBacon's voice on the phone, she immediately reminds me of a babysitter I had in elementary school, whose name was Gloria, I think. She drove a Mercury Sable and smelled like cigarette smoke and Velamints and had a gravelly voice like @LindaLikesBacon's, which, in both of them, reflected a gravelly outlook on life.

I don't ask @LindaLikesBacon right away why she told me to commit suicide. Instead, whether it's because I'm a chicken or because I want to find a way to get to know her as a full person, not just a troll, I ask her about her hobbies.

@LindaLikesBacon is into car shows and what are called "cruise nights." Which basically makes her the troll version of my dad. If you aren't lucky enough to know what cruise nights are, they're when car fanatics park their cars in a local parking lot—in my dad's case, it was usually outside the Burger King—and then walk around (in some cases with a whining preteen daughter in tow) looking at each other's cars with the hoods open so everyone can see the engines.

"What do you like about them?" I ask @LindaLikesBacon, trying to politely hide the fact that I'd rather give myself an enema with a blowtorch than go to a cruise night ever again.

"Just the camaraderie, the people," @LindaLikesBacon replies. So hate-spewing Linda, who tweeted that I'm a "carpet munching liar" and a "douche nozzle" is into camaraderie? Go figure. @LindaLikesBacon then tells me she even does "car rallies"—a.k.a. cruise nights that travel. "It's really fun," she continues, "when you have seventy-five or a hundred cars caravanning somewhere and you got people standing out in their yard waving at you."

This all catches me off guard. @LindaLikesBacon isn't the pimply basement-dwelling teenager with anger issues that I expect all trolls to be. And the more we chat, the more I have to admit she's quite likable. Which doesn't mean she doesn't also have anger issues.

I ask @LindaLikesBacon about her username. "Why bacon?"

"I guess I use that name to be offensive," she tells me.

"Uh, to people who don't like bacon?" I ask, genuinely missing the point.

"Well, Muslims who don't like bacon, yes," says @LindaLikes Bacon.

"Uh, oh. Got it," I say, trying to sound supremely nonchalant. "What about Jews who don't like bacon?" I ask this in part to be tongue-in-cheek but also because I'm curious (and Jewish and, like plenty of my Muslim friends, enjoy pork).

"They're okay," she responds. "I'm fine with Jews. I just don't like the people that want to cut my head off."

"Uh, you think all Muslims want to cut your head off?" I ask slowly.

"Well, you know, pretty much all I need to learn about Muslims I learned on 9/11."

When I press her on whether she really believes all Muslims are violent extremists, she says, yes, she really does think they are. When I ask her if she doesn't think that's being hateful to a whole large community of people, she says she doesn't think she's being hateful, just honest. And even if what she thinks of them is a little mean, it's justified, she says, by the far greater hate that they are directing at her. "I don't think that there is a moderate Muslim," she adds. For the record, @LindaLikesBacon's generalizations about the world's 1.8 billion Muslims are not only hateful but completely and totally incorrect.

Linda is offering a textbook example of what are called "attribution errors." I became a psychology major in college in large part because I was so intrigued by these quirks of the human mind. The fundamental attribution error is our tendency to believe that when someone else does something hurtful, that person is hurtful—but when we do something hurtful ourselves, it's because our action was justified by some situation or context. So, for instance, when someone else writes something hateful online, we think they're a fundamentally hateful person, that what they wrote reflects their essence. But when *we* write something hateful, it's because we were provoked—*by them!*—or maybe we just got caught up in the online vortex. It was just *the situation* making us mean, not that we actually *are mean*. So Linda thinks that Muslims are all inherently hateful, but *she's* not—she's just reacting reasonably to the hateful acts she hears about Muslims committing.

One troll I contacted wrote an explanation of why he didn't want to talk to me that could serve as a dictionary definition of "fundamental attribution error." "I call you a race-baiting hatemonger, and I cite the reasons I see you that way," one of my top trolls, @JeffMcIrish, messaged me. "To me, that is blunt and plain spoken, but truthful and, therefore, not uncivil. You post outright lies about decent people who see the world differently than you do. To me, THAT is as uncivil as it is possible to be." Then he added about himself, for good measure, "I am nice to nice people." In other words, *my* meanness is who I am. *His* meanness is situational—it's caused by *me*.

The concept of attribution errors first emerged out of a study in 1967 on political attitudes. This was not long after the Cuban missile crisis, and there was even more anti-Castro sentiment in the United States than there is today. Edward Jones and Victor Harris at Duke University had subjects read one of two essays, both called "Castro's Cuba." One version was pro-Castro; the other, anti-Castro. The subjects were told that the essayist had either *chosen* the point of view of the essay or *been assigned* that point of view. Then they were asked how much they thought the view in the essay honestly reflected the view of the writer. It made sense that when the subjects were told the writer could choose a view, the subjects believed that the essay reflected the view of the writer. But the surprise was that even when the subjects were told the essay's point of view was imposed on the writer, the subjects still thought that the writer of the pro-Castro essay was truly more pro-Castro than the writer assigned to the anti-Castro essay. The subjects knew the situational factors but nevertheless attributed the essay to the writer's essence as a person.

The effect has been confirmed in many studies since. For example, in 1977, Lee Ross and some colleagues conducted a study in which Stanford University students were randomly assigned to participate in a fake quiz show, either as questioners, contestants, or audience members. The questioners were asked to come up with ten questions based on their own knowledge, and the contestants had to try to answer those questions. Everyone, including the audience, knew this was the setup—in other words, they knew that by design the people who came up with the questions knew the answers far better than those supposed to answer them. And yet afterward, the students participating as audience members said they thought the questioners were inherently smarter than the contestants. They discounted the very obvious, staged context. Even more surprisingly, the contestants *themselves* rated the questioners as more generally knowledgeable. The mental gymnastics involved in this twist of perception are mind-boggling. And it was Lee Ross who, when he wrote up this experiment, coined the phrase "fundamental attribution error."

Then two years later, in 1979, psychologist Thomas Pettigrew took things one step further, introducing what he called the "ultimate attribution error." If we assume that the negative behaviors of other individuals are attributable to their inherent, internal disposition, Pettigrew reasoned, the same effect would be magnified in our prejudices against other groups. We all are members of in-groups and out-groups. Our family is an in-group and so is our neighborhood, while the family in the neighborhood on the other side of town is an out-group. But membership in these groups is relative. If you're primed to think about your entire town versus another town—say, during a sporting match—suddenly that other neighborhood in your town becomes part of your in-group.

And yet some demarcations between in-groups and out-groups have become cemented in our society's collective psyche. For instance, in the United States today, race and gender and immigration status and economic class and sexuality form categories of identity we're accustomed to defining ourselves in relation to, and thinking of the people in "our group" as somewhat distinct from "others." On top of this, like a giant living being, society has its own historical and collective perceptions about which of these groups usually fall in the in-group and which fall out. This is where the very meaningful, albeit complicated and sometimes even annoying, concept of "privilege" comes in—the idea that certain identities and thus certain groups are inherently favored and advantaged in the broader norms and systems of our society. That's how you end up with a dynamic where, in spite of the fact that women make up more than half the US population and more than half of US voters, more than 80 percent of those elected to Congress are men. We all ingest and imitate society's in-group and out-group biases.

So what Pettigrew's ultimate attribution error holds is that these collective in-group/out-group biases shape the way we perceive the actions of others. Take, for instance, attitudes about policing. According to a 2016 poll, 84 percent of black folks believe that black people are treated less fairly than white people in dealings with police. But just 50 percent of white folks say the same thing—which implies that the other half thinks that the way police treat black people is fair or deserved.

Now consider the fact that in a 2015 poll, 20 percent of black folks reported that they were "treated unfairly in dealings with police in [the] past 30 days" and attributed that mistreatment to their racial or ethnic background. But just 3 percent of white folks reported the same experience. There are decades of hard data to suggest that black people in the United States are systematically and unfairly overpoliced, including being pulled over and arrested more often than white people, despite the fact that black people in general commit a smaller share of crimes. But it's simply harder for white people to imagine the police unfairly stopping anyone, because it's not part of their life experience *and*, on top of that, due to the ultimate attribution error, white folks are more likely to assume that black folks are getting stopped more *because of their behavior or essential character*, not because of some situational or systemic context.

To study this bias, psychologists Rebecca Hetey and Jennifer Eberhardt presented a group of white New Yorkers with data about the racial composition of New York City jails, which is 60.3 percent black and 11.8 percent white—in large part due to racialized overpolicing. But half the subjects received false data, representing the city's prison population as "less-black" than it actually is—as 40.3 percent black and 31.8 percent white, which is closer to the demographics of the US prison population as a whole. Then all the subjects were asked about the city's "stop-and-frisk" policy—in which police detain, question, and search people on the street, often with tenuous links to any actual alleged wrongdoing. The practice has long been deployed primarily against the city's black and brown residents, not because they were necessarily doing anything wrong but simply because their very existence was often deemed suspicious, and in 2013 a judge ruled that stop-and-frisk is unconstitutional racial profiling.

Hetey and Eberhardt had the subjects read a news report about that court ruling and then answer some questions. Most of the subjects, all of whom were white, said they thought stop-and-frisk was too punitive. But when presented with the chance to sign a petition against stop-and-frisk, the subjects who thought the prison population was "less-black" were almost three times more likely to sign the petition—even though the researchers never explicitly asked about race. Meanwhile, the subjects who saw the "more-black" prison demographics reported being more worried that ending stop-and-frisk would increase crime—again, despite having just read about how unconstitutional racial profiling had unfairly shaped who was behind bars.

"I think this study further underscores the extent to which 'blackness' retains its racial stigma, even as we move far away from the time of explicit anti-black attitudes," writes journalist Jamelle Bouie. For instance, in general, about two out of five white Republicans and about one out of five white Democrats explicitly say that black people are lazier than white people. And 26 percent of

Republicans and 18 percent of Democrats say that black people are less intelligent than white people. Studies have shown that white people who incorrectly believe that blacks make up a disproportionate share of public assistance recipients also believe that people on food stamps and welfare are mostly lazy. But people who *correctly* believe that most welfare recipients are white tend to say that people getting this assistance have just fallen on hard times. These are examples of how white people blame the problems the black community faces not on society's structures and biases but on black people themselves, inherently. That's the ultimate attribution error at work.

In fact, Thomas Pettigrew also showed that because of the ultimate attribution error, when members of a privileged in-group do something good, it's assumed to reflect their inherent qualities. But when someone from the discriminated-against out-group does something good, it's assumed to be some sort of "exception," created uniquely by the context. As philosopher David Livingstone Smith puts it, "Essences give rise to stereotypical features associated with a kind. Deviations from the stereotype indicate that something is preventing the essence from being expressed or distorting its expression." Sociologists used to call this the "Cosby effect"—because white people who watched and enjoyed *The Cosby Show* didn't apply those positive generalizations to all black people but treated the Huxtables, the professionally and financially successful family on the TV sitcom, as an exception. Unfortunately, now Bill Cosby is a no longer a positive example of anything.

Harkening back to @LindaLikesBacon's username, we see attribution errors at play in her perceptions of Muslims. Partly because of media and political discourse surrounding the heinous acts of a relative handful of violent extremists, too many in the United States have tarred all Muslims as suspicious, and as harboring hate for all non-Muslims. Because of the ultimate attribution error, the hateful, violent acts of a relatively small number of extremist Muslims worldwide get ascribed to the entire out-group—which is why a significant number of people in the United States, and the West in general, believe, as @LindaLikesBacon does, that because some Muslims want to cut Americans' heads off, that means all Muslims do. Maybe if she's being generous, not all. But *most.* She thinks that's inherently who Muslims are.

Incidentally, there are an estimated 3.3 million Muslims living in the United States today. If even just 5 percent of them wanted to cut off the heads of non-Muslims, we'd definitely know it—with bands of decapitating warriors roving city streets. But that's not happening, because most Muslims are moderate and peaceful, and only want to live the best life they can, just like all the Christians and Jews and atheists in the United States. And just like most Christians and Jews and atheists, the vast majority of Muslims oppose terrorism.

Mind you, while societies and our world as a whole tend to have certain preferred or dominant in-groups versus out-groups, the ultimate attribution error is a two-way street: the people who actually are terrorists don't see themselves as hateful either. They are inclined to think that *their* particular enemies are especially, inherently hateful—that, for instance, Israelis and Americans are by nature oppressive and destructive. When an early iteration of ISIS beheaded a US citizen in Iraq in 2004, the group's statement in part read, "The mujahideen will give America a taste of the degradation you have inflicted on the Iraqi people."

I talked with Elana Duffy, who served as a terrorist interrogator in Afghanistan for the United States Army, about her impressions of the terrorists she encountered. She tells me she learned that terrorists had a range of motivations. Sometimes their hatred was ideologically driven, but often it was situational—they were poor and needed the few bucks they were paid to dig a hole and drop a bomb in, or their families were threatened with violence if they didn't comply.

"Everyone thinks that their own base motivation is good," says Duffy. "It could just be 'My family feels threatened, and I don't want my kids growing up feeling threatened. I'm going to fight against you for my children.'" In fact, to entice recruits, ISIS often uses videos that show children allegedly killed by Western bombs.

Ahmet Yayla, the deputy director of the International Center for the Study of Violent Extremism, is leading a project to interview ISIS defectors. "When you speak to them one by one, when you communicate or chat with them, you would think that they are the nicest people in the world," Yayla tells me. "They are fathers, husbands, and when you speak with them on daily matters, they are just like you and me."

So even as the extreme example of terrorists shows, people who do truly evil things have an astonishing capacity to convince themselves that they're not essentially evil people; they believe those they hate or inflict violence on are the ones who are hateful, who deserve what they get. No wonder mere internet trolls find it so easy to absolve themselves. That capacity for self-deception is in all of us.

THE ULTIMATE ATTRIBUTION error gets a powerful assist from another of the fundamental psychological habits of hate: essentialism, which is the tendency to wildly generalize about people, especially those we lump into out-groups. Essentialism is the belief that everyone within a group shares the same characteristics or qualities, generalizations we're especially likely to make—and assume are fixed—about out-groups. "Essences are imagined to be shared by members of natural kinds," writes David Livingstone Smith in his book *Less Than Human*, "kinds that are discovered rather than invented, real rather than merely imagined, and rooted in nature." But that's a myth. The distinctions between us are largely not "natural" but created. We define and demean "others" in large part because of society's biases, all of which harden into negative and unyielding judgments about others that shape the rest of our perceptions. And this, I learned, is the core of prejudice and discrimination.

So, for example, sexism is often rationalized by an appeal to essentialism—that there are behaviors and qualities that are "essentially female" versus those that are "essentially male." Which is somewhat true in terms of biological differences. But we've also used biology to justify a whole bunch of distinctions as similarly "natural"—from the idea that women are overly emotional to the idea that boys prefer playing with trucks and are better at science. These are socially constructed norms. Layer on top of that attribution errors and societal biases, and those "essentially male" qualities are interpreted as "naturally" superior and thus deserving of disproportionate power and authority.

Essentialism doesn't just play out in sexism and racism and nationalism, though. It plays out in partisanship, too. Liberals, for instance, essentialize conservatives. Consider during the 2008 presidential campaign when Barack Obama decried "bitter" Republican voters who "cling to guns or religion." Or during the 2016 campaign when Hillary Clinton referred to Trump voters as a "basket of deplorables"—lumping them all into the same category or, in this case, basket, not to mention dehumanizing them (we don't store humans in baskets!).

At the same time, when conservatives—especially white male conservatives—complain that they're being marginalized or even oppressed in our society today, there's something intensely ironic at play. A group of people who have so often objected to the argument that racism and sexism have led to differential treatment of whole groups of people in society—dismissing this view as mere "identity politics"—are now claiming that their own group is treated uniquely badly in part because of their shared identity?

When people of color point out systemic bias in policing or women critique rape culture, many conservatives accuse them of playing the race card or whining. But then the same conservatives turn around and argue that they're being discriminated against and marginalized because they're white men. Whether they realize it or not, they're giving as good as they get with the concepts of identity politics and essentialism. Our identities and experience in the world in our skin aren't the same, but can we all perhaps notice how, as the writer Anand Giridharadas says, "our very different pains rhyme"?

Meanwhile, my trolls are mean to me in large part because they've essentialized me. They have a grossly simplified view of who I am because of the ideas and identities I represent—liberal, lesbian, New Yorker, occasional recycler and noncarb dieter. But we all have an inclination, somewhere in our wiring, to draw broad conclusions about those we lump into various out-groups. Gordon Allport, the psychologist who pioneered hate studies, defined "prejudice" as "an avertive or hostile attitude toward a person who belongs to a group, simply because he belongs to that group, and is therefore presumed to have objectionable qualities ascribed to the group." And when we don't interact with people who are different from us—when we essentialize them and never get the chance to see people as individuals—our categories can become "unusually resistant to rational influence," warns psychologist Ralph Rosnow. And that, psychologists tell us, is what can ossify into prejudice and hate. Part of why it was helpful for my trolls to talk to me is that it made me not just a category but an individual. Of course, talking to my trolls helped me see them not just as categorical trolls but as individuals, too. Attribution errors and essentialism are like blinders, which stop us from truly seeing others accurately and fairly scrutinizing ourselves.

Consider the phenomenon of "affinity fraud"—through which members of the Amish and Mormon communities, for instance, have been tricked by scam artists whom the communities didn't scrutinize but, rather, trusted because they were in their same faith group. As another example, among the five stages of social conditioning terrorists use for new recruits, one is "self-deindividuation," stripping away one's own unique identity. Another is "other-deindividuation," stripping away the personal identities of others to make them a generalizable, lumped-together enemy. That's also how terrorist recruiters instill hate. So essentialism doesn't just pose dangers for out-groups but for in-groups, too.

A sense of belonging is a good thing, but when we allow our own uniqueness and the uniqueness of others to be subsumed into a forced amalgam, we lose our ability to think for ourselves. But to fight hate, we have to see ourselves and others clearly and fully. Then again, when I talked to one of my trolls—@JacksBack100—there was a point at which I literally wanted to cover my ears and crawl under my desk and hide.

My exchange with @JacksBack100 started innocently enough. In August 2016, after a segment I did on CNN, @JacksBack100 tweeted something about how he didn't know "he was gay"—the "he" being me.

I reposted his tweet and wrote, "Haha I see what you did there you so clever but if I were a dude I'd be straight bro but anyway." And then I didn't think anything more about it. I had way worse hate tweets in my feed, not to mention non-Twitter things to focus on.

What happened next had never happened to me before. @Jacks Back100 apologized. Instantaneously and pretty convincingly.

@JacksBack100 tweeted that he was sorry and that it was an insensitive and stupid joke and he meant no offense. None taken, I replied. But why did he do it? It was intriguing to me that someone would write something so mean publicly and then take it back so quickly, which made his trolling in the first place seem so casual, even accidental. Like he'd just by mistake stepped on my toe.

Over the phone, I ask @JacksBack100 about the incident. He responds slowly, lumbering, pausing before almost every word. "Yeah, I can answer . . . I can answer that. I had . . . before I did this stupid thing . . . Before I did that, I had seen you on CNN many times, and . . . I want to say this delicately . . . I . . . I was very attracted to you."

This was the last thing I was expecting to hear. Befuddled, I manage to eke out a feeble, "Uh-huh," so that he will keep talking.

"I was attracted to you . . . your physical appearance," @Jacks Back100 tells me, stumbling on. "I was attracted to your presentation. I was attracted to your intellect. I was attracted to your reason and the way you presented yourself. I just had and still have the utmost respect for you. It wasn't until I had seen you many times . . . I don't know how many times, but a number . . . numerous times . . . that it occurred to me that you were not straight."

He exhales audibly. "Is that a good way to put it?" he asks, sounding relieved that he had finally gotten it all off his chest.

I, on the other hand, do not feel relieved. I feel freaked-out. There's no handbook for what to do when the person you interview for being mean to you online suddenly professes that he has a crush on you, besides which I'm not especially well versed at fielding crushes from men in general. I can't figure out what on earth to say next—and I talk for a living!

I try a trick every therapist I've ever had has used to keep me talking and again say, "Uh-huh."

"As soon as I said it," @JacksBack100 tells me, "I said, 'Jesus Christ, one of the people who I respect and look forward to seeing on television, I just slammed.' And it just . . . I was so angry at myself that the only thing that I could do was to apologize like that."

Mind you that happened only *after* I called him out for it. I would have pointed that out during our conversation if I'd regained use of my faculties.

Then @JacksBack100 proceeds to tell me a story about his lesbian friends, which, by the way, is what most straight people do when they're trying to prove to you that they're not homophobic.

After we hung up, I thought about that scene in the movie *Big*, the one in which Tom Hanks hits Elizabeth Perkins with a rolled-up comic book, the only way the little kid inside him knows how to show he has a crush. Was @JacksBack100 just hitting me with the tweet equivalent a rolled-up comic book?

"Hate is neither the opposite of love nor the absence of love," Robert Sternberg writes in his book *The Psychology of Hate*. Or, as Chrissie Hynde of the Pretenders sang, "It's a thin line between love and hate." I really wasn't thinking about trolling as a form of flirting, but the internet—and the world—can be a very strange place.

My time at Fox News was strange on a different level. I came to realize how condescending I'd been in my views about not only the people who worked at Fox News but the people watching at home. And condescension is just a snooty form of prejudice; we are only condescending to those we feel are inherently beneath us. The more I got out of my own liberal bubble, the more I met other conservatives who were neither stupid nor hateful—or at least no more deliberately hateful than I was. Those experiences really challenged my biases and assumptions. I'm not saying that Sean Hannity is the nicest person on the planet; his political views are certainly not anywhere near what I would reasonably call nice. What I am saying is that I realized that the person I'd thought of as entirely cruel, as the caricature of a horrific right-wing monster, is actually caring and kind, and a good dad and a supportive friend. Including a supportive friend to me. That revelation is still having ripple effects throughout my life. I wonder if any of my trolls have had similar revelations about me.

Either way, the experience of getting to know and like many conservatives and at the same time receiving more and more hate mail from conservatives presented me with a choice. From here on out, was I going to believe that most conservatives were like the ones I'd worked with at Fox News, or was I going to assume that most conservatives were like the ones sending me hateful messages online? Which was the exception, and which was the rule? Honestly, I probably could have made a case either way. This was a decision that tested my core principles. I could either choose to hate most conservatives or not. I found my answer in my aunt Lucy.

In a lot of ways, Aunt Lucy reminds me of @LindaLikesBacon. I mean, I don't think Aunt Lucy has ever sent hate mail, but she has a deep love for her friends and family, a great sense of humor, and a laugh that feels like a tickle. Aunt Lucy, not her real name, by the way, lives in the middle of the country and is a conservative Republican. She also loves me and my partner and our daughter and welcomes us with open arms at every family occasion we manage to attend. The few times we've cautiously talked politics, Aunt Lucy has been curious and kind. Aunt Lucy watches Fox News, and eventually it dawned on me that most Fox viewers are probably just like her—decent, curious about the news, intending to learn and do something good with the information. I started to picture my aunt Lucy when I would go on Fox, and then when I would go on CNN, and even when I would respond to people on Twitter. It made it easier for me to think and talk and act from a place of kindness, not hate—to not essentialize the invisible people on the other side of those screens but instead to imagine my aunt Lucy, someone I love and respect.

For me, it's infinitely more encouraging, not to mention more effective, to treat conservatives as a bunch of Aunt Lucys instead of a cache of trolls or a "basket of deplorables." Nobody is going to engage in a constructive dialogue with me if they think I believe they're a bridge-dwelling gnome or a totable pile of rot. And thinking of my aunt Lucy helps undercut the dangers of essentialism.

People often ask me how they can talk to their conservative relatives at family gatherings like Thanksgiving. I actually have a handy tool, taught to me by Matt Kohut and John Neffinger, authors of the book *Compelling People*, as well as their colleague Seth Pendleton, with whom I've worked leading media trainings and public-speaking workshops.

Imagine my aunt Lucy says something about how she doesn't mean to be anti-immigrant or anything, but the economy is just really bad right now and we don't have enough jobs for the people who are already here. Now, my natural instinct is to argue: "No, you're wrong, and let me explain the three reasons why!" But what we know from neuroscience is that while we all need to use our frontal lobes to engage in a reasoned discussion—and to be open to persuasion—when we perceive an argument coming, our frontal lobes shut down and the fight-or-flight part of our brain turns on (the part of the brain, as we'll see later, that also holds our biases and stereotypes). If we want to keep the possibility of persuasion open, we have to stay conversational. Also, in her statement, my aunt Lucy isn't expressing cold hard facts so much as she's expressing a *feeling* about the facts as she understands them. And as every good couples counselor I've ever been to has told me, you can't argue with feelings. If my partner says I hurt her feelings, I can't say, "No, I didn't!" They're *her* feelings—and they're inherently valid by virtue of her feeling them.

So instead of arguing, here's a tip, which uses the shorthand ABC. The *A* stands for "affirm." First, you find a feeling that you can genuinely affirm. In this hypothetical conversation with my aunt Lucy, I might say, "I'm also really worried about the economy right now." Or, "I completely agree it's important that everyone has access to a good job." It's important that I'm not making it up. It's not some act or gesture. I mean it. I can really, authentically agree with that part of what Aunt Lucy is saying. So I start with that.

Next is *B*, for "bridge." It does not stand for "but." It also doesn't stand for "however," which is the Harvard of "buts." It's a bridge, a way of saying "and." You can actually just say "and"—or "that's why" or "actually" or "the thing is" or even "the good news is." Anything but "but." "But" basically invalidates whatever came before it. Like when I say to my partner, "I'm sorry, *but* . . ." According to those same couples counselors, that means I'm not at all sorry. Apparently, that's what my partner thinks it means, too.

Then comes *C*—"convince." This is where I put whatever I was inclined to spit out in the first place, about how comprehensive immigration reform actually raises wages and working standards for immigrant *and* citizen workers, or whatever point I wanted to make.

In my experience, ABCing is hard to do in the moment but incredibly effective when done right. It's a powerful tool for what I call "connection-speech," which not only lets you make your point but helps you make it in a friendly, respectful way that can be heard.

But beyond the ABC tool, when people ask how to talk to their own Aunt Lucys about politics, I often ask how they talk with their family members about topics *other than* politics. Do they yell and scream at their aunt if she loves some movie they think is stupid? Of course not. Maybe they get heated and say things like, "Seriously? You don't think *Dirty Dancing* is the greatest love story of all time?" But the conversation stays civil, and any outrage is secondary to the overwhelming spirit of love. I'm not going to disown Aunt Lucy for not liking *Dirty Dancing.*

Obviously, political issues are far more important. But still, I love Aunt Lucy infinitely more than I dislike Donald Trump. Remembering that helps. And frankly, I have plenty of good friends I don't see 100 percent eye to eye with but generally think are "on my side." What if I only agree with them on 90 percent of issues? Or 60 percent? Or 40 percent? Where do I draw the line between accepting we just "agree to disagree" and defining them as monstrous enemies? The thing is, I give "my people" on "my side" the benefit of the doubt. Why don't I do that for Aunt Lucy? Or my trolls, for that matter? Of course, my trolls aren't my aunt Lucy. But they also aren't Donald Trump. We often assume and act as though everyone on a given "side" is an automatic proxy for the very worst-behaving of their side's most extreme examples. Such hyperpartisanship is just another form of attribution bias and essentialism.

In fact, one of the most startling things I learned about my trolls is that many of them don't even think of themselves as trolls. Turns out they're not thinking about their trolling much at all; they're just killing time by spewing random gunk into the ether. Here I thought they were being deliberately and even strategically hateful, when they're mostly just bored.

"Do you think about the impact of your tweets?" I ask @Arlington Steve, a forty-one-year-old attorney from Virginia and another one of my top trolls. Among other things, he told me once when police had been killed, "you've got the blood of those cops on your hands," because I'd criticized systemic police brutality—and then, for added measure, he called me a bitch.

"Well, honestly, I kind of figure no one reads or cares," @ArlingtonSteve answers. "I'm just more, I guess, entertaining myself," he adds. "I admit I'll use it to vent or even, sometimes, I've been nasty to people, which I regret. Yeah, so pretty much that." Later, he sort of boasts that he has some celebrities following him, and I wonder if he's called any of them a bitch.

"Why are you on Twitter?" I ask @bmenyhert, one of my trolls who refuses to talk to me on the phone but then sends me paragraphs back and forth through Twitter's private messaging.

"Way to vent, kill time between/during classes, layovers, bathroom," @bmenyhert writes back. "Wouldn't notice if twitter disappeared tomorrow."

I ask @bmenyhert another question. "Do you think you're nicer in real life or on Twitter?"

"Hopefully everyone's nicer in real life," @bmenyhert replies.

We go back and forth a bit. Everyone's mean on Twitter, he says, so @bmenyhert is too, explaining, "When in Rome, Ma'am."

So, I ask, "do you think your behavior online is ever hateful?"

"Rude? Inconsiderate? Spiteful? Sometimes," @bmenyhert writes back. "Hateful? No."

You know, when *I'm* bored, I just read a book or take a walk or eat carbs. I don't start smearing people online. But going back and forth with @bmenyhert and talking to @ArlingtonSteve, I notice my essentialist resentment mounting as I ponder what "kind of person" or rather "kinds of *people*" do this sort of thing. And yet they both apologized to me in our exchanges together. Every coin has two sides. So, it turns out, does every human being.

I realized I had lumped all my trolls together into a vague image of pinheaded residents of Dumbfuckistan, completely essentializing them based on stereotypes of right-wingers and stripping them of human complexity—in other words, dehumanizing them. After all, trolls are monsters that live under bridges. Trolls aren't human.

But the more I talked to my trolls, the more obvious their complicated and specific humanness became. @LindaLikesBacon has a twenty-four-year-old son, who, at the time we spoke, was in rehab for meth addiction. "I just went to see him," she told me. "He seems to be doing really good. He's only got a couple months in, but he's determined to finish, so hopefully this will do the trick."

When @LindaLikesBacon said this, suddenly instead of feeling bad for myself that I was getting trolled, I felt bad for her. Here was a woman I was annoyed at for causing me a tiny bit of suffering, and she was going through so much more suffering of her own. Which I guess was ironic but mostly just felt sad.

It was surprisingly profound to realize that the monsters who were so mean to me online were just ordinary people. That they chuckle and stutter and say "uh" just like I do. That they care that celebrities are following them, just like I do. That they don't think anyone pays attention to them, which I worry about, too. That they are just imperfect, messy, complicated people, whom I have more in common with than not. Even if I still hate cruise nights, I don't hate my trolls anymore. But the more I learned, the more I did start to hate Twitter.

How much is the internet itself responsible for trolling? When the internet was invented, many believed technology would connect the world in fundamentally transformative ways—not just in terms of our ability to watch multilingual porn or to buy sneakers from anywhere in the world but at a more human, and humane, level. The idea was that having access to stories about rural farmers tending their crops in Mali and videos of children working in factories in Bangladesh would help expand our minds and our circle of compassion to become a truly global understanding. We thought global connectivity would make us more globally connected. And to an extent, that's been true. I'm still on Twitter, despite my trolls, in large part because of the things I've learned and the friends I've been able to make all over the world. And yet, the nature of technology can be inherently depersonalizing—and thus enable dehumanization. Of the over half of Americans who expect incivility to worsen in the coming years, nearly seven in ten blame the internet and social media for the current levels of nastiness in our culture. Are they right?

In a 2016 study, Justin Cheng and a team of computer scientists at Stanford had 667 people take tests. Half the subjects took an easy test, while the other half took a really hard and frustrating version. Afterward, they all filled out surveys about their mood. Unsurprisingly, the people who had taken the hard test were in a foul mood.

Then, Cheng and his team had the subjects read an article—an abridged version of a column that argued that women should vote for Hillary Clinton instead of Bernie Sanders in the 2016 Democratic primaries. The subjects were told to post at least one note in the comments section that followed the article—which they were told would be visible to others. In each case, the subjects could already see three comments that had been posted. In some cases, those comments were neutral. In others, they were troll-y.

The subjects who took the easy test and then saw the neutral responses posted trolling comments 35 percent of the time. But among subjects who had *either* taken the hard test or seen the trolling comments, 50 percent then posted trolling comments.

And among those who experienced *both* the difficult test and the trolling comments, fully 68 percent turned into trolls—in other words, they were almost twice as likely to troll as the neutral group.

In another experiment, researchers found that men who had lost an interactive video game were more likely to engage in misogynistic trolling of women who were also playing the game. Other research shows that individuals who have low self-esteem around their social identity are more likely to hold derogatory views about out-groups, and that hate-crime perpetrators actually experience a temporary boost in self-esteem. Still, is there something about the way technology uniquely shapes our experience of ourselves and others that magnifies these effects?

Yes, argues psychologist John Suler. Suler has pioneered what he calls the "online disinhibition effect"—the way in which the design of modern technology, including social media, seems to make people more inclined to "self-disclose or act out more frequently or intensely than they would in person." Suler, a professor at Rider University in New Jersey, was one of the first academics to study how we represent and express ourselves online. His online disinhibition effect, based on his own experiences in the early days of the social web, has become one of the most influential analyses of online behavior.

The question of why some people behave like jerks online first fascinated Suler about twenty years ago, when the internet was still in its relative infancy. In the late 1990s, he was involved online in something called "The Palace"—a sort of graphics-based chat room. I was in high school then and hung out in The Palace sometimes, too. The thing I most remember is a moment when I sought out a lesbian-themed room so that I could ask a bunch of naive questions to some very patient smiley faces as I was sussing out my own identity. In that sense, for me, The Palace represented the best of what the internet had to offer—information and connectivity.

But when Suler was in The Palace, he noticed people behaving differently than in real life, saying or "doing" things in this virtual community they probably would never otherwise contemplate. Suler also noticed the effect on himself. "I'm a much more talkative person online than I am in person," Suler tells me as we chatted over the phone one afternoon. "Being a clinical psychologist, I'm very introspective and I'm very much into censoring myself and being aware of what I'm doing, as far as my clinical work." But he wasn't like that in The Palace.

In fact, Suler even got involved in what he calls "slightly deviant behavior"—like playing pranks on newbies in the digital community. It was as though he acted like a different person online. "I was fascinated by how people socialize online, particularly in this imaginary world where people had avatars to represent their identities," Suler says.

Suler's online disinhibition effect has several parts. We're disinhibited online because we can hide from our real identities (what he calls "dissociative anonymity"). We don't actually see the people we're communicating with, and so we lose the normal cues of face-to-face interaction ("invisibility"). And there's a delay between when we write something and when someone reads it ("asynchronicity"), which also makes our online communication seem less like real life and therefore less connected to real-life consequences. In addition, everyone is supposedly equal online, which means everyone is equally a potential target ("minimization of status and authority"). You're not going to call a coworker an asshat, because you could get fired or ostracized by your peers, but online, you don't have status to protect and no one has authority over you.

The online world seems so different from the real world that we consciously or unconsciously believe that just like we're not our "real" selves online, neither is anyone else—that the internet is almost like a fictional realm. All of this explains why trolling and harassment are worse in spaces like Twitter, where we're often less visibly connected to—and accountable to—our family, friends, and colleagues compared with platforms like Facebook and Instagram, which are generally more personal.

"I guess it's the whole anonymous thing. Nobody knows me," @LindaLikesBacon says when I ask her how she can be so mean in tweets. "If I don't know you, I'm not going to spout off at you in person. That's just not me." But she'll do it on Twitter. "It's kind of like hiding behind an anonymous wall," she says.

"You think you're just talking to yourself," Suler explains when I tell him what @LindaLikesBacon said. "When you're talking to yourself, you're willing to say anything."

Suler calls the tendency to believe we're talking to ourselves "solipsistic introjection," by far my favorite part of his theory. It's a mental contortion that fascinates me. It turns out that when we read what somebody else writes online, we don't picture *them* saying it—especially if it's someone we don't know. We instead experience their message *as a voice within our own head*, "as if that person's psychological presence and influence have been assimilated or introjected into" our own psyche. According to Suler, that other person actually becomes a projection of ourselves—of how we would feel in the situation, or at least how we believe that the person we're writing to should be feeling. In other words, we're not considering *their* feelings; we're really thinking about *our own*.

Suler compares the phenomenon to a novelist hearing characters in her head and then writing out the dialogue as she experiences it. The characters themselves are unreal; they're just in the writer's head. The problem is, on social media these are actual human beings we're communicating with yet perceiving as sort of versions of ourselves. Hence, in aggregate, the problem.

"In real life, I wouldn't be offensive to someone just to be mean or just for entertainment value," @LindaLikesBacon tells me. But she would online.

Of course we can't just simply blame the technology—but we have to acknowledge that technology is exacerbating the problem.

What's the antidote? Suler says everyone needs to "put yourself in the place of the other person online." But, he adds, "That's not always easy to do, because you can't see people, you can't hear them. You may not know anything about their background or their identity. So it does take some well-prepared, well-tuned empathic abilities to be online and to realize that these are other people at the end of these internet connections."

That requires a deliberate, conscious approach. Susan Benesch, a lawyer and researcher who studies "dangerous speech," from genocidal propaganda to hate speech on Twitter, has proposed one such model. Benesch calls her approach "counterspeech"—but since I prefer not to define the solution only in reference to the problem, I think of Benesch's strategy as "connection-speech." According to Benesch, with this approach we can find ways to talk with one another, online or off, that facilitate deeper connection, empathy, and mutual humanity, instead of hate.

When we encounter hate speech online, most of us either ignore it or fire back with more hate. Both are understandable impulses or even instincts. But Benesch argues for responding with expressions of empathy instead, which she has shown not only interrupts cycles of hate speech but can positively transform interactions as well as people's actual beliefs. That's certainly what happened to Megan

Phelps-Roper, the granddaughter of Fred Phelps—one of the most notoriously and explicitly hateful people in modern US history.

Fred Phelps founded the Westboro Baptist Church. Maybe you've heard of it. It's the small extremist right-wing "Christian" hate group that protests the funerals of US soldiers killed in action, because Westboro members believe that military deaths are God's payback for the country's tolerance of gay rights. Westboro is probably best known for its signature slogan "God Hates Fags."

As recounted in a *New Yorker* article by Adrian Chen, in 2008, Megan created a Twitter account, and by 2009, she was regularly tweeting Westboro's messages of hate, like posting, "Thank God for AIDS" on World AIDS Day and that sort of thing. Westboro members were known for picking targets most people would find sympathetic to pummel with hate; Megan was no exception. One day, Megan decided to target @Jewlicious—a Twitter account belonging to David Abitbol, a Jerusalem-based blogger. She tweeted, "Finish this sentence: the only good Jew is a [. . .] REPENTANT Jew!" and she tagged @Jewlicious to make sure he would see it. He wrote back, "Thanks Megan! That's handy what with Yom Kippur coming up!" Because—get it?—Yom Kippur is the holiday of atonement! Megan replied with characteristically acerbic nastiness, and David tweeted back a wisecrack about Megan holding a sign reading "God Hates Shrimp."

Megan was trolling @Jewlicious, plain and simple. She was vomiting hate through her keyboard and straight in his direction. And probably no one would have blamed him if he had thrown it right back at her. But he didn't. David took the high road—and ended up taking Megan with him.

David told the *New Yorker* that his express goal was to humanize a real Jew for Megan and her hateful clan. "I wanted to be like really nice so that they would have a hard time hating me," David said.

For her part, Megan reflected, "I knew he was evil, but he was friendly." Somewhere in the space created by that "but," a sort of friendship bloomed.

There were others who helped change her mind. Graham Hughes, a Canadian college student who interviewed Megan for a paper, started corresponding with her over Twitter. They didn't just talk politics. They talked about music. "I remember just thinking, 'How can somebody who appreciates good music believe so many hateful things?" Graham said. And when Graham was hospitalized for a brain infection, Megan acted more like a friend than many of Graham's real-life friends. "I knew there was a genuine connection between us," he told the *New Yorker.*

"It was like I was becoming part of a community," Megan said of her emerging friendships on Twitter. "I was beginning to see them as human."

The people Megan met through Twitter challenged her orthodoxies and humanized for her entire groups of people she'd been taught to hate. Eventually, in the fall of 2012, Megan left Westboro—and, in effect, left most of her entire family as well.

Afterward, one of the first places she went was to a Jewlicious festival hosted by David. It was his kindness and humor that had opened Megan up to a whole new way of thinking and, ultimately, to an entirely new life on the other side of hate. And imagine that: one of the first things the former anti-Semitic "God Hates Fags" activist did was go to a giant party with progressive Jews. All because of some exchanges on usually hate-spreading Twitter!

How can we all learn to practice connection-speech? In her writings for the Dangerous Speech Project, which she directs, Susan Benesch offers a great set of guidelines. The Twitter exchange that made Megan Phelps-Roper begin to reexamine her views is an example of what Benesch calls "golden conversations."

Which makes me think of golden showers. But I love Benesch's point. According to Benesch, a successful "golden conversation" online—or presumably in real life as well—shifts hateful discourse and perhaps even beliefs, both for the person directly engaged in the hate speech as well as everyone else observing that speech as a bystander. It dovetails with the civil libertarian position that the answer to hate speech isn't curbing or infringing speech but rather encouraging *more speech*—and, in particular, constructive speech that directly combats and undermines hate.

There is something inherently unjust in suggesting that the burden to turn the other cheek should so often fall on those who have been hit hardest. Any implication that we must replicate patterns of inequality to advance the process of healing just feels deeply, intrinsically wrong, to put it mildly. And I also understand that resistance. But I also understand that if we keep waiting for the most privileged among us to make the first move, we may be waiting forever. In the face of so much violence, it was the marginalized in India and the United States and elsewhere who took up the mantle of nonviolence. And maybe it wasn't fair, but it was effective. Obviously, I have a strong bias against violence and intolerance and hate, no matter the source, and it's for that reason that I hope that even in the darkest moments and corners of the world, including those of the internet, we can all be examples of kindness and compassion. It's the possibility of such healing conversations that gives me hope, not only for Twitter but for humanity.

I've had my own experiments and small victories with connection-speech. In particular, I favor Susan Benesch's strategy of humor, which she's found to be one of the most effective connection-speech tactics. It sure worked when I joked about @JacksBack100's hate tweet, if you consider his flirtation a sign of success. And every time someone makes some wisecrack about me looking like Justin Bieber, of course I joke about it. Like, what—being compared to a hunky international pop star is an insult? Benesch writes that humorous connection-speech is especially potent in neutralizing hateful or dangerous speech that might otherwise be "viewed as powerful or intimidating."

These days, I'm less depressed or horrified by my trolls, and instead I see them—or *try* to see them—as somewhere between sad and amusing opportunities for engagement. That's not to say trolling is amusing. In fact, it can be psychologically harmful, and online threats can quickly turn into real-life concerns for safety. Sadly, I've become so accustomed to trolling that I can forget this. Faced with truly dangerous trolls, just being nice cannot and should not be the answer. We need to respond to threats and safety issues swiftly and seriously, online and off. But fortunately, most trolls aren't dangerous; they're just mean. That doesn't mean we have to be mean, too. We can choose connection-speech instead. Personally, because I've chosen connection-speech, I'm less fazed by my trolls now—and I drink less, too. Instead, I take them in stride. I style my hair with the spittle of my trolls. I also see them as opportunities to practice my humanity—and hopefully, character by character, to expand theirs.

Connection-speech, with Benesch's research supporting it, offers a ray of hope in the dark storm cloud that is internet vitriol, and vitriol in general. Because the fact is, we all say we don't like this crap. For instance, most Americans say they don't like mudslinging political ads and negative campaigns. And yet we keep voting for the mudslingers.

Ads that ran in August of the 2016 presidential campaign were more negative than ads that ran in August of the 2012 campaign, and while about two-thirds of Hillary Clinton's campaign ads were negative, almost all of Donald Trump's ads were negative. He didn't air a single positive ad. And look who won. Do we really want what we say we want? If so, we have to start actually supporting it and modeling civility ourselves. Both offline and on, if we stop fanning hate and instead practice connection-speech, that little ray of hope for a better way of interacting and even disagreeing with one another could spread. Hell, it could go viral.

But even basking in the hopeful rays of connection-speech, I still wonder if there's a larger, even darker cloud hovering over us. Sure, maybe we can mitigate a little hate here and there—but is the core problem inevitable? Is hate some inescapable social or biological imperative that we can only hope to stanch but not ever fully stop? Thankfully, I learned that, no, hate is no more compulsory than my pessimism. But both are profoundly powerful bad habits.

TWO

How We Hate: The Former Terrorist

I imagine one of the reasons people cling to their hates so stubbornly is because they sense, once hate is gone, they will be forced to deal with pain. —JAMES BALDWIN

BASSAM ARAMIN HAS a smile so broad that it reaches to his earlobes, and he speaks so softly that you can't help but want to lean closer to him to capture every word. You'd never think he was a convicted terrorist.

While internet trolling is a relatively new form of hate, in the Middle East hate seems almost synonymous with history. The tiny slip of land known as Israel today, and Palestine before that, could have been a global symbol for harmony—a place first inhabited by peaceful Arab farmers and then by Jews desperate for peace. And yet today, the land I'll call Israel/Palestine is an epicenter of acrimony, which not only defines the region but grips the globe. For many Jewish people and their allies, violent attacks against Israel echo the harrowing history of the Holocaust, and anti-Semitism more broadly. For many Palestinians and their allies, the atrocities of Israel represent the original sin of the West—settler colonialism and oppression rooted in Islamophobia. Both sides think the other overwhelmingly guilty and their own side relatively innocent, but what most everyone agrees on is that the hate is so historical and hardened that it's almost hopeless to think it can be solved. Fortunately, not everyone has given up hope.

I first heard Bassam's story through a friend, who told me how the former terrorist had eventually renounced violence against Israelis and, in 2005, founded Combatants for Peace, a group made up of Palestinians who had engaged in violence against Israelis plus former Israeli soldiers, all now working together to promote understanding between the two sides. Today, Combatants for Peace has about six hundred members. The group regularly stages nonviolent rallies, holds meetings where former combatants share their perspectives and victims of violence tell their stories, sponsors tours of the West Bank for Israelis, and rebuilds playgrounds in the territories that have been demolished by Israeli security forces.

Any story about a former terrorist now working for peace would probably have caught my attention, but in the context of Israel/Palestine, Bassam's story especially stood out. I thought that if I wanted to understand more about how hate is entrenched in human experience past and present, Israel/Palestine would be a good place to visit. And if I wanted to understand how to transform that hate into its opposite, Bassam would be a good person to talk with.

I first meet Bassam for coffee in the lobby of a Comfort Inn on the west side of Manhattan when he was in town for a Combatants for Peace fund-raiser. I guess I was expecting some sort of enlightened Buddhist type who would talk to me about the balance and subjectivity of the universe between meditative breaths. Instead, I meet a chain-smoker with a prominent limp and a wry sense of humor. When Bassam shares the story of his childhood, I am hooked.

He was born in a cave on the outskirts of Hebron in the West

Bank in 1968, the year after the Six-Day War, in which Israel defeated Egyptian, Syrian, and Jordanian forces and started occupying the West Bank, which had until then been part of Jordan. Like many families in the region, Bassam's lived in the mountains and farmed the surrounding territory. They were a large bunch, eventually including fifteen children, some of them Bassam's stepsiblings from his father's marriage to his first wife, who had passed away. I find myself picturing the cave with some sort of boho-chic vibe of fabric-draped minimalist wood furniture and strands of white Christmas tree lights crisscrossing the ceiling, like a place *Vogue* might stage a photo shoot about a hot new neocolonialist look. I catch myself, realizing that I'm trivializing, even romanticizing, Bassam's childhood to the point of being patronizing. When I later visit Bassam in the West Bank, I experience viscerally that there was nothing romantic about his youth, or about the poverty and violence still afflicting so many children in the territory all these years later.

Bassam's earliest memory is of Israeli soldiers coming to his family's cave. When he was around five years old, a helicopter landed nearby. "For me, it was something unbelievable," Bassam says almost in a whisper. "Come from the sky!" You can still hear his childlike awe. Soldiers climbed down from the helicopter. They were from the Israeli Defense Forces, which Israelis and Palestinians alike call the IDF.

"They come to the cave, these soldiers," Bassam tells me. "Very scary." His mother, his grandmother, and an older cousin were in the cave, too. The cousin was just fifteen, "But for me," Bassam says, "he was a huge man."

The soldiers talked to Bassam's family for a few minutes and then, suddenly, one of them slapped Bassam's cousin across the face. Then the IDF left. Bassam was confused and terrified by their sudden invasion and inexplicable aggression.

As he tells me the story, my mind slips to the narrative I was taught in my childhood, which often portrayed hateful, violence-prone Palestinians who must be controlled, lest another Holocaust break out. Again, I catch myself. I realize how conditioned I am to search for a justification, a reasonable explanation for the soldiers' behavior. Like a good *progressive* Jew, I can recite the facts about how Israel occupies the land of Bassam's community—and acts out that occupation in daily brutal ways that are part of a system of oppression. But even so, I figure something must have happened to justify the IDF hitting his cousin; he must have deserved it on some level. Sort of like assuming the people who get pulled over by the cops a lot must have done *something* to deserve it. Those of us who aren't subject to biased mistreatment often rationalize mistreatment as justified. I would soon learn, when I visited the West Bank, to challenge that assumption.

When Bassam was seven, he tells me, his family moved to the town nearby in order to cut down on what had been an hour-long journey each way to school and back. Then he started seeing Israeli soldiers all the time; they were a constant presence in the village. When he was twelve years old, the IDF shot and killed a young Palestinian girl near Bassam's village. A protest march was organized in response. Curious, Bassam waded into the crowd. The demonstration was illegal—it's actually been illegal since the occupation began for Palestinians to protest anything—and the IDF quickly cracked down on the march. I hear that childlike astonishment in Bassam's voice again as he describes IDF soldiers coming out of nowhere, just like they did that day in his family's cave. "Israelis come from the sky," Bassam says. "You don't understand where they come from."

Bassam says the soldiers threw tear gas canisters and the villagers started screaming and scrambling in all directions. "I found myself running in the middle of the soldiers," he recounts. "One of them hit me on my back. The other one hit me in my eyes. And I fell down." He remembers lying on the ground, dust and fear swirling around him, thinking to himself, "They're going to shoot me and I'm going to die." I try to imagine how horrifying it would be as a twelve-year-old to be lying on the street thinking you were about to be killed. But honestly, I can't. I was so sheltered and fortunate at that age. And I have been ever since.

Bassam managed to half walk, half crawl to safety, inching between the legs of the soldiers to the other side of the crowd, near where his home was. As he emerged, his hands and knees covered with stones and grit, he saw a young Palestinian standing on a hill holding a rock. Bassam guessed he was maybe eighteen or nineteen years old—the same age, by the way, as most of the IDF soldiers, who are required to serve in the military at that age.

To hear Bassam tell it, there was no way that the young man and his small rock could have hurt the heavily armed Israeli security forces. But still, as Bassam emerged from the crowd, the soldiers shot the young man on the hill. "I saw him," says Bassam. "He died." His voice is unemotional, matter-of-fact, perhaps from a lifetime of suffering.

Bassam learned to hate the IDF, and as I listen to him, I can imagine how I would have learned to hate them, too. That hate makes sense. It seems rational, even justified. Which is what makes it so incredible that Bassam would eventually reject hate. Bassam now says that peace will never be achieved unless enough people on both sides stop engaging in what conflict scholars call "competitive victimhood," each seeing themselves as the worse victims in a situation that actually hurts everyone. "I am not a victim," Bassam tells me. "No one can occupy me, because I have peace with myself in my heart."

How could someone go from being convicted of terrorism for trying to kill Israelis to such an enlightened perspective? Maybe he's not a Buddhist scholar, but Bassam clearly has plenty to teach me. When our short time at the Comfort Inn is up, I've barely scratched the surface of his story, and I ask if I can come visit him in the West Bank. He flashes his sheepish smile at me and says, "Of course!" So off I go.

I HAD LONG avoided traveling to Israel/Palestine. I grew up in Allentown, Pennsylvania, amidst a decent-sized Jewish community, which meant we had Orthodox Jews and Reform Jews and everyone in between. Some of Allentown's Jews walked to synagogue every Saturday. Some of us dropped out of Hebrew school when we were eleven years old and barely ever set foot in synagogue again. But within the diversity of what it meant to be a Jew, one thing was consistent in Allentown—we all supported Israel. Even today, I know Jews who eat pork and put up Christmas trees, but I don't know any Jews who oppose the existence of Israel.

But what it means to support Israel has been changing, including among American Jews. The universal lockstep defense of Israel I experienced in my youth has given way to a more complicated landscape of perspectives, with many Jews and allies still supporting Israel while trying to balance the rights of Israelis with the rights of Palestinians. As a young adult, I was constantly approached with offers of free "birthright" trips to Israel, sponsored by Jewish groups with unilaterally pro-Israel agendas, and I always turned them down, figuring that visiting Israel was a tacit endorsement of the country's superior position in the conflict. Now, I was ready to make the trip. In addition to visiting Bassam, I would more widely tour the occupied territories and spend time in Israel as well, interviewing both Palestinians and Israelis to try to get multiple perspectives.

Before I went to the Middle East, I brushed up on the history of the Israeli-Palestinian conflict and also read social science on the dynamics of what are called "intractable conflicts." In particular, I delved into the concept of competitive victimhood, which Bassam had opened my eyes to, and discovered the work of Israeli psychologist Daniel Bar-Tal. "Very often both sides believe that they are the victim," writes Bar-Tal with his colleagues in a paper on competitive victimhood. "The struggle over the status of the sole victim can enhance aggressiveness and lead to the employment of harsher means against the rival out-group." It's related to scapegoating, where one group perceives that its problems are the result of the other group, even if the group being scapegoated is in fact the group that is suffering *more than* and even *because of* the other.

This is how we have a dynamic in the United States today in which Christian conservatives claim they are being oppressed by the nation's incremental progress toward queer rights, despite the reality that, over decades, it was the disproportionate power and influence of those same Christian conservatives that kept basic rights from queer people. And that actually still do—it is legal for same-sex couples to marry but still also legal in most states to fire someone for being gay or gender-nonconforming. Yet the sense of competitive victimhood keeps the tension brewing—including, yes, smears from the gay community against Christian conservatives. Each side literally makes the other side suffer more to express anger over how much their side is suffering. Which is ridiculous, but there you have it.

Bar-Tal has focused his entire academic career on how to end deep-seated conflicts, and he identifies this dynamic of competitive victimhood as one of the main obstacles. It's at the heart of so many clashes all around the world, such as those between Indians and Pakistanis over the disputed territory of Kashmir and between Turks and Kurds in Turkey. It was at play in the decades of "the Troubles" in Northern Ireland and in the horrors of the Bosnian genocide, committed by Serbs. It is also a driving force in many long-brewing political battles in the US, between antiabortion and prochoice activists, gun control and gun rights advocates, and anti-globalization activists and corporatist defenders of the so-called inexorable march of globalization.

We all think we're suffering worse—and then feel justified in marginalizing those we believe are not suffering or even causing our suffering. For instance, studies suggest that bullies experience higher than average shame about their own shortcomings. And competitive victimhood also helps to explain why, according to polls, a majority of white Americans perceive that they are more victimized than black Americans. We divide ourselves up into in-groups and out-groups and then think our group has it worse.

The Israeli-Palestinian conflict is, of course, a textbook case of competitive victimhood. Palestinians generally think they suffer the most because of Israelis, and Israelis think they suffer the most because of Palestinians. In fact, I've talked to people on both sides of the conflict who think the idea that the other side suffers *at all* is preposterous. For instance, Palestinians generally articulate a version of history in which they were a peaceful people until they were invaded by Zionists, who resorted to terrorism in their colonial conquest, including the bombing of Palestinian Arab civilians in 1938, the car bomb detonated by Zionists inside Jerusalem in 1947, and the Zionist slaughtering of the people of the Palestinian village of Deir Yassin in 1948. At the same time, many Israelis dwell on a version of history in which Jews are a constantly persecuted people who merely sought solace from repeated and extended acts of world terrorism only to be victimized by Palestinians, for instance in the Arab riots during the 1920s, the Palestinian Arab revolt in the 1930s, and the Palestinian riots in Jerusalem in 1947.

To some, Jews have used their historic oppression as an excuse to oppress others, and the state of Israel is itself a terrorist organization, premised on settler colonialism, that now holds all the power. To others, Palestinian criticism of Israel reflects the inherent anti-Semitism on the part of Muslims, just as suicide bombings reflect their inherent and unresolvable inhumanity toward others.

These biases even shape both sides' perceptions of the same events. On December 30, 1947, Zionist militants threw two bombs into a crowd of Arab workers at the Haifa Oil Refinery. Six Arabs were killed. That afternoon, Arab protesters broke into the refinery and killed thirty-nine Jews. The next day, a precursor force to the IDF fired on the Palestinian Arab village of Balad al-Shaykh while the residents were asleep. As many as seventy Palestinians were killed.

Which attack was worse? Which attack was more justified? And do they all reflect hate? The litany of such attacks and counterattacks could fill a book of its own. Incidentally, I don't think it's anti-Israel to point out the oppressive nature of the current Israeli state, just like I don't think it's anti-Palestinian to point out the horrors of suicide bombings. What I do think is that if each act of violence is seen as a justified retaliation for a previous act of violence, which itself is a retaliation for some previous act of violence, any objective truth becomes buried in the blur of rationalizations. These perceptions have snowballed through decades into a rationale for enduring hate and into justifications of horrifying violence perpetrated by both sides, some of which Bar-Tal tells me he experienced firsthand while serving in the IDF.

What makes competitive victimhood so pernicious in intractable conflicts and in general is that whatever side you're on, your arguments for being the worse victim and blaming the other side seem so rational. Of course, hate isn't rational, but it *feels* rational, and therefore it feels justified. That's why we keep doing it. It's not that we're irrational; our hate is a rational reaction to our often one-sided and deeply biased perceptions. Which is why Bassam felt perfectly rational and justified when he attempted to kill Israeli soldiers.

I HAD HOPED Bassam would take me to the cave where his family lived, but the journey would have involved several hours of treacherous hiking, and Bassam has a severe limp from surviving polio as an infant. When he walks, his left leg suddenly buckles inward at the ankle and it's as though his whole leg is starting to crumble, threatening to topple him entirely. He does, however, take me on a tour of other sites of his youth, beginning at the home where he spent the remainder of his childhood, a modest cement square in the middle of the tangle of dusty streets and small cinder-block homes. There's a large pile of rocks abutting the house, which Bassam tells me are the remnants of the room his father first built for the family. The rest of the house was constructed around them, over time, as the original room crumbled. There's rebar poking out from the rocks this way and that, with some soda cans hanging from the ends, like a development project turned into modernist sculpture. He also shows me the hill where the young Palestinian he saw shot had been standing—and the building where his friends threw grenades at the IDF.

"You never conceive of yourself as a terrorist," Bassam tells me. He uses the word "terrorist" now but would never have back then.

I ask, How would he have described himself then? As a "freedom fighter"?

"Not only a freedom fighter," Bassam replies, puffing out his small chest. "We are the most humane freedom fighters on the earth. Why? Because we are against militants who try to kill us and occupy our land and our people, and we need to kill them for humanity, not for ourselves.

"It's justified," he adds.

"It's justified?" I ask. "You know it's wrong."

"No, it's *not* wrong," he says, conveying to me his mind-set when he was a teenager devoted to killing Israelis. Just like the terrorists Elana Duffy interrogated and Ahmet Yayla interviewed. They thought what they were doing was right.

Bassam formed a sort of unofficial gang with four of his friends, who were basically juvenile troublemakers in a politicized landscape. Back then, for instance, it was against the law to have a Palestinian flag, let alone display it, so Bassam and his friends would use old bits of fabric to stitch together haphazard versions of the flag. "We start[ed] our terrorism by raising the Palestinian flag on the trees around our school," says Bassam. "This was a combat mission to us. Why? Because the soldiers, when they come to the village and they see a flag, they were crazy. They did everything to put it down. They shoot it until it's burned." The little gang also scrawled graffiti against Jews, because it drove the IDF soldiers crazy. For Bassam and his friends, Jews and Israelis were synonymous, and the only members of either group they'd ever encountered were the heavily armed IDF soldiers who yelled at them in a language they didn't understand.

Bassam's anti-IDF activities grew from there. Then one day, he and his friends found a crate of unexploded Jordanian grenades in the mountains. They decided to use them to try and kill Israeli soldiers. Bassam was in full support. In fact, he wanted to throw one of the grenades himself. But his limp was a problem. Since he couldn't keep up, his friends said Bassam had to stay behind or he would slow them down if they had to escape. So when his gang of friends perched on a low roof in the village to attack an Israeli military convoy, Bassam wasn't anywhere near them. One of his friends pulled the pin and tossed the grenade, but since they were only kids with no training on how grenades worked and no internet to look such things up on, they missed their target. The grenade exploded a good distance from the convoy. No one was hurt.

Immediately after the attack, the Israeli military raided every home in the village and interrogated the residents. Bassam's family had no idea he was involved. And the police didn't know either. They were just rounding up people at random to interrogate and abuse. His brother Jamal—who is three years older than Bassam—watched from his grandfather's house as the IDF started its sweep. Jamal tells me he saw the soldiers beating random people with sticks. Eventually, the IDF raided their grandfather's house, too, and beat Jamal, Bassam's other brothers, and their uncle before hauling them off to jail, where they beat them more. Bassam wasn't there. He was hiding with his friends.

When he finally got back home and saw Bassam, Jamal told his little brother, "I want to catch this criminal who threw the hand grenade." Jamal, too, hated the Israelis, but he also hated whoever the dumb Palestinian was who threw the grenade.

"Yes," Bassam agreed. "Me too. If I meet him, I will kill him." Then a few days later, Bassam's friends threw a second grenade at the IDF.

It also missed its targets. Bassam was disappointed. He and his friends, Bassam tells me, seriously wanted to kill Israelis. They weren't manipulated by adults into throwing the grenades, nor were they naive about how deadly the weapons could be. They wanted to inflict severe, painful, and total suffering.

About a year later, in 1985, when Bassam was seventeen years old, one of the members of Bassam's gang was arrested for something else and ended up confessing to the Israeli police about the grenades. Bassam and the others were immediately arrested. Despite the fact that he hadn't been there when the grenades were thrown, and no one was killed or even injured, Bassam was sent to prison to serve a seven-year sentence for committing terrorism. His friends received longer sentences—fourteen, fifteen, nineteen, and twenty-one years.

It's important to note here that the 1999 United Nations treaty the International Convention for the Suppression of the Financing of Terrorism defines a terrorist act as one "intended to cause death or serious bodily injury to a civilian, or to any other person not taking active part in the hostilities in a situation of armed conflict." Israel signed this treaty in 2000. Under this definition, what Bassam and his friends did isn't technically terrorism; they were trying to attack a military convoy, not civilians. But "terrorism" is the word Bassam uses to describe his own acts. It's also the way his offenses were described in the charges brought against him.

But his trial was conducted in Hebrew, which Bassam didn't speak at the time, so he couldn't understand what was happening. It wasn't until years later, when Bassam was applying for a travel visa, that he saw case files from his conviction. As Bassam tells it, the charging papers said he had put "the Israeli civilians in dangerous situations"—even though there weren't any Israeli civilians for miles around the attack, just IDF soldiers.

Was this mischaracterization by the Israeli prosecution a

deliberate lie or an unconscious example of what psychologist Robert Sternberg calls "stories of hate," which we, eventually over time, unquestioningly believe? After all the mental hurdles that get us to hate, Sternberg explains, that hate ends up becoming a simplified one-sided story we tell ourselves over and over again, to the point where our biased retelling becomes more powerful in our minds than actual truth, which in turn makes it harder to take in examples or evidence that counter our story, so our own version just keeps getting more deeply reinforced.

And thus, we all rewrite history to make ourselves and our group the besieged "good guy" bravely standing against the evil enemy. Terrorists do this, too. The reality is that terrorism is not the province of purely irrational, innately hateful people, whose somehow preternatural evil existence is distinct from our own.

It's tempting to believe that. Demonizing others as irreparably evil both reinforces the fragile sense of our own inherent goodness and justifies a host of aggressive attitudes or actions against those others, to which our own moral standards would otherwise object. In other words, demonizing others reinforces our own narrative in which we are the victims of those evildoers and thus justifies hate and violence against them. But what if we're all victims and, to some extent, perpetrators of hate? And what if pointing fingers and hating each other isn't just wrong but counterproductive?

Specifically, the struggle against terrorism has been hobbled by the common belief that terrorists are psychopaths. Of course, some terrorists probably are in fact psychopaths—literally lacking the capacity to empathize with and care for others. But psychopaths are estimated to make up just 1 percent of the population. Discussing his book on psychopathy, writer Jon Ronson cited research that found that "you're four times more likely to find a psychopath at the top of the corporate ladder than you are walking around the janitor's office." Also, psychopaths by definition don't feel remorse, whereas many terrorists feel justified in their terrorism *due to* the suffering of their loved ones and community. Terrorism specialist Bruce Hoffman writes of terrorists, "Rather than the wild-eyed fanatics or crazed killers that we have been conditioned to expect, many are in fact highly articulate and extremely thoughtful individuals for whom terrorism is (or was) an entirely rational choice, often reluctantly embraced and then only after considerable reflection and debate."

That some Palestinians choose to express their political views through violence—and suicide bombings in particular—is, in context, "neither irrational nor desperate, but rational and calculated," writes Bruce Hoffman. Palestinians view such attacks as "the only way to convince Israeli decision makers that the Palestinian people will never yield to coercion."

"In the Middle East, perceived contexts in which suicide bombers and supporters express themselves include a collective sense of historical injustice, political subservience . . . as well as countervailing religious hope," writes cognitive anthropologist Scott Atran. "Addressing such perceptions does not entail accepting them as simple reality; however, ignoring the causes of these perceptions risks misidentifying causes and solutions for suicide bombing." In other words, we don't have to accept the suicide bombers' stories or perceptions as objectively real, but we have to deal with the reality that they believe them, and ideally the conditions that cause those perceptions, too.

At the same time, this supposedly "rational" calculus feeds an equally "rational" reaction on the part of Israelis to perceive the Palestinians as inherently and inexorably violent. Of course, Palestinians think that Israelis are the ones with the entrenched institutional violence problem. "If we can fulfill our goals without violence, we will do so," Mahmoud al-Zahar, cofounder of Hamas, told a reporter in 1995 just after the first intifada, a spate of violent uprisings and attacks in Palestinian territories. "Violence is a means, not a goal." Yet the violence committed by both Palestinians and Israelis for decades—whichever you think is worse—has only led to more violence, and in turn to more justifications for claiming victimhood.

The mind-changing truth that my time with Bassam Aramin and others in the region helped me to see is that the real reason we have such a persistent problem with hate is that we all do it and we all believe that our hate is justified. The vast majority of people who hate—even extremists who commit violence in the name of hate—are ordinary people who also love and worry and fear and care, and who can point to a number of what to them feel like well-justified reasons for their hatred. We don't just hate for the sake of hating. We hate because we feel under siege, and hate is our response. That's as true of terrorists as it is of bullies.

After giving me a tour of the village, Bassam takes me to the nice white stone McMansion sort of house on a hill that belongs to his brother Jamal. Sitting in the receiving room, a formal space just off the entrance where guests are entertained, with comfy overstuffed couches and a taupe-and-red plush carpet with flecks of gold thread, I'm confused. I figure that the late-night raids Palestinians keep telling me go on almost every night throughout the West Bank—where the IDF shows up unannounced, bangs on the door, and ransacks the house, and even sometimes takes over the house for a few hours or a few days to turn it into a military outpost—that doesn't happen in a nice house like this, right? So I ask Bassam's brother whether his home has ever been raided.

"Of course," Jamal answers in a straightforward way, as if I had just asked for another cup of tea.

But, I'm thinking, *not often, right?* "When was the last time?" I ask.

"Three days ago, in the middle of the night," Jamal answers, again nonchalantly. Israeli soldiers pounded on the door and inspected the home at two in the morning, apparently for no other reason than to disturb the sleep—and sense of security—of this fifty-two-year-old man and his wife. They weren't suspected of a crime, let alone an unpaid electric bill.

But a former Israeli soldier I spoke with said the main purpose of the raids, as it was explained to him during training, is just "to make our presence felt."

Later, my Palestinian translator suggests I cross the separation wall between the West Bank into Jerusalem by going on foot through the Qalandiya checkpoint. Like Jamal's home, much of the West Bank feels surprisingly normal, in spite of all the scary hype I'd heard as a kid. Cities like Ramallah and Hebron are filled with busy shopping streets and cute little cafés that could easily be mistaken for parts of downtown Brooklyn. Sure, I notice the ridiculously potholed streets and the fact that there are gleaming Israeli settlements in the middle of impoverished Palestinian villages, but I'm really not that aware I'm in a conflict-ridden militarized occupied territory until I try to leave.

The *Times of Israel* newspaper has called the Qalandiya checkpoint the region's "most infamous crossing." I shuffle through one full-body turnstile and then another, from one metal cage into another, like a cow in a stockyard. In another cage, I wait for a faceless voice to press a button so the group I'm with can go through yet another full-body turnstile and show our papers to an agent behind bulletproof glass, then put our belongings on a scanner, then wait for another turnstile and then another before we can finally exit. It's more than inconvenient; I feel dislocated and resentful.

It's midday and it's not even that crowded, yet the whole process is claustrophobic and intimidating and to move a distance of what amounts to about four hundred yards takes sixteen minutes. And I don't have to do this every single day in a land where my ancestors once were free.

"The quintessential Palestinian experience, which illustrates some of the most basic issues raised by Palestinian identity," writes Columbia University history professor Rashid Khalidi, in his foundational text, *Palestinian Identity: The Construction of Modern National Consciousness*, "takes place at a border, an airport, a checkpoint: in short, at any one of those many modern barriers where identities are checked and verified. What happens to Palestinians at these crossing points brings home to them how much they share in common as a people. For it is at these borders and barriers that the six million Palestinians are singled out for 'special treatment,' and are forcefully reminded of their identity: of who they are, and of why they are different from others."

I understand why Palestinians blame the Israelis for their suffering and therefore hate them. But to be clear, I also understand why Israelis feel justified in hating Palestinians—not just because of what I was taught growing up but because of what I directly experienced on my trip, too. At an Israeli settlement in the West Bank where I spent time, a community leader tells me how his ancestors once lived free in the land he calls Judea and Samaria, and he recounts story after story of Palestinians trying to kill Jewish settlers, explaining that the walls and security are just necessary precautions against these unprovoked threats.

At one point, when I'm touring a Palestinian refugee camp, a group of school-age kids starts jeering at me. Then a girl in the group who's maybe eleven or twelve years old, a few years older than my daughter, gets a kitchen knife and jabs it in my direction.

We're standing a hundred yards or so apart from each other. I'm not in any real danger. And she's just a kid. But my heart skips a beat. I could, in a matter of seconds, be seriously hurt. Then the guy leading my tour tsks at the kid and my translator gives her a maternal upbraiding in Arabic, and it's all over. They ask if I'm okay and I laugh it off, but the truth is I was a little scared.

I experience the competing stories that both sides tell. The problem is that aspects of both stories are true, and at the same time neither is true. So no one feels wrong, but everyone is wrong to some degree. Just like they don't feel wrong to hate, even though their hate is never truly justified.

The influential psychologist Erich Fromm divided hate into two basic types, "rational, reactive" hate, which he described as "hatred which is essentially a reaction to an attack on one's life, security or ideals or on some other person that one loves and identifies with." Then there is what Fromm dubbed "character-conditioned" hate, which he described as irrational and felt by "people who are hateful as a condition of their character." One can see how this applies through the lens of the fundamental attribution error—that *our* hate is "rational, reactive" but *theirs* is "character-conditioned." But over time, those distinctions become muddy. As Robert Sternberg writes, "According to Fromm, hatred may arise irrationally because of long-standing, deep-seated prejudices of one group against another, or rationally because of the view of an out-group as taking away economic or other resources from the in-group." But in the case of a dynamic like Israel/Palestine, past "rational" hate—for instance, over land being occupied or people being killed—ossifies into a more all-encompassing deep-seated prejudice so skewed from reality that it's "irrational."

Is the division really helpful then? The takeaway for me is that while perfectly rational people can end up being hateful and rationalizing their hate, that doesn't mean the hatred itself is actually rational. And certainly indulging in that hatred by acting on it—whether through physical violence or verbal aggression or even unconscious discrimination—is not rational or, for that matter, right. Having reasons to hate doesn't make hate reasonable. Which is the conclusion Bassam came to in prison of all places.

One might expect that going to prison, especially at such a young age, would intensify one's hatred. Indeed, incarceration often only worsens criminal behavior—one of the biggest perversions of our disastrously expansive prison-industrial complex. And in fact, initially when he was in prison, Bassam would indulge in hateful fantasies, imagining "every day, maybe, to kill thousands and thousands of Israeli soldiers." Then sometime around the middle of his prison term, the Israeli guards showed a movie about the Holocaust. Bassam decided to go watch, because, frankly, he wanted to see Jews being killed—he was sort of trolling the prison and the guards for even showing the film. "I wanted to enjoy," Bassam confesses to me, "to see someone killing and torturing them."

But somehow, witnessing the brutality of the Holocaust shocked Bassam and tore open a seam in the story of hate he'd believed up until then. The film made him weep, opening his eyes—and mind and heart—to the suffering of his enemy. Nineteenth-century poet Henry Wadsworth Longfellow wrote, "If we could read the secret history of our enemies, we would find in each person's life sorrow and suffering enough to disarm all hostility." Perhaps that's what happened to Bassam.

Startled and searching for answers, Bassam befriended an Israeli guard in the prison. "It's forbidden for him to talk to you," Bassam explains, but nonetheless he "succeeded to open a dialogue." Bassam peppered the guard with questions about Israel and religion and life in general. It was the first time he got to know an Israeli not just as a threatening apparatus of the state (though of course he was also that) but also as a human being. And it was the first time Bassam recognized the suffering of the other side.

"It's not the Israelis' fault," Bassam tells me. He has come to see "how it's difficult to grow up as a Jew everywhere around the world—everywhere," because of that deep history and psyche of persecution, believing that everyone hates your people.

"I don't hold on my shoulders three thousand years of slavery and discrimination and the Holocaust," Bassam tells me. And then the failed terrorist blows my mind. "I found it easier to be a Palestinian," Bassam says. It was as though, through a chain of events that began with that movie, Bassam not only suddenly understood the concept of competitive victimhood but also the absurdity behind it. Many others who have journeyed out of hate have experienced the same sort of sudden mind-opening inflection point, which then leads to a longer process of awakening.

When Bassam got out of prison, he enrolled in graduate school and got a master's degree in Holocaust studies. Over time, he came to appreciate the story that Israelis believe with respect to Palestine, which he articulates: "We occupied it, God gave it to us, Europe and the UK gave it to us after the Holocaust. Finally, we have this safe place, and never again. We are the weak nation. Everyone hates us. We need to survive." Bassam says he now understands why many Israeli Jews push back when challenged about their own human rights abuses. "Where were the human rights while we were going to the ovens?" Bassam says they must be thinking. And he's right.

Of course, this is a simplified version of the way Israelis, and Jews more widely, think. Bassam could write a full dissertation on the topic. But in the midst of this profoundly divided hateful context, it's striking to hear a Palestinian so succinctly and empathetically distill the perspective of Israelis. To me, it's a stunning testament to the power of compassion, and to how learning about the nature of hate—and the experience of those we hate—can help us combat the problem.

Bassam's wisdom can be hard for his fellow Palestinians to accept. Some consider him to be a traitor to their cause, seeing his vision for peace and his work together with Israelis in Combatants for Peace as a form of concession that the Palestinians will never regain control of the territories. He and other Palestinian peace activists are accused of promoting "normalization," meaning acceptance of the current conditions. Indeed, "normalization" is a dirty word I heard thrown around during my time in the West Bank, spoken as a synonym for "assimilation" or even "capitulation."

But it turns out Bassam isn't advocating for normalization. He throws me for another loop when I ask him why he decided to get a master's degree in Holocaust studies. "If you know your enemy, then you can defeat them," Bassam says to me. Wait, what?

"You still call them your enemy?" I ask.

"Of course."

"They are still your enemy?" I say, still confused, making sure we weren't misunderstanding each other.

"Yes," says Bassam. "They occupy my land, so we are enemies. We are not friends. We are not brothers."

"So you can have compassion for your enemy?" I ask.

"Absolutely." At which point, once again, my mind is completely blown.

Maybe I've been thinking about this the wrong way. I've thought that friends and allies are the people you love and enemies are the ones you hate, so if you don't want to hate anyone, that means not having any enemies. Not that I ever really believed

I could not have enemies, but I thought that was the proper aspiration. I mean, I have enemies: Donald Trump is my enemy, and so are a lot of the right-wing activists and writers and trolls who regularly attack me, and to not call them my enemies would feel disingenuous, even feckless. But I thought that considering them my enemies was a defect on my part, that I was kowtowing to my angry, oppositional instincts because the enemy construct is integral to the concept of hate.

Instead, Bassam's point suggests disaggregating the concept of enemy from the feeling of hate. After all, according to the *Oxford English Dictionary*, the word "enemy" describes a "person who is actively opposed or hostile to someone or something." In other words, by definition, it's not that *you hate them* but that *they hate you*. So even if hate is something our enemies do and cherish, something that may literally define them—it doesn't have to define us. Whatever history and rationales and perceptions we have, and however much we think the "other side" hates us, whether we ourselves choose to hate those others or not is ultimately entirely our decision. And Bassam has clearly decided to consciously and deliberately reject hate, even after suffering a tragedy that would seem to make his compassion for Israelis unfathomable.

In 2007, one of Bassam's six children, his ten-year-old daughter, Abir, was walking home from school arm in arm with her little sister. By then, Bassam and his family were living in Anata, a town in the West Bank that is technically in East Jerusalem but that is carved up by the separation wall on three of its four sides. Abir and her sister were on their way to buy candy when an IDF jeep turned onto the road nearby. As Bassam understands it, a group of other children from the school threw stones at the jeep. Through a small hole cut in the jeep's window, the IDF opened fire. Abir was hit in the back of the head with a rubber bullet from a distance of thirty yards or so. When she was shot, Abir's small body flew several feet into the air before falling sharply to the ground.

The *New York Times* reported that Abir was killed during a "clash." The Israeli government denied that Abir was killed by the IDF, claiming that she was killed by one of the stones the Palestinian kids had thrown, or even that Abir was holding some sort of grenade that exploded—trying to blame the victim and pathologize the innocent. In a 2010 civil suit filed by Bassam and his wife, and with the help of Israeli lawyers, a judge ruled that Abir had indeed been killed by a rubber bullet fired by an IDF soldier and that "that the bullet that struck Abir was fired recklessly or in violation of open-fire orders." But no criminal charges were ever brought against the officer who pulled the trigger. Like systemic police violence against black Americans in the United States, IDF violence against Palestinians is rarely officially acknowledged, let alone treated as a crime.

According to B'Tselem, the Israeli Information Center for Human Rights in the Occupied Territories, in 2007—the year that Abir was killed—Israeli security forces killed 373 Palestinians. At least 35 percent were civilians who were not taking part in any hostilities when they were killed. And of the total, fifty-three—or more than one in ten killed—were minors. This data is by many accounts incomplete, but by comparison, in the same year, Palestinians killed a total of six members of Israeli security forces and seven Israeli civilians.

As of 2014, for the almost fourteen years that B'Tselem has been tracking data, there have been 8,166 conflict-related deaths—7,065 Palestinians and 1,101 Israelis. "Put another way, for every 15 people killed in the conflict, 13 are Palestinian and two are Israeli," reports the data news site Vox. Then again, maybe trying to compare is part of the problem.

As we sit in his apartment in Anata, Bassam tells me what Abir was like as a little girl, how she loved playing with her friends, how she enjoyed school, and how on the day she was killed she'd just taken a math test she'd studied hard for. Bassam is smoking a cigarette and reaches to rub the back of his buzz-cut head, smoke curling around the collar of his shirt as his eyes well up with tears. He tells me how he fought with his daughter the morning she was killed; she left the house without saying goodbye. I think of all the times I've yelled at Willa and imagine just one of those moments being our last. Then I imagine her little body, pierced by gunfire, being jolted to the ground. As I sit next to Bassam, I feel like sobbing. I don't know how he can not hate every single person involved in even the edges of the institutions responsible for her death. I certainly couldn't do what Bassam did.

During the civil trial, he spoke to the soldier who killed his daughter. The soldier didn't apologize. Arguably, he couldn't even if he wanted to or he would be punished by the military. But Bassam said to him, "In any time in your life, if you come to ask me to forgive you, always, you will find me there. I will forgive you, but not because of yourself, at all. It's because of myself. I want to clean my heart from this anger, because I discovered that I belong to the mankind, and the human being, and because I loved my daughter very much."

Then Bassam told the soldier, "I don't ask for revenge, because I don't take revenge from victims. You are the victim.

"Believe me, it's very difficult to say, but he's a victim," Bassam tells me that afternoon, sitting in his apartment a few blocks away from where Abir was shot.

He takes a deep breath, then in a voice even more quiet than usual, almost as though it's a prayer, he says about the soldier who killed his daughter, "He is not less of a victim than his victim."

Bassam understands at some deep level what I now at least grasp intellectually: no matter how justified it seems, hate is never truly rational. We all have our reasons to hate, but that doesn't make hate reasonable. Our own suffering will never be addressed by competitively denying—or causing—the suffering of others. As Coretta Scott King once said, "Hate is too great a burden to bear. It injures the hater more than it injures the hated." Bassam doesn't just understand these ideas; he lives them.

That is admittedly a very difficult thing to do, especially for those caught up in a cycle of hatred like the Israeli-Palestinian conflict. Even his own son found Bassam's arguments hard medicine to swallow. After Abir was killed, when his son Araab was thirteen, he began playing hooky from school and throwing rocks at Israeli soldiers. After learning about what Araab was up to from his teachers, Bassam confronted him and they had a terrible fight. Araab told him, "I love Palestine, and I want to fight the occupation." And then, accusing his father, "You don't care about your daughter's blood." Bassam made him swear an oath on the Quran that he would never throw rocks at soldiers again. Though Araab did not throw rocks again, it took many more years and a visit to a Nazi death camp for Araab to embrace his father's approach.

When I visit the Combatants for Peace office in Bethlehem, I meet Araab, who is now twenty-two and works with his father in the organization. He's a tall, handsome young man with the same wide, sheepish smile as Bassam.

BASSAM'S SON WASN'T the only skeptic I encountered. In fact, I had one with me during my entire journey. Dareen Jubeh is a Palestinian freelance journalist who sometimes does work for

CNN in Jerusalem, which is how I met her. I hired Dareen as the "fixer" for my trip, to arrange my schedule of interviews and act as translator when needed.

"Bassam is not useful to talk to," Dareen told me when I first arrived in Jerusalem and we were reviewing the interview plan.

"Why not?" I asked.

"Because you say he does not hate?" As she said this, she jerked her head around and made a quiet sound with her mouth that was half disgust, half exasperation. "All Palestinians hate," she said. Dareen knew what my book was about and had agreed to help in part because I was paying her, obviously, but she didn't think I was going to get anywhere on the topic of hate—certainly not here.

"Palestinians hate Israelis. Israelis hate Palestinians," Dareen continued brusquely. "This is a fact; no one can deny it."

In a number of interviews, when I asked someone if they hate "the other side," Dareen made that same little disdainful chirp under her breath, conveying that she thought I was absolutely nuts for even asking. When people answered no, that they do not hate—including a Palestinian man whose child was killed by the IDF; an American Jew living in an Israeli settlement in the occupied territories; and a Palestinian youth activist who condones violent resistance against Israelis—Dareen made her little sound again each time.

"Of course they hate," she said to me once when we got back in the car. "Of course they do! They're just not admitting it." Everyone hates, she insisted. Basically everyone everywhere—but especially in Israel and Palestine.

Throughout our trip together, I worried that Dareen was right. Maybe everyone was just telling me what I wanted to hear and felt too embarrassed to admit they're hateful. Or maybe they were just under the influence of the fundamental attribution error and *thought* they weren't filled with hate even though they really were. I'm usually cynical enough on my own, but Dareen's cynicism was especially contagious.

Nonetheless, Bassam eventually melts Dareen. She is as drawn in by his arguments and his compassion as I am. After Bassam drops us at our car, Dareen and I head back to Jerusalem, rolling over hills dotted with communities on one side and the gargantuan separation wall on the other. Dareen turns to me as we near the highway checkpoint and says, "You were right. I agree with you about Bassam. He is a nice narrative to be part of your book, to be an example for others." She pauses, and then adds, "For Israelis *and* Palestinians."

Pausing briefly again, she smiles and professes, "I'm so happy to be in this experience."

Suddenly, I feel as though I've seen another small crack open in the giant wall of hate we're driving by. In the middle of such a deeply despair-filled place, I realize I'm feeling something entirely unexpected—a profound sense of hope. I smile broadly back at Dareen.

MANY LONG-STANDING CONFLICTS like that between Israelis and Palestinians are referred to as intractable; they seem impossible to resolve. Yet conflicts can change just like our minds and hearts can, often through a pivotal experience, as was true for Bassam watching the film about the Holocaust. It was also the case for Chen Alon, an Israeli Jew, another founding member of Combatants for Peace, and a lecturer at Tel Aviv University. As a soldier in the IDF, Chen was patrolling one of the checkpoints at which Palestinians must show permits in order to cross into Israel—like the one I crossed—when he had an epiphany. He writes:

I was asked to allow a taxi full of sick Palestinian children (who didn't have a permit) through to the hospital in Bethlehem. At the same time, I got a phone call from my wife telling me she was having problems picking up our three-year-old daughter from kindergarten.

So there I was, standing on a sand blockade talking to my wife, while sick Palestinian children were waiting in the car. I couldn't bear it any more: on the one hand I was a kind, devoted father, and on the other hand I was being so callous with these people. Were these children nothing more than potential terrorists?

My children were human, and yet we had dehumanized the Palestinian children entirely.

Soon after, Chen signed a petition against the occupation of the territories and went to jail for refusing to serve in the IDF. Later, after helping found Combatants for Peace, Chen created a "theater of the oppressed" program within the organization, borrowing from the work of Brazilian practitioner Augusto Boal, who saw interactive theater as a way to help people understand and envision social change. Chen stages performances in public spaces, which dramatize the violence of the occupation. He explains that it helps inform Israelis, many of whom have never even been in the West Bank or the Gaza Strip. "I think it's a form of knowledge, which is able to avoid, bypass or subvert obstacles such as the resistance . . . to feel for the other or identify with the other."

The public performances Chen stages and the conversations that Combatants for Peace facilitates in general are powerful forms of connection-speech. What I realized learning about their work and traveling around this intensely divided region is that connection-speech is only possible when folks are able to interact.

If we're going to have constructive connection-speech with the so-called "others" we hate, we first need opportunities to be in the same place—another piece of the opposite-of-hate puzzle that I'll call "connection-spaces."

Bassam and Combatants for Peace are creating connection-spaces by bringing Israelis and Palestinians together in intimate and even creative settings to talk and to experience each other's humanity. That's basically the same thing I inadvertently did by going to work at Fox News. That's what grassroots organizations do when they convene town halls and community picnics to talk about the issues neighbors are facing. That's even what protesters are trying to do when they use public action to command public attention, hoping that people will come together in new ways around problems they didn't previously acknowledge.

In communities persistently segregated by race and class and political partisanship and so much more, creating connection-spaces is something we have to do deliberately if we're going to give ourselves and our stories the opportunity to be challenged. We need to meet the people we hate and learn their stories, which means supporting institutions and policies that foster connection-spaces—and also creating our own. Getting outside our hate is about getting outside ourselves, breaking through the physical and mental walls of our own narratives and viewpoints. In his research on the Israeli-Palestinian conflict, psychologist Masi Noor found that the answer to competitive victimhood is "common victim identity"—using the bridge of one's own suffering to connect to someone else's suffering. For example, Jewish suffering in ancient Egypt and in Nazi Germany should help today's Jews understand the suffering of others—and identify with and prevent that suffering. Indeed, part of what has always made me proud to be Jewish is the importance Judaism places on working for the liberation of all people.

If reaching out to each other through connection-spaces is part of the answer, it makes me wonder why we even problematically divide ourselves up in the first place. Is identifying as part of an in-group and discriminating against or even hating other out-groups just part of our human nature? Before I'd even written this book, I once gave a talk about kindness and compassion and overcoming hate, and a guy in the audience came up to me and said, "Yeah, maybe hate isn't inevitable, but seeing difference is. We're always going to see each other as different. That's just human nature." Was he right? As much as Bassam, Chen, and Dareen gave me hope, my experiences in Israel and Palestine still left me worrying that we as human beings are preternaturally disposed to grouping each other, competing with each other, and even hating each other—as much as this secular bat-mitzvah-less Jew prays that's not the case.

THREE

Hating Is Belonging: The Ex–White Supremacist

The essential dilemma of my life is between my deep desire to belong and my suspicion of belonging.

—Jhumpa Lahiri

We are born to belong. "A deep sense of love and belonging is an irreducible need of all people," writes empathy researcher Brené Brown. "When those needs are not met, we don't function as we were meant to. We break. We fall apart. We numb. We ache." And, adds Brown, "We hurt others."

The problem starts when our desire to belong leads us to identify so strongly with a particular social group that we become fierce in our belonging—to the point of engaging in, or at least condoning, harmful otherizing. This capacity to otherize lies deep within us, bred into us through the long course of human evolution. As evolutionary biologist E. O. Wilson writes, "The tendency to form groups, and then to favor in-group members, has the earmarks of instinct."

Otherizing contains within it the potential for cruelty, because establishing some group as different all too readily becomes a justification for conceiving of that group as less than us in some way—less intelligent, less patriotic, less hardworking, less victimized. And that opens the door to everything from aversion to dehumanization to downright brutality. "Our bloody nature . . . is ingrained," writes Wilson, "because group-versus-group was a principal driving force that made us what we are."

Anthropologist Michael Ghiglieri notes that in human history "not only have wars shaped geopolitical boundaries and spread national ideologies, but they also have carved the distributions of humanity's religions, cultures, diseases, technologies, and even genetic populations." But, according to Ghiglieri, war vies with one other thing as the most significant process in human evolution: sex. In other words, it's not just our breaking apart that has defined human history but also our literal coming together. Both are possible; neither is predestined.

In fact, while our tendency to create groupings may be natural, *how* we create those groupings is not. It is a product of that history plus our cultures and habits that shapes how we view ourselves and others, largely at an unconscious level. For instance, for much of US history, Irish and Italian and Jewish immigrants weren't seen as white. Now they are. As biologist Robert Sapolsky, the author of several books on human behavior, writes, "Humans may be hardwired to get edgy around the Other, but our views on who falls into that category are decidedly malleable." Which means hate is malleable, too.

How does that work? How do we come to define certain categories of people and assign them to our in-group or our out-group? And what makes some people *not* as inclined to do that? If stereotypes and prejudice and other sorts of out-group classifications are baked into our society, how do they affect some of us more than others, and how do some people come to resist them or even reject them outright? These were the questions that led me to Milwaukee to meet Arno Michaelis. Arno was a neo-Nazi and a leader in the white-supremacist movement—until he left that life, and that mind-set, behind.

SOCIAL GROUP IDENTITY was a reality in North America from the moment European colonialists arrived. The fact that they even claimed they "discovered" the "New World" was already indicative of hierarchical us/them thinking—to them, the people already there plainly didn't matter. Thus it wasn't just white people who "founded" the United States but white supremacy—the fundamental idea that the white people of the planet are inherently superior to everyone else and deserve to take whatever they want and do whatever they want. Of course, the very idea of "whiteness" is a social construct; as columnist Michael Harriot puts it, it's "just some dumb shit that people made up a long time ago to build a fence around their idea of self-supremacy."

Remember that Thomas Jefferson—he who wrote in the Declaration of Independence that "all men are created equal"—owned more than six hundred black men, women, and children as slaves, apparently not seeing a contradiction between what he wrote and what he did, because, as Jefferson also once said, free blacks were "pests in society . . . as incapable as children of taking care of themselves."

The unquestioned belief in the inherent superiority of white people not only defines the founding sins of our nation but shapes the reality of life in the US today. As examples throughout this book show, everything from the way we vote, to the institutions the people we vote for serve in, to the schools our children attend and the wages and benefits they earn as adults, is inexorably shaped by the fictional superiority of whiteness and, thus, hate. In the documentary *13th*, about the racist history of the US criminal justice system, scholar Jelani Cobb says, "If you look at the history of black people's various struggles in this country, the connecting theme is the attempt to be understood as full complicated human beings. We are something other than this visceral image of criminality and menace and threat to which people associate with us."

Of course, some people have actively and enthusiastically championed the view that whiteness is superior. We call these people "white supremacists." Throughout most of US history, explicit white supremacy played a very public and powerful role in the politics, economy, and culture of the nation. It's only relatively recently that being an overt white supremacist has become more socially stigmatized. Though, again, that may no longer be the case, given the rise of neo-Nazi groups around and since the election of Donald Trump. The Southern Poverty Law Center, which monitors the activity of hate groups, counted 917 white-supremacist groups in the United States in 2016—a rise over the previous year. In particular, the number of anti-Muslim hate groups almost tripled from 2015 to 2016.

In May 2017, the FBI and the Department of Homeland Security warned that "white supremacist groups had already carried out more attacks than any other domestic extremist group over the past 16 years and were likely to carry out more attacks over the next year." Other research suggests that between 2008 and 2016, plots and attacks by the domestic far right—including white-supremacist organizations—outnumbered those by violent Muslim extremists by almost two to one. It's a statistic with which Arno Michaelis is intimately familiar.

Arno was not only a member of a white-supremacist neo-Nazi

group; he was one of the most prominent white-power leaders in North America. In 1987, Arno became a founding member of the Northern Hammerskins in Milwaukee, which evolved into Hammerskin Nation—the largest organized white-power skinhead group in the world. In addition, Arno was the lead singer for Centurion, one of the top white-power bands worldwide. But as with Bassam and my trolls, the thing that surprised me the most about Arno was that he didn't think of himself as especially hateful toward others, even when he was a leader of a bona fide hate group. He just thought he was benevolently, even heroically, looking out for his "own kind." What I ended up learning is that a lot of people who join extremist hate groups don't even really hate the maligned out-group so much as they crave approval from the in-group they've embraced. They're just looking for belonging. The hate comes later.

In Arno's case, he was also often looking for money and food. I'll admit I find it reassuring that one can't make a good living as a racist punk rocker. Arno was always broke. Usually, he would just eat cheap ramen noodles, but whenever he could scrounge together enough change, he would go to McDonald's and buy a Big Mac. And it was on one of the days that he'd found enough change that Arno's life ended up changing forever—thanks to a chance connection-speech moment that gave him a window into somewhere else he could belong.

That day, he went to buy his Big Mac at a McDonald's filled with a cross-section of Milwaukee's black and white and Latino residents, and an older black woman was working the cash register. Arno had seen her there before. She usually worked that shift. Arno ordered his burger and then reached in his pocket and handed the woman his sloppy pile of dimes and pennies and nickels. Which is when she noticed the new swastika tattoo on his finger. "What's that?" she slowly, even carefully, asked.

"It's nothing," Arno whispered, shoving his hand back in his pocket.

Which is when the black woman looked the white supremacist in the eyes and, with a kind voice and even a hint of a smile, said to Arno, "You're a better person than that. I know that's not who you are."

Arno grabbed his sandwich, turned on his heel, and fled. He never went back. But he also never saw his life quite the same way again. His views didn't exactly change overnight, but almost. In fact, one of the most jarring things about Arno's story is not only how relatively casually he left the white-supremacist movement but also how relatively accidentally he'd joined it in the first place.

Arno isn't the product of some especially dark set of life circumstances. He wasn't raised to be a white supremacist by his parents nor lured into it by some malevolent recruiter. It was mostly random happenstance.

Before I met Arno, I watched some videos of Centurion performing. One was of a track from the band's album *Fourteen Words*. "Fourteen words," incidentally, is code for the fourteen-word popular white-supremacist slogan "We must secure the existence of our people and a future for white children." In the video, Arno isn't wearing a shirt, just camouflage cargo shorts and combat boots. Tattoos cover most of his torso and creep up toward his shaved head. He stomps around the stage shouting the verses of the song incomprehensibly and then pauses dramatically, tips his head back, and pulls the microphone even closer as he growls out the band's name during the chorus—as best as I can tell, trying to make it sound like he actually swallowed the devil.

Here are some of the lyrics from the song:

Legions attack
Foes' skulls crack
We'll drown the mud
In an ocean of blood

Jewboy, tremble in fear
Your days are numbered, Centurion's here
We'll leave your kind to wither on the vine
We've made up our minds
To be rid of Jew swine

A few weeks after I watch the video, this particular Jew swine walks into an Indian restaurant in Milwaukee, Wisconsin, to meet the man who wrote those lyrics.

When you enter the Bollywood Grill on North Jackson Street in Milwaukee, there's a small Indian grocery store off to the side. I'm always early to everything, so I stand in the grocery store staring at bags of chapati flour and basmati rice as I debate whether I should text my partner my whereabouts, just in case Arno turns out to be dangerous. This didn't really occur to me when I was traveling around the Middle East, but Dareen was with me. Now I'm alone. And suddenly I wonder whether I'm also stupid. My partner knows I'm in Milwaukee to meet a former white supremacist, but I hadn't bothered telling her the details. Have I made a mistake?

I know Arno says he's left his life of violence behind, but I notice myself still feeling uneasy. This is the second time in as many months that I'm about to sit across from a person who once literally boasted about hating and wanting to hurt Jews. But this time it's going to be just me and him. Should I turn on that tracker program on my phone so that when Arno takes me on a tour later, my partner, Sarah, can find me if she needs to? Can the police track me? Even if I don't turn on that program? How does it work? Why didn't I think this through sooner? Maybe I should Google tips for meeting with former violent extremists? At least Arno chose an Indian restaurant. If he were still really a racist, he wouldn't have chosen an Indian restaurant, right? I'm taking out my phone to ask Siri about some paranoid scenario when Arno walks in.

He's massive. I'm no shrimp myself, at about six foot one, give or take, but Arno towers over me by several inches. And since he's filled out significantly since his ramen-noodle-scrounging skinhead days, the bulk makes him seem even larger. Arno has on a black T-shirt, with a long-sleeve gray thermal shirt underneath. The sleeves are pushed up, and I can see the tentacles of Arno's extensive tattooing—though the pictures are more blurred now than in the Centurion video. Because removing tattoos really hurts, Arno has had most of his white-power tattoos covered with other tattoos. "On the back of this hand, I had what was supposed to be a snake," Arno tells me later, showing me his right knuckles. Now, he says, "It looks more like a tapeworm."

We get our food and sit down. The restaurant is crowded, which is comforting, but that's also a problem. Arno is a very loud talker. Uncomfortably, awkwardly loud. And that would be bad enough were he yelling about sports or movies or traffic. But Arno is talking extremely loudly about his days as a white supremacist. In very explicit terms.

"So a white kid that goes to a mostly black school gets beaten up because of it. We flyer around the school with a swastika that says 'Niggers beware.'" Arno is recounting when he recruited for white-power groups. "Our PO box is on there, and they come to us. They send us a letter. They call our hotline. We invite them over. We get them rip-roaring drunk, telling them the tales of glory."

I'm used to white people avoiding saying the n-word. And even when they say the n-word they drop their voices and try to swallow it in a disapproving whisper. Arno doesn't do this. In fact, maybe I'm just paranoid, but he seems to say the n-word even louder than all the other loud words coming out of his mouth. I'm sitting there thinking about how I can nonverbally make clear to everyone around us that I'm completely not okay with the things Arno is saying, that I'm dying to shout out, "He's the racist, not me!" Incidentally, this is an interesting reflection of *my* craving for belonging and approval among those who self-consciously oppose hate. I'm trying to process all this while I ask Arno about his childhood.

Arno was born in Mequon, Wisconsin, in 1970. Today, as when Arno was a boy, the suburb is pretty wealthy and white—in the 2010 Census, 92 percent of Mequon's 23,139 residents were white, higher than the national average of 72 percent. And in 2015, the median income was $101,986—almost double the national average. More specifically, it's a wealthy white *conservative* suburb. In 2016, Donald Trump won 57 percent of the vote in Ozaukee County, in which Mequon is located. In 2012, Mitt Romney fared even better—winning 65 percent of the county, one of his highest margins statewide.

If connection-spaces are the answer to hate, than the lack of connection in a racially and economically segregated community could be part of the problem. But, of course, most kids from wealthy white conservative suburbs don't grow up to be neo-Nazis, so that can't be the whole explanation.

It's also tempting to paint Arno's parents as the problem. His dad was an alcoholic, and there was a good deal of emotional conflict during Arno's childhood. Arno tells me his father is "an archconservative capitalist fundamentalist," who thinks the free market can solve all problems. Arno pauses for a second, then adds, "I believe there's kind of an inherent racism in far-right political ideology."

I wouldn't put it that way myself, but much of modern conservatism in general reflects an elitism rooted in the implicit or sometimes explicit belief that wealthy white people are inherently superior to everyone else. Still, every conservative isn't an overt white supremacist, so that can't explain everything either.

Plus Arno was also exposed to far-left views at home. "My parents, who I love dearly, are a very odd couple," Arno tells me. "My mother is a quintessential child of the '60s. She's superprogressive, supermulticultural, superliberal."

One could just as easily suppose that Arno's embrace of white supremacy was a backlash against his mother's uberliberalism. But most hippies' kids don't grow up to be white-power leaders either, and I realize my own temptation to blame Arno's parents is self-protective. If I can figure out what these otherwise normal well-off white parents did wrong, then I don't have to worry that my own kid might become a hateful extremist. Just like we don't want to think we're hateful, we don't want to think that "people like us" produce hateful offspring.

Except that they do. For instance, while we might like to think that violent extremists come out of poor "broken" homes and even poor communities that somehow seem "broken," in 1994, journalist Dan Korem published a study showing that the surge in violent gang membership in the late 1980s in the US and Europe was driven by kids from "affluent, upscale communities." In his extensive studies of white-supremacist groups, Pete Simi, a sociologist at Chapman University, who is one of the foremost scholars on domestic right-wing hate groups, found that the members of right-wing hate groups come from a wide range of socioeconomic backgrounds. In fact, another study found that expressions of overt racism by whites were not really motivated by fears around economic competition but by anger about "race mixing"—in other words, not economic anxieties but cultural supremacy. Contrary to popular belief, hate and violence aren't necessarily a recourse of the poor but are sometimes a luxury of the rich. Either way, hate doesn't just fall in one income bracket.

So why then? Why did Arno become a white supremacist? One factor could be that Arno was prone to being a bully and a troublemaker, and the white-power movement embraced and encouraged those behaviors. In sixth grade, Arno actually started a little gang—called the Kids Liberation Army—to challenge how the "teachers were always bossing the kids around."

"We thought we were oppressed, because the teachers wouldn't let us beat up other kids, cheat on tests, extort lunch money—all these things," Arno says, laughing as he explains his unusual twist on competitive victimhood. But the way he remembers it, he wasn't a racist bully and his small little kid gang even had one or two black members. And when he was a bit older and got into breakdancing, Arno tells me, "I hung out with the five black kids who lived in Mequon and a couple other white kids and the Asian kid, and we started a little breakdancing crew."

Arno did, early on, exhibit some insensitivity with respect to hate. In eighth grade, he says, "There was a Jewish kid . . . whose parents had just come from Russia. I didn't care that he was Jewish, but he was a dumpy fat kid, just a target for bullying. So I started bullying him."

Arno drew pictures of a superhero character, but instead of the *S* on his chest like Superman, Arno's character had a swastika on its chest. In Arno's drawings, the "superhero" was decapitating the

Jewish student "and doing all these horrible things to him." Eventually Arno's favorite teacher, Mr. Franzen, saw the drawings.

"Arno, what's up with this Nazi shit?" Mr. Franzen said to him.

"What? I'm just fucking with him," Arno said. "It doesn't mean nothing."

"You know what this means," Mr. Franzen insisted. "You know what the swastika means. You know why that hurts people."

"Whatever. I was just having fun," Arno shrugged it off at the time. "Just getting kicks." But all these years later, Arno tells me, "I remember his disappointment in me stinging."

Mind you, Arno didn't stop bullying the Jewish kid; he just stopped putting swastikas on the drawings.

Don't get me wrong: that story is unsettling. But lots of kids do stupid and mean stuff that intentionally or unintentionally employs our society's bigoted tropes. Obviously, I'm speaking from experience here. However, what strikes me most as Arno describes his youth isn't that it was defined by any particularly strong pattern of pronounced bigotry but rather that his youth wasn't defined at all. Arno was constantly trying to figure out his relevance and find a sense of belonging—floating around from group to group, testing out how he liked them and whether they liked him, and where he might fit in. Which he never quite did.

"Everybody either loved me or hated me. You thought I was great or you just thought I sucked. There really wasn't a whole lot of people in the middle," Arno recalls. "That was my goal—to make sure there wasn't anybody in the middle. I wanted you to either love me or hate me." He says it with conviction, and loudly of course, but I don't believe him. The mom in me sees a lonely kid who desperately wanted to be liked. But Arno insists that he enjoyed annoying people and decided to embrace being an outsider. And that's when he found punk music.

Punk rock has always been deliberately countercultural. It developed in reaction to rock and roll becoming tamer and, as music critic Robert Christgau suggests, "It was also a subculture that scornfully rejected the political idealism and Californian flower-power silliness of hippie myth." Legendary punk manager and photographer Leee Black Childers once described punk as boiling down to "the un-allowed." Certainly, in the United States of the 1980s, especially among white kids, punk was the quintessential music of outsiders.

"I was just getting into the punk scene, and I knew all these thirty-year-old punk rockers all over southeastern Wisconsin and northern Illinois and Chicago," Arno tells me after we both get another helping from the Indian buffet. "I would just go find them and go take off, drink myself into oblivion, pass out on somebody's couch, and piss all over myself."

If his father tried to block the door to the house, Arno was so much bigger that he'd just lift up his father and move him aside. From what I can tell, Arno's parents did try to help him, but in response Arno started spending most of his time away from home. Eventually, he found himself drawn to the skinhead faction within the punk scene, and that led him to the white-power movement.

Skinheads, who shave their heads and wear a uniform of steel-toed boots, a T-shirt, and jeans, are a subgroup of punk rockers. The skinhead style was originally an apolitical working-class counterculture movement—a response to the flamboyant bourgeoisie of the 1970s. But by the 1980s, much of skinhead culture had been appropriated by neo-Nazis. Though not all skinheads are racist, and not all punk rockers are skinheads, racist culture and punk culture have often been intertwined.

"There's antiracist skinheads, there's racist skinheads, and then there's trans-skins in the middle, who really don't give a shit either way—they just want to drink and fight," Arno tells me. "That's who I was then." The drinking-and-fighting kind of skinhead.

"And then I heard Skrewdriver, and that brought me into the racist segment . . . I wasn't like, 'I hate blacks and I need a way to express it,'" Arno nearly shouts, and I wonder if everyone in the Bollywood Grill heard only the part "I hate blacks."

At the time, Skrewdriver was the most popular neo-Nazi band in the world. I didn't know this, by the way. But I looked it up on Wikipedia. Then I found a Skrewdriver song called "White Power" on YouTube and tried listening, but it hurt my ears, not to mention my heart. So I looked up the group on Amazon.com, where I learned that Skrewdriver's albums are still for sale and that their 1984 album *Hail The New Dawn* has fifteen reviews, all except one of which are five stars. I also learned that if you look up white-power bands on Amazon.com, for at least several months thereafter you'll get links popping up suggesting other racist albums you might enjoy. Anyway, to hear Arno tell it, before he heard Skrewdriver he wasn't a racist, and after he heard Skrewdriver he was.

At this point, as Arno keeps talking, I'm losing it inside. I find this part of his story deeply alarming. Arno is seven years older than I am, so by the time I was in high school, punk music wasn't as popular. Also, I wasn't popular. So I listened to lesbian folk. As Arno is talking about Skrewdriver, I start to wonder. Could listening to the wrong music at the wrong time have turned him into a committed, violent racist? After all, listening to the Indigo Girls didn't just spontaneously make me a lesbian, did it? *It had to have been his parents, or the Milwaukee suburbs, or his school environment. Or it was the 1980s. Is there a way to blame Ronald Reagan?* I'm trying to find anything I can hold on to that suggests that Arno's descent into white supremacy wasn't basically just contingent on a chance encounter with the wrong band.

But the more I learn about the nature of white-supremacist groups, the more I realize how plausible Arno's story is—that such random indoctrination is actually rather common. The scholar Pete Simi, who has interviewed more than a hundred former neo-Nazis and Ku Klux Klan members, explains that most white supremacists don't primarily seek to join a hate group; they're just looking for belonging. He says they "slide in" from the side, more due to camaraderie than doctrine, and they don't fully confront the movement's racist beliefs until they're already bonded with the people in the group. "Ideology is important but it's not necessarily the initial attraction that draws the person to the group," Simi writes. "The ideology is often there early on but it's not very crystallized—it's like there may be bits and pieces of the ideology that are attractive early, but rarely do you have someone who has a full appreciation for the ideology and then seeks out the group. Over time, ideology becomes more important as the person becomes more familiar with the ideas."

In fact, there's research suggesting that it's mostly through first choosing to join violent groups that members themselves then learn to embrace violence, which in turn strengthens group identification more. In early thinking on what we might now call "mob mentality," French sociologist Gustave Le Bon wrote in 1895, "By the mere fact that he forms part of an organized crowd, man descends several rungs in the ladder of civilization. Isolated, he may be a cultivated individual: in a crowd, he is a barbarian." That's a pretty extreme version of peer pressure. But Pete Simi says he has met active members of hate groups who tell him they don't even believe in all the facets of the group's ideology—or maybe even most.

Simi's account has been confirmed by other scholars. In 2002, sociologist Ziad Munson published a study of prolife activists in which he found that most didn't join the antiabortion movement because of their deeply held beliefs but, rather, deepened their beliefs by being involved in the movement. In fact, Munson found, "many individuals who become activists are at best ambivalent, and in many cases are decidedly pro-choice, in their views on abortion before getting involved."

Former federal prosecutor and congressional investigator Ken Ballen interviewed over a hundred violent Muslim extremists to understand their motives for participating in attacks against the West. More often than not, instead of finding fierce ideologues, Ballen met people seeking meaning or belonging, who said they found that in terrorist networks and *only then* became radicalized. This is why, when Ballen wrote a book based on intensive profiles of six such extremists, he called it *Terrorists in Love*. One story Ballen tells is of a young couple in Saudi Arabia who were in love since childhood but prohibited from marrying. The young girl was forced to marry a sixty-year-old man who raped her. She then attempted suicide. The young couple both wanted to kill themselves so they could be together in the afterlife, but the Islamic code of their community said they would face eternal punishment for conventional suicide. So instead, they signed up to be suicide bombers, who extremists believe are celebrated in heaven. Hard as it is to imagine, their hateful acts were motivated by love and a desire for belonging—in this case, to each other.

But the nagging question remains: Why find belonging through hate? If the people who fall into hate groups are just normal human beings searching for connection, what the hell is wrong with humanity that we find connection by deliberately disconnecting from and even disdaining others? And don't think this just applies to neo-Nazis. Isn't laughing at a racist joke a kind of hate bonding? Or sitting around a dinner table talking about how stupid the other half of the country is? If we think about it, we all have examples of trying to blend in with one crowd by talking smack about another in large and small ways. "Group processes, like individual processes, are dynamic, not static—changing, not changeless," writes scholar James Waller.

Overall, it's a good thing that we, as humans, like to connect with one another. Indeed, I'm suggesting that *more connection* is an integral part of the solution to hate. But we also need to address the dark side.

For some reason, whenever I think about tribalism, I think about the summers I spent as a preteen at the Jewish Community Center Day Camp outside of Allentown, where every summer we would have color wars. The camp was divided into teams—red and blue and yellow and green—and we would "fight" each other in swimming races and games of capture the flag. I especially remember competing every year in a match to see who could eat a giant handful of saltines and then whistle first. I was really good at that. The color wars were mostly fun, but we kids took them seriously—including wearing clothes in our designated team color for the week and taunting the other-color teams with name-calling and pranks.

I always thought it was fascinating how a group of kids who were otherwise friendly with each other, even close friends during the rest of the summer, could suddenly be turned into viciously warring factions just because we were randomly assigned blue or yellow. Then I read about the Robbers Cave study and it all made sense.

In 1954, social psychologist Muzafer Sherif invited twenty-two white Protestant middle-class boys around the age of twelve to spend three weeks at a free summer camp staffed by University of Oklahoma faculty. Robbers Cave was the name of the campground, and thus the study. Sherif divided the boys into two groups, and for the first week, neither group met the other. In fact, for several days, they had no idea another group was at the camp; they were carefully kept apart by the researchers.

During that time, the boys roamed the property, picking their favorite activities—one group spending a lot of time at a swimming hole; the other, canoeing in a creek. The groups were intentionally given a number of tasks that required them to work together for a common goal, and as Sherif and his team stood back and watched, the boys cooperated in their groups and established norms dividing up duties, like who would carry the canoes or who would gather wood for the campfire. The kids even decided to name their groups. One group called themselves the Rattlers, and the other called themselves the Eagles.

Then, after a few days, Sherif had the groups learn about each other's existence. In one case, the staff told the boys. In the other case, the boys overheard the other group playing baseball. Immediately, both groups asked the staff if they could compete with the other group in games. Sherif wrote that their discovery of one another "heightened awareness of 'us' and 'ours,'" and that it led to "an intense desire to compete with the other group." That's not all it led to. One boy in the Eagles group was overheard referring to the Rattlers as "those nigger campers," though he hadn't yet seen them and all the kids were white anyway. But apparently, in that little white kid's mind, blackness went with otherness.

In the second week of the study, Sherif indeed pitted the groups against each other in a number of athletic competitions, and the animosity heated up, spreading beyond the playing field. After the Rattlers won a baseball game and then a tug-of-war contest, the Eagles stole the Rattlers' flag, set it on fire, and then rehung the charred remains. The next day, when the Eagles won a game, the Rattlers ransacked their cabin. The Eagles threatened to collect stones and attack the Rattlers, but the adults stopped them. Still, by the end of the week, the two groups were starting fistfights and calling each other "dirty bums" and "sissies"—not incidentally, insults tinged with classism and sexism.

What Sherif showed is that merely separating children with otherwise extremely similar backgrounds into arbitrary groups and then putting them in competition against each other was all it took for them to start hating the "other." In Sherif's words, their hate was "experimentally produced from scratch." Yet there was one more week to go in the study—and curiously, it's this last part of Sherif's research that's least often reported on. What happened next is as encouraging as the first two weeks were depressing. But we'll come back to that.

In a completely different study, conducted in 2007, Katherine Kinzler and her colleagues at Harvard showed that our tendency to identify with an in-group to a large degree begins in infancy and may be innate. Kinzler and her team took a bunch of five-month-olds whose families only spoke English and showed the babies two videos. In one video, a woman was speaking English. In the other, a woman was speaking Spanish. Then they were shown a screen with both women side by side, not speaking. In infant psychology research, the standard measure for affinity or interest is attention—babies will apparently stare longer at the things they like more. In Kinzler's study, the babies stared at the English speakers longer. In other studies, researchers have found that infants are more likely to take a toy offered by someone who speaks the same language as them, and that even among those speaking the same language, infants prefer the accent of their own family to a "foreign twang." Psychologists routinely cite these and other experiments as evidence of our built-in evolutionary preference for "our own kind."

But a major takeaway from first two weeks of Sherif's Robbers Cave study is that while our inclination to divide the world into in-groups and out-groups and to be hostile toward out-groups may indeed be innate, the way we devise those groups is not. "Human beings are consistent in their codes of honor but endlessly fickle with reference to whom the codes apply," writes evolutionary biologist E. O. Wilson. In distinguishing between in-groups and out-groups, Wilson continues, "the precise location of the dividing line is shifted back and forth with ease."

There's actually a field of academic study, called "minimal group theory," that shows how readily we can apply our in-group/out-group instincts to otherwise nonsensical categories. For instance, neuropsychology researcher Jay Van Bavel conducted a study in which white subjects were first tested for racial bias and then randomly assigned to mixed-race groups—which were nicknamed the Lions and the Tigers. Van Bevel then retested the white subjects, and they showed lower rates of racial bias—just because they suddenly had this incredibly thin identification with a multiracial grouping. What Van Bevel found was that "merely belonging to a mixed-race team triggers positive automatic associations with *all* the members of their own group, irrespective of race."

So while kids as young as six have shown a strong preference for their own racial group, just as important is research that shows that kids before that age *don't* show racial bias. And even with older kids who do show racial bias, scientists can readily induce artificial in-group biases that quickly override racial prejudice.

Case in point: in 2001, psychologist Rebecca Bigler and her colleagues at the University of Wisconsin–Madison conducted a series of experiments with elementary school kids during a summer program that lasted three to six weeks. At the start of each experiment, the researchers gave some of the kids yellow shirts and other kids blue shirts to wear. Again, I think of color wars . . . but this was different. In a control group, the kids just wore the shirts and went on with their summer program activities as usual. In one experimental group, the teachers never discriminated against the kids based on their T-shirt color but simply gave labeling cues. For example, the teachers would have the kids line up according to T-shirt color or use the shirts to form groups for activities. Then in another version of the experiment, there were motivational posters displayed around the classroom that mainly showed kids in blue shirts in the victorious roles—winning a race, being elected class president, and so on. All the students in that experimental group were told that the posters reflected the accomplishments of kids in the prior year's program.

So what happened? Perhaps not surprisingly, the kids who saw all the blue-shirt motivational posters developed significant pro-blue-shirt bias by the end of the experiment. But even in the version when the colors of shirts were simply pointed out in supposedly neutral ways, the kids still developed biases. They consistently assigned more positive traits to their own color group. They also essentialized each other, seeing less variation among individuals in the groups than the kids in the control class did. "Kids started to think the blue was different from the yellow," Bigler writes. "What comes very quickly after that is, 'the blues are better than the yellows.'"

Artificially created minimal groups can induce in-group bias and out-group discrimination in adults, too. In 1973, social psychologist Henri Tajfel conducted a "minimal group" study in which groups of teenage boys were shown several paintings and then told (falsely and at random) that they had demonstrated a preference either for the art of Paul Klee or for works by Wassily Kandinsky. Then later, when they were tasked with distributing resources, the

Klee lovers discriminated against the Kandinsky lovers—and vice versa—even though there was no real benefit to themselves in discriminating. The study, Tajfel wrote, "established social categories on an explicitly random basis without any reference to any such real similarity."

It's safe to say we don't have a baked-in biological instinct to deny resources to fans of turn-of-the-century Russian artists, just like these studies and plenty of others show that we don't have biological instincts to categorize each other by skin color or ethnicity or race, let alone discriminate against people accordingly. Those categories are also made-up—but they're made up by our entire society, instead of just some research team.

Racial justice advocate Bryan Stevenson, who was one of my professors in law school, often says, "Slavery didn't end in 1865. It evolved." In particular, says Stevenson, the narrative of racial difference—of inherent white superiority and inherent black inferiority, which justified slavery and segregation and all manners of violence past and present—has never been fully repudiated. "While we passed civil rights laws, we never confronted the damage that this narrative of racial difference did and continues to do," Stevenson says.

The tendency to form groups may be written into our evolutionary DNA, but the groups we actually see and give meaning to—and thus the divisions around race or other categories that we perceive—are products of the historical and cultural DNA of our nation. That means they are deeply ingrained in us, but that doesn't mean they are inherent or inevitable. "We might have natural biases to favor some groups over others, but apparently we are not natural-born racists," concludes cognitive scientist Paul Bloom in his review of the research in this area.

In fact, salient though our historical and cultural in-group and out-group tendencies may be—especially around identities like race or sexuality or economic class—it's incredibly profound to realize that even these deep societally forged and reinforced categories of hate can be overruled in a matter of minutes by a researcher saying that you're in the Kandinsky group or you're one of the Tigers. Thus the inverse is also, thankfully, true. Even though our brutal, hateful history may prime us toward certain patterns of otherizing, we have the capacity to change.

So while Arno Michaelis certainly has—and takes—personal responsibility for his racism, he's the product of the same biology and social conditioning as the rest of us. There's something equalizing about that but also terrifying—remember that Arno wasn't looking to be a white supremacist but rather was looking for belonging and "slid into" explicit racism. And the fact that he could slide into racism says just as much, or even more perhaps, about our society's propensity for replicating racial bias and hatred than it says about Arno. Also, Arno isn't the only person who, in searching for belonging, "slid into" being a neo-Nazi.

Angela King is now the deputy director of Life After Hate, a group of former American right-wing extremists who now counsel others on escaping hate movements. Two decades ago, Angela was a member of a racist skinhead group and eventually went to prison for participating in the armed robbery of a Jewish-owned store. Angela tells me over the phone that as a child she was horribly bullied, and so she became a bully to protect herself: "I pretty much told myself that if I'm the one doing the bullying, no one can ever humiliate me again." From there, she became socially isolated. "I didn't have people to count on," Angela says. "I didn't have a solid group of friends. I didn't feel like I was accepted." Angela searched for belonging everywhere she could find it, including joining a local gang. But when she was raped, she fled and fell in with a group of Nazi skinheads. She says she wasn't looking for hate. She was looking for somewhere she could feel safe and connected—and she found it in a hate group.

Angela's friend Tony McAleer is on the phone, too, and he chimes in: "It's meeting the wrong person at the wrong time in a state of vulnerability." Angela, Tony says, was "looking for something to latch on to."

Tony ought to know. For years, he was a recruiter for the White Aryan Resistance, and when he was recruiting young people into the movement, he didn't try to hook them with overt racist messaging but instead by addressing their need for belonging. He sees the same strategy in ISIS today. "If you look at ISIS recruiting techniques for kids in Europe," he said in an interview with *Vice*, "it's not like they sell it on the idea of becoming an Islamic scholar. They find these kids who are almost delinquents, and they sell them on the sense of purpose and a sense of meaning that they can find through the group."

Still, why not join a chess club? Or if you're into violence, some sort of weird kinky sex group? Does our desire to belong to some in-group have to lead to hating some out-group? No, evolutionary biologists say. Whatever groupings we define, we have the biological capacity to hate those groups or help them. We're hardwired for both.

Maybe just like sex and violence sell in Hollywood, they also sell, so to speak, in anthropology museums—because whenever I take my daughter, Willa, to some natural history museum or another, there are always sprawling dioramas of prehistoric humans decapitating each other or something equally brutal. But undoubtedly, off to the side in a tiny cabinet, is a collection of the tools they worked together to fashion and a rendering of the primitive villages they built. Even the Greek and Roman history displays seem to emphasize war and violence way more than ideas and architecture and art. Why is it that we pay more attention to the history of competition than the history of cooperation?

The fact is that for hundreds of thousands of years as we evolved from apelike knuckle draggers into the modern upright creatures we are today, we lived in nomadic tribes where different members of the group took responsibility for either hunting or gathering or protecting everyone from predators. "Modern groups are psychologically equivalent to the tribes of ancient history," writes biologist E .O. Wilson, and our preference for our in-group could be like an evolutionary nod of gratitude.

Some experts on human evolution have tried to argue that intergroup violence was common in this early era, and thus that violence toward out-groups is also probably innate, supposedly the root of war and of mass atrocities as humanity evolved. But increasingly, scientists agree that human beings are not—or at least not only—naturally inclined to be hateful and violent, and that our tendency to form groups is not necessarily correlated with any tendency toward violence.

In fact, we humans also have as strong, or even stronger, instincts toward empathy, altruism, and cooperation with others. Having conducted an exhaustive study of the evidence about early human violence, cognitive scientist Steven Pinker concluded that, "Human nature may embrace motives that lead to aggression, but it also embraces motives like empathy, self-control, and reason, which, under the right circumstances, can outweigh the aggressive impulses."

"Humans have a capacity for warfare—nobody's denying that," anthropologist Douglas Fry says. "But to make it a central part of human nature is grossly out of contact with the data."

Additional evidence for this view comes from our closest

biological relatives, chimpanzees. Psychologists Martin Schmelz and Sebastian Grüneisen in Leipzig, Germany, trained a group of chimps to play a sharing game. On the one side of the game was a young female chimp named Tai, and Tai had a choice of four ropes to pull. One rope would give just Tai herself a banana pellet; one would give another chimp a pellet; one would give them both pellets; and the last rope would allow Tai to skip her turn and instead let the other chimp choose which of the four ropes to pull.

But here's the thing: unbeknownst to the other chimps, the researchers had trained Tai to always pull the last rope, thus giving her turn to the other chimp. So what did the other chimps do? Fully 75 percent of the time, they pulled the rope to give both themselves and Tai a banana pellet—in a sense rewarding Tai for her behavior.

But the real test of cooperation came next. The team repeated the experiment, but after Tai gave up her turn, the other chimps had the option to give themselves four banana pellets and none to Tai or give both themselves and Tai only three pellets. So giving Tai pellets would mean getting *fewer* pellets themselves. In a control test, the subject chimps shared the pellets just 17 percent of the time, but when they saw that Tai had forgone her turn and given it to them, the chimps shared the pellets 44 percent of the time—even though it meant they got fewer pellets themselves. This study, and many others like it, confirm that even our mammalian ancestors are hardwired for the sort of reciprocity that Schmelz and Grüneisen call the "landmark of human cooperation."

And so are we. In another study, thirty-six chimpanzees and thirty-six eighteen-month-old humans were each placed in a room with a human stranger and some object the stranger pretended to clearly want. The object was out of reach for the stranger—but not for the chimps and toddlers. When the stranger reached for the object but clearly couldn't get to it, the majority of chimps and toddlers would help the stranger by handing him or her the object, even if the chimps and toddlers didn't get any rewards for their kindness themselves. "The only species difference found," the researchers report, "was that the helping of human infants was faster." The toddlers were even quicker to altruistically help the stranger.

Psychologist Frans de Waal, who has spent his career studying primates and comparing their behavior to human nature, argues that this sort of compassion and kindness traces back through ancient evolution—"probably as old as mammals and birds." So while the desire for belonging may be part of what draws people into hate groups, that innate pull toward empathy turns out to be a powerful antidote to extremist hate. Just as the search for belonging brought Arno into white supremacy, finding that sense of belonging elsewhere was what helped him escape.

First, Arno became a dad. He had met a woman named Cassandra. "Cassandra was one of the original Chicago Area Skinheads, which was the first white-power crew in the country," Arno explains. "She looked like Scarlett Johansson. She was just absolutely fucking drop-dead gorgeous, and I was just like, 'Whoa.'"

Apparently, more than "whoa" was exchanged between them, and, a year later, their daughter was born. They named her Mija, the Nordic spelling of Mia—a proper Aryan name. But soon, Cassandra had addiction problems. She and Arno split, and he got custody of Mija. Suddenly, he was a single father.

And then a close friend of Arno's in the neo-Nazi movement went to prison, and another was shot and killed. Especially as a new father, those events left Arno jolted and questioning the life he was leading. So he started searching for a new life.

"I left the movement in 1994," Arno tells me, "and by 1996, I was in a filthy, dilapidated warehouse on the South Side of Chicago at four in the morning on a Saturday, shaking my ass to house music with three thousand people of every possible ethnicity, sexual orientation, and gender identification on earth—and like full of MDMA, and fucking loving every second of it."

Arno felt accepted. "I'm sitting on the floor, spun out of my mind on ecstasy," Arno recalls. There's a woman sitting next to him. "We're giving each other back rubs and doing ecstasy stuff." Which I guess means the touchy-feely stuff one apparently does when on ecstasy; I wouldn't know.

"She's holding my arm in her lap, and she's going like this on the swastikas," Arno says, caressing his own forearm.

"She's like, 'What is that?'"

"I'm like, 'I was a skinhead. I feel really bad about it.'"

"She's like, 'Not anymore, are you?'"

"I'm like, 'No, not at all.'"

"She's like, 'Oh, okay.'"

And then Arno jerks his head and shoulders back and forth to imitate dancing and makes a techno-music *doosh, doosh, doosh* sound to show that it was that easy—that was all it took—and they went back to dancing. "That's how everybody was," Arno says.

"Gay black people, and transgendered people, and people who I would have attacked on sight—they all accepted me and filled that gap, that hole in my life that the movement left there. And it was so much nicer."

There's at least one lesson here: ecstasy and hot girls are more enjoyable than cheap beer and drunken brawls. I'm not speaking from personal experience myself, but I'm pretty sure this is true.

"Once I took a step out of this ideological box I had placed myself in, it became a run," Arno tells me. He ran from his old life and embraced his new one with the same zeal.

"What about the rest of your social scene?" I ask. "All of your friends?"

"It was all replaced within a year by the rave scene."

Being a white supremacist had given Arno a sense of belonging, but it turns out so did raves. And the music was better, the drugs were better, and he liked the people more. Almost as quickly as he'd slipped into the neo-Nazi scene, Arno slipped out—and found another place he could belong. These days, Arno is off booze and drugs altogether and is a practicing Buddhist. Really.

If Arno's transformation strikes you as frighteningly, even ridiculously, casual and accidental, I'm right there with you. At first, all it took was the wrong *band*, and now just the right *party*? The control freak in me wants both entering and leaving hateful extremism to be significantly more deliberate—like something involving a roving band of jackboot-clad recruiters, who are as easy to identify as their targets and, thus, easy to distance yourself from or disrupt. Hearing Arno's story makes me think about people I know who've had heroin or crack addictions. You imagine that doesn't happen to "normal" people, and then you realize a bunch of normal people you know are suffering or even dying. The things we don't think can happen to "people like us" are often already happening all around us.

Activist Michael Skolnik made this point about white supremacists in the aftermath of a pro-KKK march in Charlottesville, Virginia, in 2017. "White people, it is time for us to have a serious conversation with our families, our friends (past and present), our co-workers, college roommates, high school classmates, sports teammates, our neighbors, our church congregations and youth groups, our fraternity brothers and sorority sisters." What he means is that it's not *those people* who are participating in these most explicit and extreme forms of hate—it's *our people*. And sometimes *us*. We have to help lead the way out.

For Christian Picciolini, another member of the Life After Hate organization, his mind-set started changing when he opened a record store that sold white-power music but also punk and ska and metal, too. Suddenly, he was interacting with a wider range of people. "They were black people and Jewish people and gay people and Hispanic people," Christian says about his customers. "I couldn't deny the fact that I started to bond with them over things like music and the neighborhood."

It was through music that Megan Phelps-Roper and @Jewlicious bonded, too.

As for Angela King, her life changed when she was convicted of robbing that Jewish-owned store and met black and Latino women in prison. "I was shown kindness and compassion from people I felt I least deserved it from," Angela tells me. "I was disarmed by their kindness. I had no idea what to do with it." And for Tony McAleer, like Arno, a big part of his transformation was becoming a parent. Tony recalls "feeling safe to love again because it's safe to love a child. They can't reject you," he says. "They can't shame you."

Our innate desire for belonging can be harnessed for bad or good—for altruism or for hate. Belonging to a family, belonging to a compassionate community, even belonging to a hopped-up mess of techno dancers, can lead to inclusion and equity and justice just as much as the desire to belong can lead to hate. This is where connection-spaces are important—creating opportunities for us to get out of our proverbial bubbles, either accidentally or deliberately.

But to be clear, connecting over our essential human sameness doesn't mean ignoring or papering over the differences between us. Just like the hometowns we come from and the sports teams we root for, our gender and sexuality and ethnicity are important and valuable parts of our identities. For example, some conservatives like to suggest that even acknowledging racial classifications—say, for purposes of pointing out inequity and proposing solutions—is tantamount to racism. Yet sociologists like Eduardo Bonilla-Silva, author of *Racism without Racists*, argue that the idea of "color-blindness" functions as an ideology that actually makes us blind to the less visible but still insidious forms of bias in ourselves and the institutions around us.

Remember that in Rebecca Bigler's study of elementary school kids, it wasn't just wearing the blue T-shirts or yellow T-shirts that created biases but the fact that the kids were treated differently because of their T-shirt colors. Now imagine that the differences aren't shirts you can take on and off but rather skin color—with all the history and habits of either privilege or discrimination inextricably woven in, such that the kids with dark skin get *treated* differently than the kids with light skin. Is the answer to ignore the problem? If, for instance, teachers are treating kids differently because of their society-imbued identities, how can we solve that if we're not even supposed to talk about those identities? As Justice Harry Blackmun wrote in a 1978 Supreme Court ruling upholding affirmative action, "In order to get beyond racism, we must first take account of race. There is no other way." Connection-spaces must be used to facilitate thinking that helps us identify and thus start to unravel patterns in our discriminatory perceptions, from which discriminatory treatment flows. We can understand and respect each other's differences while simultaneously recognizing our common humanity.

Which, in a nutshell, is what Muzafer Sherif found in the final stage of his Robbers Cave experiment. Recall that during the first week at the camp, the two groups bonded and formed distinctive group identities as the Rattlers and the Eagles. When they learned about each other, they were eager to compete, and when Sherif pitted them against one another in various games, such as tug-of-war, and offered them prizes, they went on the warpath. But in the third and final week of the study, Sherif changed the terms of their situation yet again. And just as easily as he had artificially created us/them distinctions, fierce competition, and even hatred, Sherif then made all of that no longer matter.

All it took was a few shared experiences—situations that forced them to work together to solve problems. At first, Sherif and his team blocked a pipe so suddenly that both the Rattlers and the Eagles had a water shortage they had to solve. The next day, the staff said they could rent a movie to watch, but only if the all the campers could help pay for it. Then, en route to an overnight camping trip, one of the vans "broke down." The kids all pitched in to fix the van, and the next day when it "broke down" again, all agreed they could share a van for the rest of the trip. By the last night of camp, the boys were sitting all mixed together "with no regard for Rattlerdom and Eagleness." Sherif, who had been conducting opinion polls of the boys throughout the study, found that "overwhelmingly hostile sentiments about 'the others' had been replaced by overwhelmingly positive feelings." After camp ended, on the ride back to Oklahoma City, the van stopped for snacks. The Rattlers, who had extra prize money from their contest victories, spent it to buy malts—for themselves and the Eagles.

Of course, real life is infinitely more complex than the situation of a group of boys sequestered at a summer camp for a few weeks. But like those boys, we can use our instincts to form and bond with in-groups to fan resentment and hate toward out-groups—or to broaden our sense of in-groups, redefine and expand our circles of moral inclusion, and ignite mutual understanding and empathy.

Incidentally, Arno Michaelis still thinks of himself as white. He didn't disguise or ignore his identity; he just stopped being a white supremacist. Our identities aren't the problem. The choices we make around those identities—the meanings that we and society give them—that's the problem. Arno made one choice for part of his life and then changed his mind and made a different choice. We can also make different choices and turn away from hate.

We've mostly been talking about explicit, conscious hatred—like the kind embraced by overt white supremacists. As I've said, though, my definition of hate is much broader and includes unconscious bias, too. Perhaps it's obvious that explicit hate isn't inevitable—we've thankfully seen it wane at times in our history. But unconscious bias and hate seem harder to solve, in part because they're more pervasive and because, by definition, we may not even be aware of them. How should we think about and address the hate that we may not even know we have?

FOUR

Unconscious Hate: The Trump Supporter

If you love peace, then hate injustice, hate tyranny, hate greed—
but hate these things in yourself, not in another.

—Mahatma Gandhi

It would be comforting to think that the only kind of hate in the world is the conscious, explicit sort we see in overt white supremacists. Then we'd know exactly what we were up against and could target it equally explicitly, like publicly calling out neo-Nazis when they march in the streets (something a lot of people, though not Donald Trump, were quick to do after the Charlottesville demonstrations and violence in 2017). We've been recently reminded that there are plenty of carbon copies of the old Arno Michaelis, plus more modern mainstream versions, like the so-called "alt-right," and that many political leaders and organizations in the US still openly express explicit hate toward immigrants and Muslims and transgender people. But in a country literally built on the enslavement of black people, which later instituted segregation policies and condoned lynching, overt hatred is thankfully not as widely socially acceptable nor politically embraced today as it once was. That's why so many white Americans have been surprised by the recent surge in white supremacy.

Let me be clear. I believe that most Americans today really don't consciously subscribe to racism or most other overtly bigoted beliefs. Even still, African Americans are incarcerated at five times the rate of whites and receive harsher sentences for the same crimes. Women earn less than what men earn for the same work. LGBT youth are disproportionately more likely to be homeless. Unemployment rates for black and Latino Americans are almost double those for whites. If we're no longer, by and large, overtly bigoted, how do these blatant injustices persist?

A large body of research assigns some of the blame to our unconscious biases—or, as the academic community calls them, "implicit biases"—the attitudes and misperceptions that are baked into our minds due to systemic racism and pervasive stereotyping across society. As products of a sexist society, we all have a bias in favor of men and masculinity and against women and femininity. As products of a racist society, we all have a bias for white people and against people of color. As products of a classist society, we all have a bias for rich people and against poor people. And so on. We don't consciously hold these beliefs; they're like deep-down reflexes we've habituated to over time. They're encoded in our brains and, in turn, they play out in ways that then reinforce society-wide bias.

Writing about persistent racial inequities, sociologist Eduardo Bonilla-Silva observes, "The main problem nowadays is not the folks with the hoods, but the folks dressed in suits. The more we assume that the problem of racism is limited to the Klan, the birthers, the tea party or to the Republican Party, the less we understand that racial domination is a collective process and we are all in this game."

Systemic racism, though, can be hard for white folks to see, because it's not targeted at them and we don't talk about it as a society. As Bonilla-Silva points out, while most whites believe that racism is synonymous with overt or explicit prejudicial thinking or action, for people of color, "racism is systemic or institutionalized." Communities of color live out the myriad effects of systemic racism on a daily basis. Many of us who are white don't acknowledge the realities of systemic bias partly because we don't really understand the experiences and perspectives of those communities we're biased against, and partly because we don't want to. It can be unpleasant to admit our own biases.

Also, some people use overt bias to argue that implicit incarnations aren't the problem, as if to say: "See that inequality you're complaining about. It's that really racist guy's fault, not mine." Doing so makes us feel better about ourselves—at least we're not as bad as *that guy*! But the fact that blatant racism persists doesn't negate the fact that unconscious bias is real and widespread, or that our social and political institutions are warped by it.

Is it appropriate to call implicit bias a form of hate? Yes, I argue that it is. Hate doesn't have to be conscious. Actually saying out loud that women are inferior to men and should be treated as such is clearly hateful, but what if you just think it but don't say it? Or what if you think it but don't realize you think it? Is that just as hateful? Certainly all of these biases are rooted in the same history and habits of hate in our society, and certainly they all in turn shape our attitudes and behaviors, and the world around us. It's not all the same kind of hate, or even as awful, but still, unconscious bias is hate. In making this argument, Bonilla-Silva and I have an unusual ally—my friend the Tea Party activist and prominent Trump supporter Scottie Nell Hughes.

"How do you define racism?" I ask Scottie Nell one night over dinner in California, where we're speaking together at a conference.

"Hatred," she replies easily.

"Say more."

"Racism—it's valuing one person's life over another because of a physical feature or preference," Scottie Nell explains.

"Consciously or unconsciously?" I ask. "Does it have to be conscious?"

"I think it's both," Scottie Nell answers. "I think hate can be unconscious." Here, we agree. But then things get tricky. Acknowledging that some people subconsciously hate others is one thing, but admitting that "some people" includes ourselves is harder. Maybe it's because I'm particularly self-deprecating that I have less difficulty admitting that I, personally, have unconscious hate, and that over time I've learned to notice it in my perceptions and actions. That's where Scottie Nell and I diverge. While Scottie Nell agrees that unconscious bias is real and that it constitutes hate, she doesn't necessarily agree that everyone is biased. Certainly she doesn't think that *she* is biased.

SCOTTIE NELL WAS one of the most prominent Trump supporters in the news media during the 2016 election as an on-air commentator and colleague of mine on CNN. I first met her at the Conservative Political Action Conference (CPAC) in 2012, when I was still at Fox News. I'd been invited to speak at some side event, and I went because I'd always been curious about the annual gathering of what I considered the "presentable right"—the strong right-leaning part of the conservative movement that wear bow ties and work in think tanks. Like a lot of political conferences, CPAC sets up a media row in a big room, with booth after booth of the usual suspects. As I was strolling the hall, I heard a squeal in my direction. It was Scottie Nell Hughes. She ran over from the Tea Party News Network, where she was news director at the time, to say hello. We'd been on air a few times together at Fox but never in the same room, so this was our first chance to meet in person.

We exchanged hugs and pleasantries and took a selfie. I remember Scottie Nell defending me to a handful of other conference-goers, who were leaning away from me like I was poison.

Since appearing on CNN seemingly every other day or more during the 2016 elections, often debating Scottie Nell or other Trump supporters, like Kayleigh McEnany, Jeffrey Lord, and Betsy McCaughey, strangers on the street constantly come up to me and ask how I stop myself from punching them in the face. The honest answer is, I've never wanted to.

Sure, I'll admit that once or twice, or maybe six dozen times, I've wanted to scream at them—like when Scottie Nell said that it was sexist of Hillary Clinton to say that she's showing little girls they can grow up to be president, too. Clinton, according to Scottie Nell, was trying to "tear down" boys in order to "build up" girls. At which point every nerve ending in my body wanted to ring out: *Dear God in heaven, are you fucking kidding me? Hillary makes one tiny comment alluding to 270-plus years of institutional inequity, and for that you wanna call* her *sexist?!?!* But I didn't say that. Nor did I hit Scottie Nell. Although I did hold hands on camera with my fellow panelist, writer and activist Michaela Angela Davis, as both of us tried desperately to keep our composure. Scottie Nell Hughes doesn't think she is being sexist, nor that Donald Trump is sexist, but Hillary Clinton *is*? Seriously?

In fact, as Hillary Clinton told CNN's Fareed Zakaria in the wake of the 2016 election, "I think sexism and misogyny are endemic in our society." She would probably say everyone is guilty of gender bias to some extent. And she'd be right.

By comparison, during the first presidential debate, NBC's Lester Holt asked her, "Do you believe that police are implicitly biased against black people?"

Hillary Clinton answered, "Implicit bias is a problem for

everyone, not just police. I think, unfortunately, too many of us in our great country jump to conclusions about each other. And therefore, I think we need all of us to be asking hard questions about, you know, 'Why am I feeling this way?'" Clinton also said, "We've got to address systemic racism in our criminal justice system."

The right wing exploded. Days later, Donald Trump said that Clinton was "suggesting that everyone, including our police, are basically racist and prejudiced." Then vice presidential candidate Mike Pence, in his own debate comments, laid into Clinton. "Enough of this seeking every opportunity to demean law enforcement broadly by making the accusation of implicit bias whenever tragedy happens," Pence fumed. Pence went on to note that some of the shootings of unarmed blacks were by black officers. His implication was that disproportionate police violence against the black community can't be due to implicit racial bias, because black cops do it too. But Pence is wrong on this. Everyone is biased.

"There's way too much research on implicit bias to deny its existence," conservative columnist William Saletan wrote in response to Pence. "'Implicit bias' isn't an accusation. It doesn't mean you're bad. It means you're normal." And because implicit bias is normal, normal people have it. That means black people, too.

This is one of the things that white college students have in common with black police officers—they're all biased. Why? "Blacks and whites receive the same narratives and images that perpetuate stereotypes of black criminality and flippancy while synonymizing white culture with American values," writes Theodore R. Johnson, a former navy commander who is a fellow at the New America think tank. In an article in the *Atlantic*, Johnson writes about discovering his own implicit antiblack bias as a black man after taking the Implicit Association Test (IAT), the test most commonly used to measure implicit bias. Johnson writes, “My own hidden biases punched me in the gut.”

As I was eating dinner with Scottie Nell, I thought back to a trip I’d taken with her a year before. It offers a stark reminder of how biases and stereotypes are ingrained in our minds but how hard it can be for any of us to see them.

In October 2016, Scottie Nell and I find ourselves together in Farmville, Virginia. Vice presidential candidates Mike Pence and Tim Kaine are at Longwood University for their one and only debate during the election campaign, and Scottie Nell and I are both there for CNN’s coverage. Long before this debate, Farmville played a far more important role in US history. In 1951, black students at Robert Russa Moton High School staged a walkout to protest the intolerable conditions of their segregated school, and to challenge segregated education in general, a vestige of Jim Crow laws that persisted in Virginia and nationwide. Ultimately, the Moton High walkout helped lead to *Brown v. Board of Education*. When the Supreme Court struck down school segregation in 1954, three-fourths of the plaintiffs in the case on which they ruled came from the Moton school. But it wasn’t until 1959—and only under federal pressure—that Virginia finally started the process of integration.

Prince Edward County—where Farmville is located—didn’t want to integrate its public schools, so the country just shut them all down instead. For five years, Prince Edward County had no public schools. White kids flocked to all-white private schools that were being created in response to integration. The county’s black students crammed into churches and living rooms as volunteers from the community and some teachers from up north tried to give the students the education they were missing. It took another Supreme Court case to force the county to reopen its schools in 1964.

The school is now a museum, and Scottie Nell and I have a little downtime. Side by side, we walk through the halls of the former Robert Russa Moton High School without speaking. Each room captures a snippet of history, with photographs and text that explains what happened then, but the history you can't see in each room, what that space represents, is palpably heavy. We're both trying to read as much of the wall texts as we can, taking it all in.

After a long while of moving from room to room in silent contemplation, I finally speak. "This is just so awful," I blurt out. I don't know what else to say, but I want to say something.

"Yeah, it really is," Scottie Nell replies. And then we both take a deep breath at the same time, followed by more silence. Because really, what more is there to say?

Then, maybe a minute later, Scottie Nell adds, "But thankfully it wasn't everyone who supported this."

"Huh?" I respond. "What do you mean?"

"Well, I mean, thankfully most of the white people thought this was wrong," Scottie Nell says. "It was just some bad apples who supported it."

"No, Scottie Nell, it wasn't," I say, trying to sound earnest but probably sounding as shocked as I feel. "It was *most* of the white people. The *vast, vast majority* of the white people supported and defended segregation." A 1942 poll confirms this. It asked Americans whether "white students and Negro students should go to the same schools." Only 30 percent of Americans—nationwide—said yes. In 1956, the same question was asked, and support for integration still fell below 50 percent. And that's just the people who were willing to admit it to the pollster.

I turn and face Scottie Nell. "I like to think that if I'd been alive back then, I would have fought against segregation," I say. "But the odds are, I wouldn't have. That's just a reflection of the reality of the time that I would have been a product of, just as much as anyone else."

"You don't know that!" she says, raising her voice and becoming more and more visibly upset. "You don't know what your ancestors thought or what they believed."

Clearly, Scottie Nell has never met my racist grandfather, but that's not the point. The point is statistics. "I know that the vast majority of white people back then supported segregation, and the odds are that I would have been one of them," I say.

Not because I'm an evil person but because that's how hate works—when it's all around us, we soak it in and regurgitate it. In the case of the US in the 1950s, we're talking about explicit aggressive racism, but the same is true of unconscious bias.

"I wish that wasn't true," I say to Scottie Nell, "but it is."

This statement about the past seems to bother Scottie Nell in the same way as Hillary Clinton's statement about the present—the implication that it's not just a fraction of white folks who prop up injustice but, somehow, all of us. Scottie Nell feels that when I and pretty much everyone on the left use terms like "implicit bias," we're really just calling her a racist.

I try to never call anyone a "racist," because the word can be "triggering" (another word I try not to use, because it, well, triggers people's reactions). Being called racist instantly puts people on the defensive. In 1950s Virginia, the term was certainly widely called for, and even now, colloquially, we tend to think "racist" refers to someone who is a deliberate, explicit bigot.

Let me say for the record that I don't think Scottie Nell Hughes is a deliberate, explicit bigot. And I don't think the vast majority of

Americans—right, left, and center—are deliberate, explicit bigots. But I do think all of us need come to terms with the fact that we all hold unconscious ideas about the superiority of some groups and the inferiority of others—ideas that may not be expressed like they were in 1950s Virginia but that come from that same history and hateful legacy. And when I say all of us, I really do mean everyone. Myself included. And you, too.

Some brilliant work in neuroscience has explained why. Jennifer Kubota, a professor of neuroscience at the University of Chicago, has focused her research on implicit bias and the brain. Kubota explains to me how stereotypes are encoded in our brains. In particular, Kubota points to the little structure deep in the brain called the amygdala. It's composed of two dense clusters of nuclei, one on each side of the center of the brain, each cluster shaped roughly like an almond—*amygdala* is Latin for "almond."

While the amygdala has sometimes been characterized as the brain's emotion center, and often more specifically as the fear center, that's not quite right. The amygdala doesn't itself generate feelings, Kubota clarifies, and there is no one "center" of emotion. Rather, she explains, the amygdala is involved "in learning about important or threatening or novel things in our environment." And then, when we need it, the amygdala quickly recalls what's been learned so we can just as quickly evaluate whatever situation we're in and respond accordingly. Think of the amygdala like an efficient filing cabinet for everything society has taught us that our brains have absorbed. The amygdala takes in whatever messages are around it—including the endemic racial stereotypes—that percolate through the media and our education practices and our families and every other single aspect of our existence.

So, for instance, if Kubota asks a diverse class of freshmen to list the stereotypes about women in the United States, she says,

"It's pretty remarkable how much consensus you'll get." Everyone can regurgitate the same narrative, "even if they don't personally believe that . . . That associative information is kind of stuck in the system." And the women in the class know the stereotypes as well as the men. In other words, biases are stuck in society's system and, in turn, get stuck in all of our brains—particularly in our tiny almonds. The amygdala doesn't mean to be hateful. It learns to hate from a hateful society.

The unconscious "makes associations based on frequency," explains john a. powell, a law professor at the University of California, Berkeley, who has extensively studied the research on implicit bias. So, for instance, because the news overreports black crime, "at an unconscious level," explains powell, "we'll create a neural linkage between crime and black"—whether or not we even personally, consciously believe black people are more or less likely to commit crime. Implicit biases are like projections of society's biases etched into our unconscious. And it happens to all of us. "It's the air that we breathe," says powell. "You breathe that until you're an adult, you're going to have those associations. Whites will have them. Blacks will have them. Latinos will have them."

Those associations have shown up clearly in brain studies. Most brain research nowadays is done using functional magnetic resonance imaging (fMRI). Blood activity in the brain is scanned, using MRI technology, to measure degrees of brain activity prompted by various stimuli, such as looking at photos. The "functional" part is that it happens in real time; in other words, researchers will say or do something to subjects and watch the subjects' brains "light up" according to which parts are involved in processing the given information. The more a part of the brain lights up, the more actively engaged that part is.

New York University neuroscientist Elizabeth Phelps and her

research team conducted an important study in 2000 that identified the neural signature of negative stereotypes. They built on earlier work that found that the amygdala is activated more when subjects are shown photos of people with fearful facial expressions than when they are presented with photos of people with neutral expressions. This detection of danger, in turn helping trigger fear, is one of the most well-established functions of the amygdala, and neuroscientists have long believed that greater amygdala activation is due to a greater perceived threat.

Phelps's study followed this same basic procedure, but with a twist. Her team hooked subjects up to an fMRI machine and then flashed random yearbook photos of white people and black people, all of whom had neutral facial expressions; none were fearful. The results? "The majority of White subjects," Phelps reported, "showed greater amygdala activation when viewing unfamiliar Black compared to White faces." In other words, seeing unfamiliar neutral black faces triggered fear. Phelps and her team then compared the same people's amygdala activation to their scores on an implicit bias assessment, which they'd taken before the fMRI study. They found that the more implicit bias people had, the more their amygdala lit up.

Her team also used another common measure of unconscious fear to evaluate the white subjects' reactions to the two sets of faces. Called the "startle response," it looks at the magnitude of a person's eye-blink reflex, which is another indicator of fear. The people with higher implicit bias and higher amygdala activity also had more intense startle responses.

How did scientists interpret those results? Their conclusion was that greater amygdala activity indicated that subjects perceived a threat when viewing the black faces. A wealth of subsequent fMRI studies have produced similar evidence of implicit antiblack bias, and, as Elizabeth Phelps and her colleagues sum up the findings, "work on measures of implicit biases has shown that they are pervasive and robust."

A great deal of research has revealed the pernicious effects of implicit bias in people's lives. As john a. powell and a group of other researchers write in a comprehensive report that summarized this work, titled *The Science of Equality*, studies have shown that bias is operating in our schools, our business offices, our medical institutions—and, yes, as Hillary Clinton said, in our criminal justice system.

In the case of medical treatment, studies have revealed that white doctors spend less time, on average, with black patients, discuss their conditions with them less fully, involve them less in the decision-making about their treatment, and exhibit bias in referring them for procedures and treatments and prescribing medications to them. For instance, one study showed that black patients who reported chest pain were 40 percent less likely than white patients to be referred for cardiac catheterization, a standard procedure for measuring heart function. Other studies have shown that black patients are "systemically undertreated for pain relative to white patients."

One of these studies, which examined an extraordinary 60 million cases of pain medication prescriptions written for patients between 2007 and 2011, found that "a black patient with the same level of pain and everything else being accounted for [meaning factors such as age, socioeconomic level, and type of insurance] was much less likely to receive an opioid prescription than a white patient with the same characteristics."

There are equally troubling findings regarding bias in the criminal justice system. One study, published by Stanford Law School professor Jennifer Eberhardt and colleagues, found that "defendants whose appearance was more stereotypically Black" (i.e., darker-skinned, with a broader nose and thicker lips) were sentenced more harshly and, in particular, were more likely to be sentenced to death than if their features were less stereotypically black. The authors explain: "A growing body of research demonstrates that people more readily apply racial stereotypes to Blacks who are thought to look more stereotypically Black," and that "the more stereotypically Black a person's physical traits appear to be, the more criminal that person is perceived to be."

Concerning biases in interactions between police officers and people they stop, another Stanford study made use of footage from police body cameras. The researchers found that "officers on average spoke less respectfully to black residents than their white counterparts," meaning that they were "less likely to be addressed with a formal greeting, titles such as 'sir' or 'ma'am' were infrequent, sharp commands were more common and apologies or expressions of gratitude were rare." They conclude that, "The issue is not overt expressions of racism . . . It is believed that, many times, [the officers] simply do not realize that their words sometimes harm those on the receiving end, who must then determine whether they are the subject of a racist police confrontation."

In studies of classroom interactions between teachers and students, researchers have found that teachers tend to devote less attention to black students and ask them fewer questions in class, as well as offering them less feedback on their work. As reported by *U.S. News & World Report*, multiple studies have also shown that "in college, professors are less responsive to inquiries from students of color, and implicit bias can influence the grades professors give students whose work is identical."

Regarding bias in the workplace, a number of studies have shown that among job applicants with closely comparable skills and experience, white job seekers received 50 percent more calls for interviews than black and Latino job candidates. In one of these studies, researchers sent in résumés they had written that listed exactly the same set of skills and same job experience to over thirteen hundred advertisements for jobs. The only differentiating feature of the résumés was that half of the ostensible applicants had stereotypically black names, such as Lakeisha Washington, and half had stereotypically white names, such as Susan Baker. The résumés with the "white" names received 50 percent more callbacks for interviews. We might expect that some of this bias was actually explicit, but in the main, the researchers assert that the stereotyping of blacks was unconscious.

Often, unconscious bias can be hard to point out, let alone measure. But anecdotally, there are glaring examples. In 2016, when African American high school student Adia Brown entered the room at her school in Denver where she was to take the ACT exam, the proctor, who had never met her and knew nothing about her academic background, told her, "Special education students are tested down the hall." Also in 2016, African American ob-gyn Tamika Cross was on a Delta Air Lines flight when a passenger fell ill. When Cross went to help the passenger, the crew wouldn't allow her to, because they did not believe she was a doctor. After Cross wrote about the incident on Facebook, the hashtag #WhatADoctorLooksLike was started in response, with multitudes of women doctors of color posting photos of themselves in their medical uniforms.

I could write about countless more such experiences of bias, including the subtle acts of discrimination and mistreatment often called "microaggressions," which may be genuinely unconscious to those who commit them but are acutely observed by those they're directed against and have a profound impact on those individuals and our society. As john powell and his colleagues write, they are "replicated in everyday micro-behaviors demonstrating that race affects social perception—such as the clutched purse when a black man enters the elevator, the assumption that a black lawyer works in the mail room or as a secretary."

Thinking that finding a way to specifically measure implicit bias would support better research and documentation and raise public awareness about the problem, psychologists Anthony Greenwald and Mahzarin Banaji created the Implicit Association Test (IAT) in 1998. You can take the IAT for free on the website of Project Implicit, which Banaji and Greenwald run. I did, and I found the design of the test ingenious. The basic procedure is that you're asked to respond to a series of words or pictures flashed on a screen, and the computer measures how quickly you make associations between them. The theory behind the test is that the more quickly we're able to match concepts, the more closely those concepts must be associated in our minds. For instance, we'll associate "ball" and "tennis" more quickly than "ball" and "checkers." That's not because "ball" and "checkers" *can't* be associated—they are, after all, both games—but the association between "ball" and "tennis" is for most people stronger, and therefore happens more quickly in our minds.

The idea at the core of the IAT is that the speed with which we make these unconscious associations can be measured, and then compared, to determine relative bias. So, for instance, the racial bias IAT has you use computer keys to sort pictures of faces as being either "white" or "black." Then you use the keys to sort words like "excellent" and "joy" and "nasty" and "hate" as either "good" or "bad." Then comes the real test—the computer flashes pictures of faces along with either positive or negative words, such as a white face with the word "nasty" and a black face with the word "excellent"—and you have to sort them into one of two categories, "white and bad" or "black and good."

The results from more than two million test takers show that people *of all races* tend to more quickly make associations between "white" and "good" and between "black" and "bad." In the end, the test gives takers a score, ranging from having "little to no automatic preference for white people compared to black people" to a "slight," "moderate" or "strong" preference. Greenwald, Banaji, and their colleagues have since created IAT tests that also attempt to measure bias around gender, sexuality, religion, and more, all of which are available to take on the website.

The reality of implicit bias was understood by the scholarly community well before the creation of the IAT. But this innovative way to measure implicit bias led to an explosion of new research and public debate. The American Psychological Society's magazine called the IAT "A Revolution in Social Psychology." And Malcolm Gladwell, in his best-selling book *Blink*, wrote, "The IAT is more than just an abstract measure of attitudes. It's a powerful predictor of how we act in certain kinds of spontaneous situations."

Yet the IAT has been criticized by some researchers and scientific journalists. The arguments aren't about whether implicit bias is a real phenomenon; on that, there's broad agreement. Even Hart Blanton, a social psychologist at the University of Connecticut, who is one of the leading critics of the IAT, told a reporter for *Wired* magazine, "In general, researchers are comfortable with the idea implicit bias is a problem and word needs to get out."

Rather, critics argue that the IAT is not accurate enough for a person's score to be considered a reliable predictor of the way people think and behave. Critics point out that people may in fact end up with different scores if they take the test multiple times. Anthony Greenwald and Mahzarin Banaji have actually conceded that the test isn't that sort of precise diagnostic, and they caution on the Project Implicit website that people should not consider their scores a firm indication that they necessarily act in biased ways. They say the test should instead be considered a tool for becoming generally more aware of the negative stereotyping that has made its way into all of our minds to some degree. And I'll vouch for it being quite revelatory in that sense. It was for me.

I think that's the vital point about implicit bias that has been obscured by the controversy. The whole point is to just be more self-aware—and that doing so can actually help counter any bias. As neuroscientist Jennifer Kubota stresses, implicit bias absolutely does not *have* to dictate our behavior. If we *are* acting with bias, becoming aware of the problem allows us to consciously work to counter that.

A group of researchers studied the effects of what they called a "prejudice habit-breaking intervention" that involved teaching people about their implicit race bias, and the results were that "people who received the intervention showed dramatic reductions" in their bias. I believe the IAT can do a world of good by helping people simply see what are otherwise hard-to-see biases. For what it's worth, Arno Michaelis, Scottie Nell Hughes, and I all took the race IAT. And we all showed a preference for white people over black people.

DURING MY DINNER with her in California, as we polish off a plate of cheese and tomatoes, Scottie Nell tells me, "You're wanting change by only focusing on the negatives."

"No," I say, "I don't think it's a negative to acknowledge my own bias."

"What are you biased against?" Scottie Nell asks, putting her fork down and staring incredulously at me.

"I'm biased against the exact same things we all are," I answer.

"What?" Scottie Nell presses.

"Well, I'm biased in favor of men against women," I say.

This statement is just too much for Scottie Nell to take. Especially because of the whole me-being-a-lesbian thing, I think.

"Wait a minute. You're in favor of men?" she half says, half laughs.

"Yeah," I say.

At this point, the waitress interrupts to see if we want dessert. No, of course we don't want dessert. We're two women on television, both overly concerned about our weight. And also we're finally getting somewhere in this conversation.

"You mean to tell me you are biased? You're sexist?" Scottie Nell asks again when the waitress leaves.

"Obviously. Of course I am." I regularly assume that men are more qualified and knowledgeable on subjects than women are. I often wonder how my female colleagues got their jobs but don't even think to question the credentials of male colleagues. I try to notice it and catch myself and counteract it, but those biases are there. Not to mention the fact that I'm a butch lesbian who dresses in men's clothing and ostensibly benefits from masculine power and privilege because of how I present in the world—but I didn't think Scottie Nell was quite ready for that level of reflection. So I brought up a different example of my own bias.

"I live in a neighborhood that's segregated block by block but is fairly racially diverse," I tell Scottie Nell. According to US Census Bureau data, New York City is the second-most diverse city in the nation (after San Jose, California), and my zip code is in the top quartile of the most diverse in the city.

"I'll tell you. I mean, I catch myself doing it and try not to do it," I say to Scottie Nell, "but if I see a white person in a Mercedes, I don't even think about it. I just assume they're a doctor or a lawyer or whatever. I just assume they're rich. But if I see a black person driving a Mercedes, I notice it and I wonder why they have that car. That's bias. My bias."

I could try to explain that away as my psyche merely absorbing the statistical patterns of the racial wealth gap, and to some extent, that might be true. There are definitely more rich white people in the United States, and in New York City, and therefore more rich white people likely to be driving a Mercedes. But what my unconscious is doing, when unchecked, is applying that assumption to every case—even when it's completely unjustified or, in fact, discriminatory. I'm not even assuming that 10 or 5 or even 3 percent of the black people with a Mercedes are doctors. If I'm being honest, I'm wondering almost 100 percent of the time if they're drug dealers. That's bias. It's the same bias that made the people on the Delta flight not believe that the black ob-gyn was really a doctor.

In other words, in response to Scottie Nell's question, yes, when I say everyone is biased, I am definitely including myself. Because I grew up in a nation where the news media disproportionately reports on black crime and portrays black people accused of crimes as more sinister, those biases are inscribed on my unconscious. I inherently believe boys are better at science and more aggressive, that girls are sensitive and more creative, also because of society's patterns and messages. All of which, in turn, are regurgitated and replicated in my attitudes and assumptions and actions. Unless I do something about it.

This is where fault and responsibility become complicated. I don't think it's my fault that the United States has a racist, sexist, hate-filled history. But I do think it's my responsibility to do something about it. It's here that my conversation with Scottie Nell breaks down again—and again I think back to that trip to

Farmville in the fall of 2016. Scottie Nell had brought up a story about when she was a freshman in college at the University of Tennessee at Martin in the late 1990s. There was a new program to pair white freshmen with black freshmen as roommates, which we both agreed was a good thing. Coming from a small rural white town, Scottie Nell said she was excited to expand her horizons.

But, as Scottie Nell told the story, even though her black roommate and she came from similar working-class backgrounds, Scottie Nell had to work two jobs during college to pay her bills while her roommate got a full scholarship. And, said Scottie Nell, "That wasn't fair."

I responded, "You're assuming she got the scholarship because she's black, and that's why you feel resentful."

Scottie Nell agreed. "Yeah," she said, as if the point was blazingly obvious: *of course* that's why she got the scholarship! But how did she know the award wasn't based on her roommate's academic performance? Or that her roommate wasn't involved in more extracurricular activities? If her roommate had been white and gotten a scholarship, Scottie Nell probably would have assumed her roommate somehow deserved the scholarship. Why did she *not* assume that because her roommate was black?

But perhaps most significantly, it seems never to have dawned on Scottie Nell that *she*—along with all whites in the United States—might be the one who unfairly benefited from racial discrimination. Founded in 1927, the University of Tennessee admitted white students only for the first thirty-four years of its existence. Those students didn't get in because they were better than black students but because they got a leg up from an exclusionary racist system, in which they didn't have to fairly compete. Exclusion of black students from university admittance compounded the historic economic oppression of black families, further preventing black kids from getting higher-quality jobs and thus continuing to leave generation after generation with little wealth. The result was that by the time Scottie Nell and her roommate were attending college, the national net worth of white households was on average $100,700 higher than the net worth of black households.

It seems not to have occurred to Scottie Nell that the great economic injustice that has been inflicted on black families, and continues to this day, demanded some sort of solution—and that perhaps giving one black student a scholarship to attend one historically white university was a good start. When I brought up the historic injustices that faced her black roommate and her roommate's ancestors, Scottie Nell replied, "Why is that my fault? Why should she be given an advantage over me?"

Now, in California, in the thick of our dinner discussion about bias, she returns to the story with the same plea. Scottie Nell doesn't think it's her responsibility to right those past wrongs. Many Americans feel the same, because in the story they tell themselves about society and everyone's place within it, it just doesn't seem fair. But perhaps that story itself is what's wrong.

In 2016, sociologist Arlie Russell Hochschild published *Strangers in Their Own Land*, a book based on her time immersed with Tea Party members and Trump supporters in rural Louisiana—folks just like Scottie Nell. In it, Hochschild details what she calls the "deep story" that these folks believe, not necessarily a true or factual story but a "feels-as-if" emotional story that is the "subjective prism" through which they see life and the other side of the political spectrum. Here is an excerpt of how Hochschild sums up that deep story:

> You are patiently standing in a long line leading up a hill, as in a pilgrimage. You are situated in the middle of this line, along

> with others who are also white, older, Christian, and predominantly male, some with college degrees, some not.
>
> Just over the brow of the hill is the American Dream, the goal of everyone waiting in line. Many in the back of the line are people of color—poor, young and old, mainly without college degrees. It's scary to look back; there are so many behind you, and in principle you wish them well. Still, you've waited a long time, worked hard, and the line is barely moving. . . .
>
> Look! You see people *cutting in line ahead of you!* You're following the rules. They aren't. As they cut in, it feels like you are being moved back. How can they just do that? Who are they? Some are black. Through affirmative action plans, pushed by the federal government, they are being given preference for places in colleges and universities, apprenticeships, jobs, welfare payments, and free lunches . . . Women, immigrants, refugees, public sector workers—where will it end?

Hochschild shared a longer version of this "deep story" narrative with her many Tea Party interviewees, and they said it summed up their perspectives. And I heard Hochschild's "deep story" in my conversations with Scottie Nell, in her belief that her college roommate was cutting in line with her scholarship while Scottie Nell was being punished simply for being white. How Scottie Nell got to the middle of the line to begin with is largely invisible—she doesn't think about how her ancestors not only cut in line but may have literally beat, enslaved, and killed the people at the back of the line in order to do so. Even if her ancestors didn't hurt anyone, the history and meaning of her whiteness put her in line ahead of others to begin with, just like men were systematically put ahead of her. Still, even if Scottie Nell does think about any of that, she doesn't think it should matter now.

The way Scottie Nell tells the story about her college roommate, it's like a fresh wound, like some moment in the past that is even more painful—and pertinent—today. The line is the way it is. And maybe having to suffer centuries of slavery wasn't fair then, but cutting the line isn't fair now. It was the Italian political theorist Antonio Gramsci who pioneered the concept of "cultural hegemony," whereby the worldview of the elite becomes the accepted social norm. The historically dominant view in the United States that white people should rightfully have more privilege and power is a form of cultural hegemony. And groups who benefit from hegemony don't see their own bias—they just think that's the way things *should be*. As the saying goes, "When you're accustomed to privilege, equality feels like oppression." But to Scottie Nell and so many others, concepts like "privilege" and "implicit bias" are really just politically correct code words for telling people like her to go to the back of the line, and not to feel angry about it, but guilty.

In Scottie Nell's telling, racism isn't what elected Donald Trump. And she's not entirely wrong. Explicit racism played a role—the KKK voters and the alt-right and such—but, thankfully, it isn't embraced by a majority of Trump voters. And yet support for him was run through with white racial resentment and implicit bias. Donald Trump, as writer Ta-Nehisi Coates observes, "is a white man who would not be president were it not for this fact." The white presidents before him "made their way to high office through the passive power of whiteness," Coates writes, "that bloody heirloom which cannot ensure mastery of all events but can conjure a tailwind for most of them." Coates continues:

> Land theft and human plunder cleared the grounds for Trump's forefathers and barred others from it. Once upon the field, these men became soldiers, statesmen, and scholars; held court

in Paris; presided at Princeton; advanced into the Wilderness and then into the White House. Their individual triumphs made this exclusive party seem above America's founding sins, and it was forgotten that the former was in fact bound to the latter, that all their victories had transpired on cleared grounds.

There is an ugly reality to the myth of these individual triumphs. And within that lies an alternative "deep story"—one that is arguably far closer to the truth. In the deep story of many people of color and progressive whites, the American Dream is more like a dog pile than an orderly line—and certain groups of people clambered to the top by stepping on others throughout history and still today.

White families don't have twice as much wealth on average today as black families because white people are smarter or harder-working but because of slavery and segregation and discrimination, through which generations of white people exploited black people for their sole gain. And, yeah, their great-great-grandkids don't own slaves or believe in separate water fountains, but they're still born at the top of the pile because of their race. It's not necessarily that their parents and grandparents handed them places on top because of their disproportionate wealth or education or good jobs, though that certainly happens for some. But the shape of the hill, and who is generally on top versus on the bottom, has been contoured by that bias, which, in turn, actively shapes our lives today.

The people who aren't at the bottom of the dog pile think they got where they are not because of history or luck but because they deserve to be there. And the irony is that these are the people who believe the other "deep story" myth, the one about the orderly line.

The people in the middle and top of the dog pile often *believe* life is an orderly line—when in fact, that's all that the people at the bottom are asking for. The people at the bottom are desperate for the world to work the way that the people at the top insist it already does, for opportunity to be truly equal and for achievement to be merit-based. It seems we can all agree on the ideal. What we disagree on is whether we've already achieved it or not.

That doesn't mean there aren't white people who struggle and even people of color who make it to the top. Of course it's not that simple. See, for example, Barack Obama and Oprah Winfrey. But still, women and people of color and immigrants and poor people and queer folks and people with disabilities see that the deck is stacked against them more than it is for others. Because objective evidence shows it is. And that's what's not fair. Whereas taking away from others the unfair advantage that they've wrongly enjoyed throughout history is, in the grand scheme of things, fair—even if it always doesn't feel that way.

So while I agree with Scottie Nell that it's not her fault or my fault that our ancestors probably would have supported—and certainly benefited from—white supremacy, I think it *is* our duty to do something about it going forward. Sure, it's kind of like having to clean up a mess someone else made. Spend as much time as you want resenting that. But the fact is that a lot like air pollution, that mess is making us all sick. The American Dream has been broken for a long time. Lots of people are seeing their jobs disappear, their wages stagnate, their housing values implode, and their children's prospects dim. In the conservative deep story, we're all viciously competing with one another. In the progressive deep story, we all rise together—or fall.

"What if your roommate had been white and she'd gotten a

scholarship and you hadn't?" I ask Scottie Nell as we continue our dinner. "Wouldn't you then just chalk it up to her somehow deserving it more, or being lucky?"

"Probably," she replies.

One thing I appreciate about Scottie Nell is her honesty. That's basically like admitting that she thinks other white people deserve to be next to her in line, or even ahead of her, but that black people must be cutting. And that right there is implicit bias.

During another one of our conversations, Scottie Nell goes off on Chicago's black community for tolerating poverty and drug use and violence.

"What makes you think they tolerate any of that?" I ask.

"Because they haven't *solved it*," she retorts. Her implication is that the black community caused the problem, and it's their problem to solve, too. I asked Scottie Nell if she thinks that joblessness and drug abuse in the rural white Rust Belt is white people's fault. She gets defensive and insists, "That's different!"

Is it? Ta-Nehisi Coates nails this central hypocrisy in how biased whites misperceive reality: "Black workers suffer because it was and is our lot. But when white workers suffer, something in nature has gone awry." That's the ultimate attribution error playing on our deep implicit biases.

And again, lest you think I'm judging Scottie Nell alone, let's be clear—we all do this. Recently, there was a conference I wanted to speak at, and I wasn't invited. But four white guys and one black woman were. I caught myself thinking that the black woman was only invited because she's black—but, mind you, it never dawned on me that the four white guys were only invited because they're men. Automatically, I assumed the white guys are as equally qualified as I am but the black woman wasn't quite, that she got the slot not also because she was equally as qualified as me but because of her race. That's exactly the same thing Scottie Nell was doing with her roommate, baked-in biases playing out as subtle or not-so-subtle resentment.

Similarly, I've had plenty of "well-intentioned" white friends bemoan not getting into graduate school or not getting hired for some job because "they probably picked a person of color instead"—but of course they're good liberals who support affirmative action, so they quickly add something like "but that's a good thing" after their resentful complaint. I'm sure I've done that, too. Again, there were probably dozens or even hundreds of other white people who were picked instead of them, but the unexamined assumption is that *numerically many more* white folks were *actually* qualified whereas a single person of color would *only* or primarily be chosen because of their race.

"I don't think we're free in America," says criminal justice reform advocate Bryan Stevenson. "I think we are burdened by our history of racial inequality. We have a history of horrific mistreatment of people based on color. And I think that narrative of racial difference that was cultivated to justify that mistreatment has created a kind of smog, and we have all been breathing it in."

Of course, unconsciously perceiving black people to be, say, more dangerous is different than explicitly wanting to subjugate all black people because you believe they are fundamentally and collectively inferior. "People can have implicit racial bias and not have explicit bias," john a. powell tells me. And yet, he continues, "The conscious and unconscious is not disconnected." People who demonstrate explicit bias are also likely to show high levels of implicit bias, powell explains. The biases in society that we absorb into our unconscious are vestiges of the legacy of explicit bias and hate, in which our history is steeped. Pretending otherwise is either self-protective white fragility or denial.

Psychologist Mahzarin Banaji, codeveloper of the IAT, who runs Project Implicit at Harvard, suggests a helpful way of thinking about the relationship between unconscious bias, explicit hate, and society in general. "It would be disingenuous, if not in flagrant opposition to the evidence, to hold that if prejudice is not explicitly spoken, it cannot reflect a prejudice," Banaji writes with IAT research colleagues Anthony Greenwald and Brian Nosek. Instead, Banaji proposes that we think about "the thumbprint of the culture."

"Perhaps we behave in ways that are not known to our own conscious awareness, that we are being driven to act in certain ways not because we are explicitly prejudiced but because we may carry in our heads the thumbprint of the culture," Banaji tells NPR's Shankar Vedantam. And as the research on discrimination clearly shows, that thumbprint leaves a very tangible mark.

In civil rights and nondiscrimination law, intentional discrimination is known as "disparate treatment"—which is basically when an employer or business or government agency explicitly, knowingly treats an individual or group differently because of their gender, race, or religion, etc. But in 1971, the Supreme Court ruled in *Griggs v. Duke Power Co.* that the 1964 Civil Rights Act "proscribes not only overt discrimination but also practices that are fair in form, but discriminatory in operation." In other words, discrimination doesn't have to be intentional to be illegal.

Again, perhaps we can argue that explicit discrimination is on some moral or philosophical level worse, but in *Griggs*, civil rights advocates successfully argued that discriminatory *impact* matters as much or more than discriminatory *intent*. We might make the same argument with respect to bias. Sure, explicit bias is overt, but what matters most is impact—which can be just as pernicious whether rooted in implicit bias or explicit hate.

Undetected hate hiding deep in our brains is still hate. Just like a little cancer is still cancer. You don't want even a smidgen inside you.

Thankfully, researchers are coming up with more and more evidence that interventions work. And so we arrive at the next part of the formula for countering hate, what I'll call "connection-thinking"—the conscious effort to neutralize the stereotypes embedded in our amygdalae. Researchers generally call this "debiasing," and they're getting promising results.

Consider this study: New York University psychologists Daniel Yudkin and Jay Van Bavel had subjects play a game online with other people. In certain cases, the subjects saw one of the other players—actually a member of the research team—steal another player's money. The subjects were then given the choice to punish the thief by taking some or taking all of the thief's money and ejecting that player from the game. What the researchers manipulated was the identity of the thief. Sometimes the subject believed the thief was a fan of the same football team as the subject, but sometimes the thief was a fan of a rival team. Or sometimes the subject and thief were from the same country; sometimes not. Perhaps not surprisingly, given what we've already learned, Yudkin and Van Bavel found that people punished members of out-groups more harshly and went easy on in-group members—whichever way the groupings had been defined. But even more interesting and encouraging was that when the researchers asked subjects to *reflect* before making their punishment decisions, their biases basically went away. They handed out equal punishments to everyone, whether they were in their in-group or their out-group.

In another experiment, Princeton University psychologist Susan Fiske used a simple strategy to erase people's bias. When Fiske showed pictures of unknown black faces to white participants, their amygdala activity predictably spiked. But when Fiske instructed the research subjects to guess the favorite vegetable of the people in the pictures, their amygdala activation remained the same, whether they were shown pictures of white people or black people. Just thinking about what vegetable these unknown folks might enjoy, having to engage in the process of trying to take the perspective of the other, was enough to break down bias.

And remember the study in which Elizabeth Phelps and her team showed people random yearbook photos of black and white people with neutral facial expressions? After observing that most of the white subjects' amygdalae lit up more when shown pictures of black faces, Phelps and her team tried a different experiment. They showed the white subjects the faces of well-liked famous people, both white and black. And this time, their amygdala activation was significantly lower. So, in other words, just knowing people, just having more real-life exposure to "others" changes the way our brains activate in response. That's more great support for the importance of creating more connection-spaces that then help foster connection-thinking.

These are all studies conducted in labs, of course, and life is not a controlled experiment. But one more study I'll cite shows promising signs that if we will acknowledge that we have implicit bias, we can consciously train our minds to disregard it. Talma Hendler and other neuroscientists at Tel Aviv University hooked subjects up to a fancy computer that allowed them to monitor their fMRI results themselves, watching in real time as their amygdala activation rates were being tested. With a little bit of coaching and a lot of encouragement, when they were shown stimuli that were meant to trigger their fear mechanisms and at the same time were shown a screen where their amygdalae were lighting up, people could deliberately lower their amygdala stimulation. Just getting that feedback helped people regulate their own unconscious mental processes.

What that study indicates—and what neuroscientists have been learning through a massive volume of research in the last few decades—is that like a computer, our brains are made up of hardware and software. The amygdala is part of our hardware and performs the same basic functions in all of us—like a processor or memory card in a computer we all buy from the same store. But what each of our particular amygdalae learns to fear or even hate, that's what therapist Athena Staik calls "soft-wired" information—specific coding written by our lives and the society around us. Which means it can be reprogrammed. Doing so starts with awareness.

According to Yudkin and Van Bavel, "Acknowledging the truth about ourselves—that we see and think about the world through the lens of group affiliations—is the first step to making things better." So the answer isn't to ignore biases, as with arguments about "colorblindness" or attacks on identity politics, but rather to acknowledge them and keep working at consciously countering them. We're not going to change our stereotyped thinking overnight, and we certainly won't change it long-term simply because we imagine someone's favorite vegetable. But with concerted effort over time, we can make great headway.

When I was a baby activist in the late 1990s, working in the LGBT rights movement while finishing up college, a group of scientists was trying to prove the existence of a gay gene. These scientists themselves were gay and believed that objections to equal rights laws could be overcome by proving gayness to be immutable. There was a problem though. The idea that "no one would choose to be gay" was implicitly rooted not in equality but *inferiority*, and the inference was that rights should be extended out of pity not principle. That's not justice. For example, religion is definitely not genetic and it's usually consciously chosen, but no one ever argues we shouldn't protect religious freedom.

In the end, gay gene research fanned preexisting debates about the biological worth of gay people in particular, and it fed into what were then scientifically popular notions that our character as human beings could be boiled down not only to biology but to *fixed and unyielding* biology. A society that had for centuries built itself around subjective hate was increasingly trying to objectively rationalize that hate with junk science, arguing that certain communities were biologically prone to criminality and promiscuity and poverty, and then arguing that hate itself wasn't subjective and immoral but rather also biologically predetermined, a hardwired reaction to the world.

Thus at every turn in the gaping injustice and inequality in US society, someone or another has tried to "prove" that such injustice and inequality has "natural" roots—to absolve the rest of us from our role in perpetuating and prospering under the imbalanced status quo. Sure, to some extent, our minds have the raw capacity to hate. But who we hate and how we hate is "soft-wired" into our systems by society. And in the middle of that, we get to choose what we do. Just like my being gay isn't solely the interplay between some unknown biological predilection and society's social pressures and counterdynamics—I get to choose how and to what extent, every day, I'm going to be, and act, super-duper gay—you also get to choose whether to hate me. That's your call. You don't get to blame neurobiology or society.

As it happens, near the end of my dinner with Scottie Nell, she and I get into a heated debate about nature versus nurture—how much inequality is just baked into humanity as opposed to how much is "soft-wired" by society and our biases.

"You have to at least acknowledge that we have a problem with racism in this country, and we continue to systematically treat black people as less than," I say to Scottie Nell. "If you don't acknowledge that, then you're never going to solve it."

"We're not in the 1950s," Scottie Nell replies. "We're not in the 1960s. We are not even in the 1970s or '80s. This is now."

"Why do you think black people have less wealth and lower graduation rates?" I ask.

Scottie Nell's reply is decisive: "I think that's something they need to address within their own community."

I point out that, statistically, white high school dropouts have on average a higher net worth than black college graduates. Which has only two possible explanations. "It's either that we have a longer, bigger problem of some kind of hidden unconscious racism as a society that we're not addressing," I say, "or these lazy black folks just haven't tried hard enough and that's why they're poor."

"I don't agree with that," Scottie Nell replies.

"Which? Which part?"

"Either," she says.

"So what, then?" I press.

"I think you have to look at the environments and what's been the focus of those environments," Scottie Nell replies.

"You're saying it's their fault," I say.

"No," Scottie Nell says, "I'm saying you look at the culture of hip-hop music. And I have hip-hop music, I love hip-hop, I love urban music. But the culture that exists in their pop music—of degrading women, encouraging violence against police, encouraging violence against each other—versus a country music song!"

“There’s no misogyny in country music songs?” I ask her.

“Name one,” she says.

“I don’t know. I can’t,” I confess. “I don’t know country music songs.”

“You can’t!” she triumphs.

“Mind you, I can’t name a hip-hop song either,” I add.

“Okay, well, there’s a big difference,” Scottie Nell continues. “The hate that is in that pop culture, that environment, is a reflection sometimes of what is going on, or else it wouldn’t be popular. You would not have certain songs . . .” Her voice trails off, and then she adds, “This has been going on since the ’80s!”

Well, something’s been going on, but maybe not what Scottie Nell thinks. In 1999, social psychologist Carrie Fried published an innovative study on this very question. She took the lyrics from an obscure folk song by the Kingston Trio, a song called “Bad Man’s Blunder,” which told the tale of a young man who intentionally shoots and kills a police officer. Fried printed out a section of the song’s lyrics on paper and gave them to research subjects, most of whom were white. Half the subjects were told the lyrics were from a country song. Half were told the lyrics were from a rap song. And that made all the difference. Subjects who thought they’d read rap lyrics rated the song as significantly more offensive and dangerous than subjects did when they thought they were country lyrics. In other words, perceptions about the music—and overall “culture”—weren’t governed by objective reality but by unconscious bias.

“Race is an idea, not a fact,” explains historian Nell Irvin Painter. Yet what is a fact is that our history and our minds, past and present, are irrevocably shaped by our country’s unique idea and expression of race. Implicit bias is also a fact. We can see it in our brains and in our reflexes, in our assumptions and our institutions. And if we don't see our biases—all of our biases—and do something about them, we're at risk of those biases being manipulated, twisted, and turned toward even darker ends. In fact, while it may be hard to think about and grasp our unconscious biases, the consequences of those biases being exacerbated and exploited on a systemic level can be truly horrific.

FIVE

When Hate Becomes Pandemic: The Genocide

Forgiveness is not forgetting. Forgiveness is freedom from hate.

—Valarie Kaur

When I step out of the airport in Kigali, Rwanda, in November 2016, the air smells like burning trash. I'm told that if I'd been there twenty-two years ago, it would have smelled like rotting flesh.

Of course, as an American, I wouldn't have been there then—every embassy worker from the US and every other country's diplomats, and most of the rest of the foreigners in the country, fled. During a period of one hundred days in 1994, Rwanda's Hutu majority killed approximately eight hundred thousand of the nation's Tutsi minority. The Rwandan genocide is, in fact, often described as the fastest genocide in world history—a breathtaking average of eight thousand people were murdered every day, many by their own friends and neighbors. Thousands and thousands of ordinary people—it is estimated that at least two hundred thousand Hutus participated in the genocide—became, in the words of genocide scholar Daniel Goldhagen, "willing executioners." This is what happens when hate, like wildfire, is deliberately spread nationwide.

When evil reaches a massive, pandemic scale, most of those who are not the direct victims just look the other way. It's as though if genocide isn't happening to us personally, we feel bad, but we don't feel connected—like it has nothing to do with us, our history, our hate. Too often, especially those of us in the West think genocide is some unusual thing that only happens to unusual people in unusual places. We think it can never happen to us, or *because of us*. How wrong we are.

When the Rwandan genocide began, John Giraneza, a Tutsi, was twenty years old. John grew up in the Bugesera District, in eastern Rwanda, in a village about an hour's drive from Kigali, the country's capital. The area around his village is called the Rweru sector, which is a lush valley named for Lake Rweru, which straddles the border with Burundi. Rural Rwanda is a study in stark contrasts; lush green avocado, mango, and citrus trees sprout in clusters like mirages out of an otherwise relentless topography of dirt and dust. I drive to John's village with my guide Solange Uwera, a young Rwandan woman with a heap of braids, worn sometimes on top of her head, sometimes cascading down her back. When we pass the villages on the way to Bugesera, groups of tiny children are running around in the fields and through the streets. I notice that all the boys *and* girls have their heads shaved. It's expensive to care for hair in Rwanda. Solange's braids are a luxury.

Eventually, our driver turns off the main road and we bump along a dirt one for several miles, passing lines of women in colorful kente-fabric wrap skirts and T-shirts, large nylon sacks balanced on their heads. They are probably carrying beans or rice, Solange tells me. One of the women has an extra cloth tied around her waist, and I can see the head of a baby just peeking out the back and gently bumping up and down as she walks. Then we pass a camel and, like a kid on a safari, I point excitedly and whip out my phone to take a picture. But so do Solange and the driver. Laughing, they tell me they've never seen a camel in Rwanda, or anywhere in sub-Saharan Africa, for that matter. They have no idea what the hell it's doing here. In the spirit of the apparent absurdity, I decide to tell that joke that the one sloth tells the other sloth in the movie *Zootopia*: "What do you call a three-humped camel? . . . Pregnant!" Solange doesn't laugh. When she translates it to our driver, he doesn't laugh either. Apparently, a camel is funny in Rwanda, but I'm not.

While camels are an anomaly in rural Rwanda, cows are everywhere—including on everyone's mind. Coming from the United States, where we can buy mass-produced, albeit chemically loaded, beef for $1.99 a pound, it's hard for me at first to grasp the important role of cattle in Rwanda. The country is historically, and epically, cow-centric.

"Rwandan obsession to cattle rates back to history when a man's wealth and manhood were considered by the number of long horned cattle he possessed," reads an article in the *New Times*, Rwanda's English-language daily. Cows were the only acceptable form of dowry and are still the best present to give a friend. Not only do Rwandans name their cows, but some even name their children after cow-like attributes. There are kids with names like Munganyinka ("she is as valuable as a cow"), Zaninka ("bring a cow") and—my favorite—Nzamukosha ("I will exchange her for a cow"). "All these are names meant to show the great significance of cattle in the Rwandan culture," I learned from the article in the *New Times*.

During my interviews, in every rural village I visited, everyone talked about cows in the context of the genocide—how so-and-so Tutsi had so many cows that others were jealous, or how a Tutsi gave a cow to his Hutu neighbor to try to prevent the Hutu from killing him. In Rwanda, cows are both powerful symbols and hard currency.

John Giraneza is from a Tutsi family that had cows. A lot of cows. More than two hundred. His father was very wealthy by village standards. John's father also had a lot of wives—ten, to be exact, each with her own home. The homes weren't fancy by Western standards, but they were as nice or nicer than those of most Hutu families, who had only one.

John's father didn't have as many children as he had cows, but he had a lot of children, too. John had thirty-six brothers and sisters spread among the ten wives and some other women. John's own mother was not one of his father's wives, and after John was born, she left. John's father kept him, and he was raised by the ten mothers. At mealtime, he and a gaggle of his siblings would start out eating at one mother's house and then go to another and then another until they were full. At night, he could sleep in whichever house he wanted. It sounds like a pretty fun childhood, actually. Or a reality TV show. Incidentally, because I'm sure you're wondering, too, John's father would spend two nights in each wife's house in a scheduled rotation.

Life was good for John, until suddenly it was not. John's father was killed in the lead-up to the genocide, and on the second day of the genocide, the rest of his family was slaughtered.

The killing was done with intimate sloppiness. I'd heard that the Rwandan genocide wasn't committed solely by the Hutu-run military or even the *interahamwe*, trained armed militias of civilian Hutu extremists, but also by Hutu civilians, who picked up the machetes in their backyards and hacked their neighbors to death at close range—close enough for slayer and victim to look into each other's eyes.

Before I went to Rwanda, I figured it must not really be true that Hutus killed their actual friends. I imagined what the historians meant was the equivalent of my suddenly attacking that guy who lives up the street, someone I say hi to regularly when I walk by but whose name I don't know, or anything else about him, so we aren't technically friends. Which would, of course, be plenty horrible by itself. But I soon learned that in many cases the Hutus and the Tutsis they killed really were friends. Close friends. I met several Hutu perpetrators who were the godparents of their Tutsi friends' kids and had family dinners together every weekend. In fact, in some mixed Hutu-Tutsi families, people were killed by their own husbands or wives.

Whenever I bring up the Rwandan genocide in conversation—I promise, I really am fun at parties—no one thinks they could ever slaughter their neighbors, let alone family members. Lots of people I talk with are against trolling and bullying and political incivility but can at least recognize the germs of that same hatred inside themselves. With enough pondering, they can imagine extreme life circumstances that could have turned them into a racist like Arno or a terrorist like Bassam. But slaughter their neighbors? People who do that must be monsters, right?

In truth, what makes mass atrocities like the Rwandan genocide so hard to fathom is that so many perfectly "normal" people not only look the other way at the horror but often actively, even enthusiastically, participate. In Rwanda, hundreds of thousands of people were massacred, hundreds of thousands more were raped and maimed, and millions of lives were destroyed and displaced—not because a few evil monsters did unspeakably evil things but because, by and large, good, even loving, people did unspeakably evil things. I met many of them, and they were not monsters.

Equally disconcerting is that the killing can't be attributed to the Hutus losing their minds in a mass spasm of uncontrollable rage. As fast as it was, the slaughter continued for one hundred days. The Hutu perpetrators I met told me they had not lost either their consciousness or their conscience during the horrors they were committing. They knew, in the moment, what they were doing was wrong. Some of the perpetrators even helped rescue and hide Tutsi children or friends while simultaneously killing other Tutsis. A Hutu gang member recounted to a journalist: "If, by misfortune I caught sight of an acquaintance, like a soccer comrade, for example, a pang pinched my heart, and I left him to a nearby colleague. But I had to do this quietly, I could not reveal my good heart." His "good heart" could call out to him—and yet he could also keep right on killing.

Former US ambassador to the United Nations Samantha Power titled her book about genocide *A Problem from Hell*. But while the French philosopher Jean-Paul Sartre wrote, "Hell is other people," the American playwright Tennessee Williams argued, "Hell is yourself." American ethicist Nel Noddings warns, "Evil does not have a stomach-turning stench, nor does it signal its presence with palpable cold and darkness. We do not fall haplessly, nor does it entrap (possess) us. Rather, we often act willfully in complicity with it."

Such mass atrocities can happen only because many fundamentally decent human beings participate and many other decent people fail to intervene. When we take that in, we realize that genocide is terrifying not only because it happened to *them* but because it could also happen to *us*—and that we could just as easily be the victims or the perpetrators.

In every genocide, some people do resist. Many know of Paul Rusesabagina, a Hutu who, as concierge at the fancy Hôtel des Mille Collines in Kigali, helped to hide and protect over twelve hundred Tutsis and Hutus. His story was the basis for the movie *Hotel Rwanda*. There were other rescuers, but the exact number isn't known. An estimated twenty-five thousand to forty-five thousand Hutus were killed in the genocide. But many of them were killed simply for being moderates who didn't support the extremist government, not because they intervened to save Tutsis. Others were killed because they looked Tutsi.

As of 2016, there were less than fifty confirmed examples of rescuers during the genocide. As heartening and instructive as it is to know that these brave souls existed, they constituted a tiny fraction of Rwanda's overall population of 5.95 million Hutus in 1994. Similarly, during the Holocaust, active resisters of Nazi atrocities against Jews are estimated to have made up just half of 1 percent of the entire civilian population.

We might all like to believe, as Scottie Nell Hughes did in my conversation with her at the Moton Museum, that had we been the ones faced with that moment in history, we would have done the right thing. But the problem is, as the numbers starkly show again and again, most people don't.

The question about Rwanda is: What lessons does the genocide hold for those of us who want to stop the spread of hate in our culture? How can good people be so willingly recruited to serve the interests of hate, even when the consequences are so extreme? I wanted to understand what genocide can tell us about how such intense hate systemically engulfs a whole society and how its spread can be systemically prevented. What I learned is that a combination of long-stewing resentments, explicit dehumanizing propaganda, and official sanctioning of violence fuel explosive hate. A genocide doesn't just spontaneously erupt, even one as ferociously fast-burning as the Rwandan genocide was. The flames are strategically, societally fanned. And what I find deeply troubling about the lessons of Rwanda for the United States and the rest of the world is that the embers of hatred are being stoked in so many places today in so many similar ways.

During the 2016 presidential election in the US, I meet Yannick Tona, a young Tutsi who survived the Rwandan genocide and was attending Texas Christian University on a scholarship. Yannick immediately starts our conversation on a foreboding note. "Oh my God, you guys are doing what we were doing twenty-five years before the genocide in my country, or ten years before the genocide," Yannick says, almost jumping out of the couch he's sitting on at the school bookstore lounge. "Maybe not on the same level or as extremist as in my country at that time, but it is just all these elements, and I'm like, 'What's going on in this country?' The more I live here, the more I get depressed about it. Like, 'Oh my God, this is worse than I thought.'"

Yannick, three-fourths of whose extended family was slaughtered in the Rwandan genocide, is now warning us that the same thing can happen here. Maybe Rwanda and Nazi Germany and Cambodia and the former Yugoslavia weren't bizarre aberrations but merely examples of how any culture in any country might turn monstrous.

I'm not suggesting that I think the United States is at risk of genocide anytime soon. At the very least, though, Americans should be terrified that a survivor of the Rwandan genocide hears the same type of hatred that lit his own country on fire being spewed here. As should Europeans, about the mounting hatred being voiced there. After all, history's worst genocide didn't happen in Africa or the Middle East but in Germany. The Rwandan genocide speaks volumes about the dangers of manipulatively pitting social groups against one another, as thought leaders in spreading hate are so avidly doing in the US and around the globe, which can have truly disastrous consequences. It's also a lesson about how our own forms of hate, which we might think of as trivial, can become deadly.

The resentments between Hutus and Tutsis resulted largely from colonial meddling. While Hutus and Tutsis had long been distinct identity groups, and Hutus tended to be farmers while Tutsis herded cattle and thus did enjoy a higher status, the groups were not in heated conflict until the late 1800s, when German and then Belgian colonial powers seized control of the region. In fact, Philip Gourevitch, the author of *We Wish to Inform You That Tomorrow We Will Be Killed with Our Families*, about the Rwandan genocide, explains that prior to the colonial conquest, Hutus and Tutsis intermarried to such an extent that "ethnographers and historians agree that Hutus and Tutsis cannot properly be called distinct ethnic groups." As a UN report on the genocide describes it, "Prior to the colonial era, Tutsis generally occupied the higher strata in the social system and the Hutus the lower. However, social mobility was possible, a Hutu who acquired a large number of cattle or other wealth could be assimilated into the Tutsi group and impoverished Tutsi would be regarded as Hutu."

During the so-called "Scramble for Africa," the nations of Europe saw fit to divide the continent among themselves, and eventually the region that included the Kingdom of Rwanda was "given" to Germany. Through a twisted history of deeply condescending and fundamentally racist otherizing, the Germans officially designated Tutsis as superior to Hutus, and they awarded more local ruling power and economic privilege to Tutsis. After World War I, the League of Nations "gave" Rwanda to Belgium, and the Belgians not only maintained the ethnic divisions of power established by the Germans but took them a sinister step further, issuing identity cards that labeled Rwandans as either Hutu, Tutsi, or Twa, a minority pygmy tribe that makes up less than 1 percent of the country. The Germans and Belgians turned ethnic distinctions into major economic and political divisions.

The history of identity politics in Rwanda echoes the history of how social group identities have been invented and employed elsewhere in the world to serve the interests of the powerful. For instance, much of the Zionist justification for dominating the totality of the land of Israel centers on a specious claim that there was no historic Palestinian identity before the State of Israel was formed. The implication is that a people who didn't *categorize* themselves as a people don't deserve their own political sovereignty. Similarly, the cultural identity of the people of East Timor was partly crystalized as a reaction against Portuguese colonization and then occupation by Indonesia; the emerging independent identity that was defined in reaction to such oppression increased simultaneously with the desire for political independence. Remember that while tribalism may be inherent in human beings, the way those "tribes" are shaped—and how they are set against other groups—often stems from the purposeful, political manipulation of tribalism.

The handiwork of the colonial powers in Rwanda led to lasting social unrest. "Hutus in Rwanda had been massacring Tutsis on and off since the waning days of Belgian colonial rule, in the late fifties," writes Gourevitch. During Rwanda's struggle for independence in the 1960s, tens of thousands of Tutsis were killed and an estimated 40 to 70 percent of the remaining Tutsi population fled the country, many across the border into Uganda.

In 1959, the Hutu-led independence movement took charge of the newly independent Rwanda. Over the years, the Tutsi exiles kept trying to invade and overthrow the Hutu government. One incarnation of that effort was the Rwandan Patriotic Front (RPF), which in 1990 invaded Rwanda and took control of some territory in the country's northeast.

To those watching ignorantly from the outside, the Hutu genocide against the Tutsis came across as a spontaneous outbreak of pure insanity. Indeed, that's how the extremist Hutu government that directed the killing later tried to portray it. But Rwanda's Hutu president, Juvenal Habyarimana, and his wife, Agathe, had been plotting annihilation of the Tutsis since Habyarimana seized power in a 1973 coup. Agathe Habyarimana coordinated the group of Hutu extremists who meticulously planned the genocide, including recruiting and training the interahamwe militias. In 1992, the Hutu extremists conducted a dry run of their genocidal plans. They killed several hundred Tutsis around the country. John Giraneza's father was one of them.

John was eighteen years old at the time. "I was coming home from school when I met a group of attackers on the road," John recalls. "They said to me, 'We will attack your home and kill you.'" That night, the group came to John's house and slaughtered his father with a machete, but they harmed no other family members. John's father died the following morning as the next phase of full-blown genocide was being birthed.

State-sponsored propaganda increasingly targeted Tutsis. One popular radio station mixed popular music with hours and hours of venomous lies about the RPF and, by association, labeled all Tutsis *inyenzi* ("cockroaches"). In an extremist newspaper, Hutu activists printed a list of the "Hutu Ten Commandments," which included statements like "Every Hutu should know that every Tutsi is dishonest in business. His only aim is the supremacy of his ethnic group." While the Hutu extremists were winding up the machinery for genocide, they were also fomenting a murderous mind-set.

On August 6, 1994, President Habyarimana's plane was shot down and Habyarimana died. Propaganda radio broadcasts instantly pinned the blame on Tutsis. Who shot the plane down is actually still in dispute, but the claim that Tutsis had done it was the spark that started the fire. Within hours, Agathe Habyarimana's posse gave the order to the Hutu-extremist-controlled military and the interahamwe to begin mass killings. Propaganda radio issued explicit commands for Hutus to find Tutsis and "stand near this place and encircle them and kill them because they are there."

It was just one day later, on April 7, that John Giraneza returned from tending cattle to find the rest of his family being massacred. A combination of the government military, the interahamwe, and other Hutus from his village had launched the attack. As John hid in the hills, he saw attackers repeatedly rape two of his sisters. Afterward, their attackers shoved wooden posts through each girl's vagina until they pierced their skulls. Another group of attackers buried one of John's younger brothers alive in the ground and then stood watch over the mound of dirt to make sure the child didn't escape death. "Our houses had been set on fire," John recalls slowly, between deep breaths. "Grenades were exploding. And cows were screaming."

When it was over, all ten mothers and twenty-seven of John's brothers and sisters were murdered. There was nothing John could have done to stop the slaughter. The gang of killers was large, well armed, and well trained. John could only keep himself hidden and watch in agony. Then he fled farther up into the hills to search for other Tutsis. He wanted to form a group of Tutsis to fight back.

Many Hutus and Tutsis rightfully blame the propaganda for whipping up the genocide. But why was it so effective?

While clearly, interethnic animosity had plagued the country for decades, the fact is that most Hutus didn't start out as enthusiastic executioners. I met many Hutus who had participated in the killing who told me they had not hated those they murdered. One of those was Leonard Rucogoza.

I was introduced to him in the living room of Marie Izagiriza, a Tutsi, who lives in the same village as John Giraneza. She lost her husband and five of her eight children in the genocide. It was Leonard who slaughtered Marie's husband and then pushed two of her children, who were six and nine years old, down a well, then stood guard, making sure they didn't escape, as they slowly starved to death. Up until that moment, their families had been friendly, including enjoying holidays and celebratory meals together. Like John Giraneza's father, Marie's husband was wealthy; he owned many cows. So many, in fact, that he had given cows to some of his neighbors, including Leonard.

As we sit together in Marie's home, Marie tells me, "I never felt hate between Hutus and Tutsis before."

Leonard is one of those who blames the radio propaganda, saying that it taught "us that Tutsis should be killed." He insists, "I didn't feel hate against Tutsis during the entire period."

I gasp. "Really?" I say, trying to hide my cynicism.

"Really," Leonard says. Then he raises another motivation that fueled the killing. "I felt, you know, I should kill them. We were taught if you kill Tutsis, you can take their property. You should kill him so you can freely take his belongings." After Leonard killed Marie's husband, he took the family's cows.

Many Hutu perpetrators and other Hutus I spoke with also try to tell me the killing was motivated more by greed than hate. Marie-Jeanne Uwimana is among them.

Marie-Jeanne was ten years old when the genocide started. She lived with her father and mother and sister a mile or so from John Giraneza's family, not in the same village, but close enough that she knew of John's family and he knew of hers. Eventually, John and Marie-Jeanne would become even closer—but only after the genocide tore apart both their lives.

Marie-Jeanne's father was a farmer, and she has fond memories of her childhood, of helping him sell his avocados. Marie-Jeanne remembers her father coming home at night with new things for her and her sister—things he had stolen from the Tutsi families he'd helped slaughter. One Tutsi her father killed was a family friend who used to give Marie-Jeanne's family land for farming.

I ask Marie-Jeanne why she thinks her father participated in the killing.

"Imagine killing someone who used to give you a living," she tells me. She concedes that "it is true that they had been trained to kill"—whether formally through the interahamwe or through propaganda. "But mostly those who took part in the genocide were driven by greed," Marie-Jeanne says definitively.

Still, I can't help wondering if that's not the explanation she gives because it's better to be a thief than a monster. How can greed explain why Leonard killed two young children? Or the widespread brutality against women who controlled no property?

Yannick Tona, the Tutsi student at Texas Christian University, was just four years old when the genocide began. He hid in his grandmother's house with his mother and three siblings, as well as aunts and uncles—sixteen in total. Eventually, they fled the house, thinking their best bet was to hide in pairs and try to escape. Only Yannick, his mother, his sister, and his uncle survived.

Yannick tells me that his grandmother stayed with his baby brother, taking cover in her backyard. But the baby cried.

"He was one year old and just making baby noises," Yannick says as we talk in the atrium of the university bookstore.

The Hutu attackers heard Yannick's baby brother and found him and his grandmother.

"My grandmother . . . was raped." Yannick speaks stoically, but tears well in his wide eyes. "And my brother . . . they took him and beat him on the wall, beat his brains to bits, and they forced my grandma to drink the blood."

Then they killed his grandmother.

Yannick tells me that the attackers "were neighbors who my grandmother's family had lived with for generations."

At one point during my time in Rwanda, I visit a church in Ntarama, a village on the way to where both John and Marie-Jeanne grew up, in the Bugesera District. When the genocide started, the Tutsis from the surrounding area sought sanctuary in the church. But like other expats, the Italian Catholic priests fled the country—leaving their flock to defend themselves.

Thousands of people locked themselves in the small church in Ntarama, hoping that together they could ward off the Hutu militias—or that, somehow, God would help. It was in a small outbuilding that used to be the Sunday school where all the babies were sheltered. Hutu militants used a grenade to blow a hole in the side of the Sunday school building and then, one by one, killed the babies by holding on to their legs and swinging their heads against a wall at the front of the room. There is still a dark patch of stained bricks on the wall.

While greed seems certainly to have played a part in the genocide, and certainly economic resentment overall fueled much of the ethnic tension Hutus felt toward Tutsis, what happened in Rwanda can't be boiled down to just greed alone. The genocide was a perfect storm of out-group otherizing, a terrifying testament to how readily intense feelings of competitive victimhood, anger, and disgust toward demonized social groups can be fomented toward extremely deadly ends.

Crucial to the story is that with its propaganda and training of militias, the government established that killing Tutsis was the *responsibility* of Hutus. The government established a new social norm that Hutus felt duty-bound to conform with. Just like racial discrimination and violence was the norm in North America in the 1750s and 1850s and 1950s. Brutality was made normative in Rwanda, and that explains why "normal" people like Leonard Rucogoza could kill people they didn't hate. Leonard, and human beings generally, have an inclination to conform to social norms—which is deeply troubling when the norms themselves are hateful.

To HELP WRAP my head around how brutality can become so normative—in fact, so normal—I spoke with philosopher Elizabeth Minnich. She was a student and protégé of one of history's most renowned philosophers, Hannah Arendt, who turned the world's understanding of evil upside down.

Arendt was born in Germany in 1906 and escaped the Holocaust, eventually resettling in the United States. In the 1950s, she published two important works—*The Origins of Totalitarianism* and *The Human Condition*—both exploring the theme of freedom as it relates to the individual, society, and political regimes. But it was in 1961 that Hannah Arendt became a household name. That year, the *New Yorker* magazine sent her to Jerusalem to cover the trial of Adolf Eichmann—who had been a lieutenant under Adolf Hitler during the Holocaust. Eichmann designed and managed the logistics for deporting millions of Europe's Jews into concentration camps, where most were killed.

What Arendt reported back to the United States and the world was shocking. Eichmann, she said, wasn't a monster but a pretty average person, who was mindlessly following orders. But if Eichmann wasn't a monster, how could you explain his monstrous acts? In offering an answer, Arendt coined the phrase "the banality of evil." She meant not that the evil Eichmann committed was banal but that *he* was banal—an ordinary person who did extraordinarily awful things.

About Eichmann's banality, Arendt wrote, "It was sheer thoughtlessness—something by no means identical with stupidity—that predisposed him to become one of the greatest criminals of that period." Eichmann had "a curious, quite authentic inability to think." What Arendt particularly emphasized was that Eichmann didn't seem to have questioned in the slightest the new norms of brutality being established by the Nazi party—norms that, like the dehumanization of Tutsis in Rwanda, were carefully spread over time. Arendt argued that it's an individual's responsibility to challenge social norms and, when need be, defy them. She called such independent-mindedness "thinking without a banister." But more often than not, Arendt argued, we cling to norms in the way we grip a banister on a treacherous flight of stairs.

The focus of Elizabeth Minnich's work has been to try to deconstruct this banister-clinging mode of thinking. Minnich writes in her book *The Evil of Banality*, "Since my first encounters with dramatic injustices . . . I have increasingly felt that understanding thinking—and so also thoughtlessness, and so also banality in its many forms—is for me the most pressing moral and political quest."

Now a senior fellow at the Association of American Colleges and Universities, Minnich helped me understand what she calls "extensive evil," which she differentiates from individual crimes of desperation or passion—like robbing a bank or killing a lover. "Basically, there are two kinds of evil," she tells me over the phone from her home in North Carolina. "One is intensive—it begins and ends pretty quickly and is surrounded by a normalcy that makes us so shocked when it's violated." Intensive crimes include random physical attacks and murders. "The other type of evil," Minnich explains, "is extensive—it involves mass crimes, committed not by individuals or small groups of offenders but whole communities or societies."

Her point is that while intensive crime is plainly wrong and abhorrent to everyone else observing it, extensive evil is not. "Extensive evil may indeed shock and horrify us" from a distance, she says, "but the fact is that it's normal for its time."

When Minnich says this, I get goose bumps. The idea that genocide could in any way be seen as normal initially seems outrageous, but then I realize she means normal in the sense of normalizing, of creating a social norm—like the norms of discrimination about which Scottie Nell and I wrestled in Virginia.

"Once initiated, violence generates an evolution in perpetrators," Minnich continues. "Social norms, institutions, and culture all change in ways that make greater violence easier and more likely."

This is also the diagnosis of psychologist Donald Dutton, another expert on genocide. "Behavior towards the victims that would previously have been considered inconceivable," he writes, "now becomes acceptable and 'normal.' Eventually, killing the victims becomes the 'right' thing to do."

As genocide scholar James Waller puts it, "Perpetrators of extraordinary evil are extraordinary only by what they have done, not by who they are."

Observing war crimes tribunals after the Bosnian genocide in 1995, Croatian writer Slavenka Drakulic observed:

> You sit in a courtroom watching a defendant day after day and at first you wonder, as Primo Levi did, "if this is a man." No, this is not a man, it is all too easy to answer, but as the days pass you find the criminals become increasingly human. Soon you feel that you know them intimately. You watch their faces, ugly or pleasant, their small habits of yawning, taking notes, scratching their heads, cleaning their nails, and you have to ask yourself: what if this *is* a man? The more you know them, the more you wonder how they could have committed such crimes, these waiters and taxi drivers, teachers and peasants in front of you. And the more you realize that war criminals might be ordinary people, the more afraid you become. Of course, this is because the consequences are more serious than if they were monsters. If ordinary people committed war crimes, it means that any of us can commit them.

As I reflect on how normal genocide can become, I think about the history of the United States. During our colonial era and early history as a nation, collective evil was also a norm—from the mass slaughter of native peoples to the mass enslavement of Africans. Later, between 1877 and 1950, at least 3,959 black people were killed in racial terror lynchings—which Paul Robeson and other civil rights activists argued met the definition of "genocide" under United Nations conventions. These lynchings weren't just shamefully carried out in the shadows but as public celebrations. "Large crowds of white people, often numbering in the thousands, gathered to witness pre-planned, heinous killings that featured prolonged torture, mutilation, dismemberment, and/or burning of the victim," the Equal Justice Initiative reports in its extensive documentation of lynchings in the United States.

As Tuskegee University sociologists Stewart Tolnay and E. M.

Beck reported in their book about lynchings in the South, "White press justified and promoted these carnival like events, with vendors selling food, printers producing postcards featuring photographs of the lynching and corpse, and the victim's body parts collected as souvenirs." The white folks in the audience, like the white folks actually committing the lynchings, likely thought themselves to be good people. White parents who brought their kids to watch—which they did—likely thought themselves to be good parents. They were participating in—and perpetuating—what had become the norm. That doesn't make them innocent. What it makes them, for that time and place, is *normal.*

THE FRIGHTENING POWER of our desire to conform even to dangerous norms was shockingly—and I mean that literally—demonstrated in a set of famous experiments conducted by psychologist Stanley Milgram in the 1960s. Disturbed by Hannah Arendt's reporting about how supposedly normal Adolf Eichmann was, Milgram decided to test the degree to which people would obey authority figures who instructed them to commit violence.

When subjects arrived for Milgram's study, they were put in pairs and drew straws to find out who would play the "teacher" and who would be the "learner." Except the draw was actually fixed; the subjects were always the "teacher," and one of Milgram's research assistants was always the "learner." Each subject saw the "learner" put in a room and strapped to a chair with electrodes attached to his arms. Then the subject was brought into a room next door, which contained a machine that appeared to generate electric shocks applied to the "learner." The machine was "marked from 15 volts (Slight Shock) to 375 volts (Danger: Severe Shock) to 450 volts (XXX)." The machine was actually a fake; it didn't really do anything. But the subjects thought it was real.

The subject "teachers" were supposed to teach a list of word pairs to the "learner" and then quiz him. Every time the "learner" got answers wrong, the subjects were told to administer a shock. The learner gave wrong answers most of the time, on purpose. And if the subjects refused to administer a shock, they were given prompts like "The experiment requires you to continue" and even "You have no other choice but to continue."

Milgram hypothesized that maybe 10 percent of the participants would go so far as to administer the supposedly lethal shock level of 450 volts. In actuality, 65 percent did. And every single one of the subjects went to at least 300 volts. Ultimately Milgram carried out eighteen versions of the study, all with similar results.

But that was then, right? Unfortunately, no. Ethical standards in academic research in the United States have gotten tougher since the 1960s, in part because of studies like Milgram's. But in 2017, a group of researchers basically replicated Milgram's experiment, in Poland—where I guess they don't have such strict standards. In that experiment, 90 percent of subjects were willing to apply the highest voltage shock.

Milgram argued that his studies revealed how intent so many people are to be obedient to authority. Before him, another researcher, Solomon Asch, whose work Milgram had drawn on, showed that authority figures don't even have to be directly involved to induce conformity. Peer pressure is enough. In the 1950s, Asch conducted a groundbreaking experiment, which, as with the Milgram studies, is one of the most widely cited in social psychology. Each subject was brought into a room with people who they thought were other subjects but who were actually part of the research team. Asch showed them all three lines of clearly different lengths and then a fourth line that was obviously the same as one, and only one, of the first three.

Everyone was supposed to say which it matched, which was basically a stupidly simple task. The correct answer was really obvious. But when the confederates in the room deliberately gave the wrong answer, the subjects would also answer incorrectly 32 percent of the time. Across twelve similar experiments, 25 percent of the subjects never conformed, but 75 percent of subjects gave the wrong answer at least once.

What was going on in their minds? Were they aware that they were conforming to the norm, just going along to get along? Or did they honestly think they were giving the correct answer? A half century after Asch's experiment, psychiatrist Gregory Berns and a team at Emory University replicated Asch's study while subjects had their brains scanned with an fMRI machine. In this case, they were comparing what looked like Tetris pieces—drawings of two different 3-D objects. The subjects were told to mentally rotate the objects to determine if they were the same or different. Again, the correct answer was superclear. But when the accomplices in the room gave the wrong answer, the subjects also answered incorrectly 41 percent of the time.

Berns figured that if the subjects were lying, the part of the brain associated with conscious deception would light up. But it didn't. Instead, the parts of the brain associated with visual perception and spatial awareness lit up. In other words, the subjects weren't lying. The data suggest their minds were genuinely modifying their actual perceptions to conform with the group: if the rest of the group insisted that they saw a triangle, the subjects who went along with the group literally "saw" a triangle too. Meanwhile, the subjects who went against the group showed brain activity in the right amygdala—suggesting that there's an emotional toll, potentially even fear, associated with standing up for one's beliefs.

Notably, when Berns and his team performed a version of the

experiment in which subjects were tested against computers instead of human researchers, the amygdala didn't light up. The research team concluded that it's not taking a stand in general but going against one's peers that causes emotional distress. Psychologists Christian Crandall and Amy Eshelman studied 105 different kinds of prejudice as they played out in different scenarios—like job discrimination or laughing at hateful jokes—and found that prejudice was highly correlated with the need for social approval from the dominant group. Which apparently can occur subconsciously.

Let's be clear, our tendency toward conformity isn't necessarily bad. Societies depend on a degree of conformity. If 25 percent or even 10 percent of us decided on a regular basis to disobey traffic lights, we'd have a serious problem. It's conforming to harmful norms that we want to resist.

In Rwanda, some people acted with remarkable courage. At the all-girls Sainte Marie School, Hutu and Tutsi students refused to follow a militia's orders to separate themselves into ethnic groups, and so all the girls were killed—taking a stand together. Over the course of the genocide, Josephine Dusaminama, a Hutu woman, hid thirteen Tutsis in her home and then secretly ferried them on boats across the border to the Democratic Republic of the Congo. Another Hutu woman, Olive Mukankusi, rescued three Tutsis, hiding them in a pit in her backyard that was used for making banana beer. Mukankusi knew the risk she was taking. As she told NPR, "I was ready to die with them, whatever would happen to me or my family."

What would make it likely, in those moments, for more of us to demonstrate such nonconformist courage? There is no simple answer, but one clue could be in what genocide scholar Erwin Staub has found—that many rescuers are themselves on the margins of society, like members of a minority religion or people with multiethnic heritage. For instance during Rwanda's genocide, most Hutus among Rwanda's Muslim minority not only didn't participate in killings but helped hide and rescue both Muslim and non-Muslim Tutsis.

Social psychologists Aurelia Mok and Michael Morris have produced strong research evidence that supports Staub's observation. They presented Asian American subjects with pairs of 3-D objects like those in the Berns fMRI study—two Tetris shapes that were clearly exactly the same or different. And as in the Berns, Asch, and Milgram studies, Mok and Morris had researchers pretending to be subjects—who would then give the wrong answers. Remember that in Asch's study, 75 percent of subjects went along with the obviously incorrect answer at least once.

But Mok and Morris got different results. They found that Asian American subjects who demonstrated "low bicultural identity integration"—meaning that they don't see their Asian and American identities as fully compatible and integrated into one social identity—were more likely to resist peer pressure and give the correct answer, no matter what the confederates did. This makes the case that the way to stop us from discriminating against or hating various identity groups isn't actually to pretend that those different identities don't exist. The lesson is not that we need some people who feel like outsiders or who haven't fully integrated their sense of cultural affiliation into a seamless whole—indeed, having low bicultural identity integration is associated with greater rates of anxiety and depression. The lesson is that we need to combat negative otherizing without forcing assimilation or conformity. We can still have groups—the problem is when they are pitted against one another as dominant versus inferior.

Research by anthropologist Jennie Burnet suggests that fostering values of mutual humanity and respect can also counter hate.

That certainly was the case, Burnet found, in Rwanda, where she extensively interviewed Hutus who were rescuers. "They almost all said it's what any decent human being would do," Burnet reports. They all saw themselves as a "certain kind of person."

As one rescuer told her, "The first reason why some people saved others is because they understood that every person is like themselves—and that, if he was being hunted today it's maybe because you could also be hunted the following day, that if he dies today, you can die tomorrow. . . . We understood that no one has [the] right over another person's life."

Another rescuer said, "The one who had a beastly heart didn't save the person, but the one who had a merciful heart, which understood that a human being is a human being, saved that person. That's how we saved people."

Several other studies have suggested that genocide rescuers are more compassionate and altruistic than average.

"Dehumanization isn't a way of talking. It's a way of thinking—a way of thinking that, sadly, comes all too easily to us," writes philosopher David Livingstone Smith. But the challenge, as Elizabeth Minnich teaches, isn't just to replace one set of banisters with another—like some uniformly enforced kumbaya assimilation crap that erases individuality. Rather, the question is how we as people and as societies help make habits out of independent thinking—how can we use the spaces in which we come together, from schools to churches to nations, to simultaneously understand how we're all connected to each other and at the same time learn how to think independently. That's a tall order.

HIGH IN THE hills near his village, John Giraneza found other Tutsis who had fled. And they, too, wanted to mount a resistance. But they were untrained and poorly armed, and before long, Hutu militants found John and his group. The Tutsis fought as hard as they could, but most of them were slaughtered. John was shot in the head, and his leg was severely cut by a machete. He fell to the ground, unconscious. The Hutu militants assumed John was dead and left him among the other corpses. Eventually, another group of Tutsis came across the scene and noticed John was breathing. They brought him to a hospital in Kigali. John remained in a coma for 135 days. He woke up just weeks after the genocide ended.

He'd survived. Seven out of ten Tutsis in Rwanda would not be as lucky. And after the genocide, there were ninety-five thousand orphans in Rwanda.

When John awoke from his coma, he had nothing. Most of his family was dead and all of their property was destroyed or looted. Only twenty years old, John became what Rwandans call a "street boy"—a homeless kid wandering Kigali. "I lived in Nyanza landfills, where I was eating garbage," John tells me. Hotels and hospitals would dump their trash wrapped in big tarps, and John and other street boys would string the tarps across trees for shelter and then forage the trash for scraps of food. This is how he lived for fourteen years.

"It was a life too hard to live," John says as his eyes look toward the ground. "I attempted to commit suicide on ten occasions but was unsuccessful, because God knew I would be here with you today." He looks up at me, his saucerlike eyes sadly smiling. "It was very hard," he says, "but finally my heart was healed."

A year after the genocide, Bishop Gashagaza Deo—who everyone calls Pastor Deo—started Prison Fellowship Rwanda, a group that opposes violence and promotes reconciliation. Pastor Deo had grown up in the Democratic Republic of the Congo with his Tutsi family, who had fled Rwanda in 1959. In 1994, when the genocide ended, Pastor Deo went to Rwanda to find his other relatives. But they'd been killed. He cried for three days, then heard a voice that said, "Do not cry. You'll be my instrument for reconciliation."

Pastor Deo tells me this with a smile that suggests he knows I might be thinking he's crazy, but in this deeply religious country, no one bats an eye about hearing messages from God.

Pastor Deo went into Rwanda's prisons, thinking he might find the people who killed his family and also test the message he'd received. He ended up ministering to Hutus in prison. They wanted Pastor Deo to pray for their forgiveness. And, he says, they also wanted his help.

"One day if I am released," one *genocidaire* asked, "how can I live in my home when my victim has nowhere to sleep?" And so reconciliation villages were born.

In 2005, Pastor Deo and the Rwanda Prison Fellowship constructed their first reconciliation village—a community of homes half for genocide perpetrators, half for survivors. Pastor Deo's idea spread, and eventually the Rwanda Prison Fellowship built eight such villages.

When construction started on one in the area where John's family had once lived, community members told Pastor Deo about John and that they'd heard he was now living on the streets and barely surviving. Pastor Deo and his team set out to find John.

"They started coming to visit me," John recalls. "However, in the first few days, I tried to hide myself, in fear that they were with policemen." In Kigali, the police would regularly harass and arrest homeless people.

But soon, John realized the people who came back day after day asking around for him were from his village. "Then we started interacting," says John.

Pastor Deo and the reconciliation village offered John a house, a place to live in the new village near his family's old home, for free.

John was skeptical. Wouldn't you be? Also, he wanted nothing to do with Hutus. He was terrified of them.

After he finally relented, out of desperation, and moved to the reconciliation village, he kept a machete next to his bed at night, convinced one of his Hutu neighbors would try to murder him in his sleep. He was that afraid of them and, understandably, angry.

The reconciliation village in which John lives is a grid of a hundred or so tin-roof houses, with walls made of mud bricks that have been plastered over with concrete. Each house has three or four rooms with walls and doorways between them, but no doors. In most of the houses I visit, there are bedsheets hung in the doorways. The houses have pit latrines but no running water. Near the center of the village is a well that everyone uses, lugging five-gallon yellow plastic jerry cans filled with well water back to their homes.

The floors are dirt. The yards are dirt. The streets are dirt. When school isn't in session, the kids from the village pool in little groups and spend most of the day playing in the dirt, poking it with sticks, crawling through it on their knees. I thought of Willa and wished she was in the village with me so she could realize how lucky she is and not whine the next time I refuse to get her a bazillionth stuffed animal at the toy store.

When I visited John, I brought his village the first soccer ball they'd ever had. It cost me six dollars. Half of Rwandans live on less than two dollars a day.

And almost 90 percent of the country attends church. Soon after he moved into the reconciliation village, John started attending church services led by Pastor Deo. A month in, John heard Pastor Deo give a speech. "He said that if you don't forgive, you will not be forgiven by God," John recalls. That was it. John decided he was ready. "As soon as I pronounced that word, 'I have forgiven,' my heart became clean," he tells me. And he says that he went from seeing the Hutus around him as potential killers to seeing them as nice people.

"Really?" I ask incredulously.

Like with Arno Michaelis and Bassam Aramin, this swiftness is hard for me to process—even more so given the extreme horror John has been put through. John suffered to a degree I can't even fathom. Which makes me feel indignant for him, and for all of the Tutsis who lost their loved ones and their own lives. It just seems unfair that John should have to forgive anyone. In the face of that kind of hate, hating maybe isn't only justified but just.

If you don't hate, are you a hero—or a sucker? And is it ridiculous, possibly even offensive, to suggest that someone like John should be celebrated and held up as a role model for shouldering the burden of forgiveness? I can't help thinking that the Hutus who live around him should be groveling at his feet with apologies every single day, that something about praising John for being so magnanimous puts too much of a burden on him and lets the killers off the hook.

Forgiveness is a complicated thing. The philosopher Friedrich Nietzsche wrote that forgiveness is weakness. Going a step further, writer Audre Lorde suggests that forgiveness is injustice: "Black and Third World people are expected to educate white people as to our humanity. Women are expected to educate men. Lesbians and gay men are expected to educate the heterosexual world. The oppressors maintain their position and evade their responsibility for their own actions. There is a constant drain of energy which might be better used in redefining ourselves and devising realistic scenarios for altering the present and constructing the future."

Personally, I realize that anger makes those holding the anger sick—it weakens our body's immune system and leads to higher blood pressure, stress, and anxiety. Yet forgiveness sometimes feels to me like a perversion of justice disguised as spiritual grace; expecting the oppressed to forgive the oppressor feels like yet another burden to put on the oppressed.

So as I listen to John tell his story, this forgiving thing feels messed-up. Which I mention to John. He shrugs in response, as if to say that I can think whatever I want to think, but this is what's right for him. John adds that it was not only Pastor Deo's preaching that affected him. "It is also worth mentioning that what they [the Prison Fellowship] were doing for me contributed to my change." The members of the Prison Fellowship community had opened their hearts to John, and that, in turn, helped John open his heart to the community—Hutus included.

And then in walked Marie-Jeanne Uwimana, the Hutu woman John had known of only as a small girl who lived in the next village.

"It is during the church services that I heard her name, and I became so curious that I asked people where her family lived," John says about Marie-Jeanne. He's a bit coy telling this part of the story, almost bashful. What's clear is that even though their age difference was more pronounced when they were younger, John had fond notions of Marie-Jeanne.

One night, he continues, "God showed me Marie-Jeanne." He means in a dream, it seems, but either way, no one else blinks at this notion either.

John decided to go court her. Three days later, he proposed. John and others tell me that such speedy courtship is common in Rwanda, especially in the countryside. And after you've been through so much pain, I understand wanting to rush toward love. But there was one other detail I found almost impossible to fathom: Marie-Jeanne's father had led the Hutu militia that slaughtered John's family—and John knew it.

Marie-Jeanne also knew that her father had something to do with the murder of John's family, but she didn't know the details. Either way, she didn't let that stop her. "When I saw him," she tells me about the day John showed up on her doorstep, "I immediately thought that he had come to propose." And she said yes.

But she also told him she had to talk with her family.

"When I shared the idea with my family members, they could not believe their ears," she recounts. Her mother and sister told Marie-Jeanne exactly what her father had done. They told her everything. Still, she was undeterred. Her family pleaded with her that she couldn't marry John, that he was only proposing to her for revenge and would mistreat her in retaliation.

In a phenomenal example of thinking without a banister, Marie-Jeanne says, "I told them that if my father wronged John's family, I was not the one to blame. I came to the conclusion that this had been my father's business, not mine."

Marie-Jeanne says she told herself, "If he really loves me, nothing will stop me from marrying him."

As the American feminist Robin Morgan writes, "Hate generalizes, love specifies." Through love, we challenge and let go of all kinds of assumptions. And whatever cynicism I'd had about John and Marie-Jeanne's rapid courtship was melted away by seeing them together.

In the fall of 2016, when I travel to Rwanda and meet Marie-Jeanne and John, they are living in the same home John was given, in Pastor Deo's reconciliation village. They've been married for ten years. Their four absolutely adorable little kids keep trying to hide behind the table legs and sneak a look at the gangly white lady with the iPhone and the notebook. Meanwhile, John and Marie-Jeanne's obvious affection for each other is purely enchanting.

Marie-Jeanne tells me that her mother and sister "have been

amazed by the way we live happily together. It is something beyond their imagination."

But what of Marie-Jeanne's father, I wonder. Marie-Jeanne has been trying to find him. She believes he's living in Uganda, trying to escape persecution for his crimes during the genocide. Whenever anyone she knows visits Uganda, Marie-Jeanne sends them with whatever scraps of details she has about her father's whereabouts and asks them to try to find him and urge him to come back home. "I do not hate him," Marie-Jeanne tells me. "I cannot hate him." She explains that he was a good dad and a good person as she knew him.

And what about John? Does he hate his wife's father, the cause of so much of his suffering? No, John insists. He seems to have learned a transformative kind of love that perhaps few of us can ever attain. "I really love him so much," John tells me. "The only problem is that I don't have strong legs. If I did, I would even uplift him to show him how much I love him." John hoists his arms enthusiastically in the air to show how high he would lift Marie-Jeanne's father if he could.

"Nothing is easier than to denounce the evildoer, nothing is harder than to understand him," wrote Fyodor Dostoyevsky. Loving the evildoer who massacred your entire family seems downright impossible.

Then a smile fills John's whole face. "I really love the man who gave birth to my beloved wife," he declares.

"I feel that John and I will live together forever," Marie-Jeanne tells me as she smiles back at her husband. "People should know that all human beings are to be treated the same way. My desire is to see people love each other the way we do."

Genocide scholar Steven Baum dedicated his book, *The Psy-*

chology of Genocide, to those who acted as resisters and rescuers during atrocities, whom he refers to as *alles goeie mensen*, a Dutch phrase he translates as "those good people who live above hate." John and Marie-Jeanne have learned to love above hate. Their story would be heartwarming anywhere in the world, but in a nation that once burned so hot with hatred, Marie-Jeanne and John are like two phoenixes rising from the ashes, taking the hope for Rwanda's future under their wings.

AND HOW HAS Rwanda fared postgenocide? Not exactly as well as Marie-John and John. Though by many accounts, great strides have been made, tensions and resentments remain.

The genocide ended when RPF forces, led by Paul Kagame, overthrew the Hutu government and established an RPF-dominated coalition government. Kagame has been president since 2000, having won a landslide reelection in 2017. He is hailed as a savior by some but condemned as a tyrant by others. Some of the steps the government has taken to bring about reconciliation have been widely praised. Others have been harshly criticized.

The ringleaders of the genocide were tried in the International Criminal Court. But for the hundreds of thousands of others suspected of participating in the killing, the government set up *gacaca* courts. "Gacaca" roughly translates as "sitting down to discuss an important issue." The courts were overburdened and imperfect; many alleged perpetrators died awaiting trial. But in addition to determining guilt and punishment for those convicted, the gacaca courts created a public process for community members to hear what had happened to their loved ones, and for communities in general to engage in accountability and healing.

Many Tutsi survivors told me that they only found out where

the bodies of their family members were buried because of the gacaca process. And Hutu perpetrators told me it forced them to take responsibility, not just serving their time in prison but fully facing what they had done and the people they'd done it to. As a Hutu man named Frederic Kazigwemo explained to me, "During the gacaca courts, there were Hutus who were together during the genocide—they were refusing to say that they took the properties of Tutsis. For me, I was judging them, because I saw them. And so I said, 'You took this! You took this! I was seeing you!'"

More controversial, however, are the government-created *ingando*—national reeducation camps designed to foster national unity and discourage ethnic distinctions. As Hutu prisoners have been released, they've been required to attend the camps, as have most of the nation's Hutu and Tutsi youth. But the government plan calls for every Rwandan to eventually attend. The idea is to create spaces where Hutus and Tutsis together learn about their connections and combat the hateful ideas spread by genocide propaganda, "to share from a common dish—to eat and sleep together—this would build confidence . . . that we could in fact live together," as the director of National Unity and Reconciliation Commission once explained it.

Yet some have criticized the ingando as projects of pro-RPF propaganda—"a dangerous undertaking in a country in which political indoctrination and government-controlled information were essential in sparking and sustaining the genocide," writes Fordham University professor and human rights lawyer Chi Mgbako. And there are troubling aspects to the government's promotion of pan-ethnic nationalism. As Mgbako argues, "*ingando* is dangerous because instead of teaching tolerance for 'difference,' it leads to an obliteration of 'difference.'" One Rwandan journalist told Mgbako that the camps are basically "brainwashing"—and that, yes, it's important for people to put the common good or even the nation above ethnic identity, but the journalist added, "it is wrong to tell people not to identify as what they are."

Plus remember the research showing that those who preserve their distinct identities are more likely to resist groupthink? We must foster group bonds not by imposing a homogenous identity on everyone but by building a sense of shared humanity that not only respects but actively appreciates everyone's differences, especially because those differences help us resist dangerous groupthink banisters.

Has the Rwandan government merely been imposing other types of dangerous conformity? For instance, it's now a crime in Rwanda to point out that as part of their efforts to defeat the Hutu extremist government and take over the country, rebel Tutsi forces also committed atrocities during the period of the genocide. Those atrocities committed by Hutus against Tutsis were unarguably several orders of magnitude worse, but if you go to the genocide memorials and museums in Rwanda, the staff now officially talk about the "genocide against the Tutsis" as a matter of government policy. And, as the *New York Times* reported, a university professor was sentenced to prison for five years after a student reported the professor had said something critical of Paul Kagame.

Coming from a country that has never engaged in a national truth-and-reconciliation process to atone for its founding sin of ethnic cleansing and its sins of slavery and segregation, I'm in no position to point fingers here. I think the progress Rwanda has made in light of its history is remarkable, and despite imperfections, the impact thus far seems positive. I met a number of Tutsis living together peacefully, as neighbors, with the Hutus who had killed their loved ones—like Leonard Rucogoza and Marie Izagiriza—and even, slowly, carefully restoring their friendships. That's beyond incredible.

Still, Rwanda serves as a cautionary tale, not only about how readily people can be provoked to commit horrific violence but also how easily governments, opposition groups, media, and other aspects of society can undermine our ability to think without banisters. This is why—while each of us can and should play our own part in shoring up civility, repudiating hate and rejecting the banisters that lead to ugliness—understanding how hate is fostered systemically, in overt and covert ways, and how deeply hate can be embedded in our institutions, is an integral component of combating pandemics.

SIX

Systems of Hate: The Big Picture

The chain reaction of evil—hate begetting hate, wars producing more wars—must be broken, or we shall be plunged into the dark abyss of annihilation. —Martin Luther King Jr.

When Grace Bell Hardison was born in North Carolina in 1916, black women in the US didn't have the right to vote. In fact, no women did. Even after the Fifteenth Amendment passed in 1870, it granted voting rights only to African American men. So it wasn't until the Nineteenth Amendment was adopted in 1920 that women—including black women like Grace—could vote.

Despite those constitutional guarantees, when Grace reached voting age in 1934, disenfranchisement of black voters was still widespread. In many southern states, including North Carolina, where Grace has lived her whole life, the government mandated literacy tests for voters. These were harder for black folks to pass, because they had been discriminated against in the education system. And states adopted poll taxes, requiring voters to pay a fee in order to cast a ballot, another barrier aimed at disenfranchising black voters, who were disproportionately poor.

If it wasn't clear enough that these laws were meant to inhibit black voters, they included "grandfather" clauses. If your father or grandfather could vote prior to 1867, you were exempted from the poll taxes and literacy tests. Of course, there were no black voters prior to 1867; the Fifteenth Amendment hadn't been passed yet. This was just a loophole so that poor illiterate white folks could still vote. It's also a prime example of how an allegedly race-neutral law can be actually extremely discriminatory when taken in context.

Meanwhile, the few black citizens who did manage, in spite of all this, to successfully register to vote would find their names published in the local newspaper, which would alert local KKK gangs to then show up at their homes and threaten them with violence. For instance, in 1922, members of the KKK reportedly flew over Topeka, Kansas, and dropped postcards in black neighborhoods warning against voting. If black people did nonetheless manage to try to vote, they often found out that the KKK would make good on their threats.

The 1965 Voting Rights Act was supposed to fix all this, specifically outlawing literacy tests and, more generally, prohibiting states or the federal government from enacting any voting laws that had either the intent or effect of discriminating against race or language minorities. And the law established federal oversight for communities in which more than 50 percent of the nonwhite population had been stopped from registering to vote. This way, the Department of Justice could keep an eye on states that had historically engaged in widespread disenfranchisement.

So the problem was solved, right? Not exactly. The Voting Rights Act did make a huge difference in shifting public norms while creating vital oversight and accountability. But that didn't mean voter suppression stopped.

For instance, in the 1980s the Republican National Committee created the National Ballot Security Task Force, in which off-duty police officers armed with their loaded service revolvers patrolled polling stations in black communities. The party was sued in 1982 for violating the Voting Rights Act. But then just four years later, a leaked memo from the Republican National Committee detailed how a new "ballot security" program in Louisiana would "keep the black vote down." Sure, Republicans had a partisan motivation in suppressing the Democratic vote, but they could have also tried to suppress the *white* Democratic vote. Arguably, other bias and bigotry was at play here in choosing to suppress the black vote in particular. And perhaps Republicans thought they could get away with it in a society with a history of not caring about black people and their rights. Questioning the legitimacy of white voters would seem preposterous, but who would bat an eye at questioning the legitimacy of black voters, whose very humanity, let alone voting rights, had already been questioned by US society and politics for so long? This tangle of laws and norms and causes and effects is systemic hate.

In 2013, Shelby County, Alabama, sued to overturn the sections of the Voting Rights Act that had put its electoral practices under federal oversight. The county won. In the landmark ruling *Shelby County v. Holder*, which gutted major parts of the Voting Rights Act, Chief Justice John Roberts declared, "Our country has changed."

Yes, but how much? A year later, Alabama passed a strict requirement that all voters show ID—and then it shut down DMV offices in 80 percent of the state's blackest counties, making it harder for black residents to get the IDs they were now required to have to vote. It's the kind of move the Voting Rights Act wouldn't have allowed, had it still been fully in effect.

All of which brings us to 2016, when the state of North Carolina tried to disenfranchise Grace Bell Hardison. A mailing sent to Grace's home by a mayoral candidate was returned as undeliverable—because Grace used a post office box for her mail. But Republican activists used the returned mailing as evidence to try to have Grace removed from the voting rolls altogether, along with 137 other North Carolina voters they similarly targeted—two-thirds of whom were, like Grace, black and registered as Democrats. Fortunately, Grace fought back—and through her family and the local National Association for the Advancement of Colored People (NAACP) chapter, got the attention of the media and even then-president Barack Obama. "It is a shame that I had to experience this ordeal at 100 years old, and over 50 years after the Voting Rights Act was signed into law," Grace wrote in a letter to President Obama. "It is also disappointing that other African-American voters are being targeted in the same way."

What does any of this have to do with hate? Efforts to disenfranchise black voters today are inextricably linked to the past—to slavery and the fact that for centuries black people weren't recognized as full *human beings*, let alone citizens with equal civil rights. And then, amidst whatever the other excuses or explanations may be, that systematic marginalization plays out in other forms, from who gets threatened with violence to whose legitimate right to vote is questioned at all. Grace and I have the same exact voting rights, but Grace faces more barriers to voting, because of systemic hate.

Grace Bell Hardison did manage to cast her vote in the 2016 presidential election. An election official brought a ballot to her as she sat in the passenger seat of a car parked at her polling place—she's one hundred years old, after all. A photo of Grace sitting in the car, proudly wearing an "I Voted" sticker, quickly spread around social media, and for good reason. But the photo shows only Grace's individual triumph. What it doesn't show is all the systemic hurdles that Grace and so many other voters have had to maneuver over, and that still prevent many people—especially people of color—from voting.

Voting is just one example of how hateful otherizing and inequity can be embedded in and fostered by policies and institutions. We see the same embedded history of hate in everything from schools to health care to the criminal justice system and more, and not only in terms of discriminating against black people or women. For instance, as we'll see, systemic hate in our institutions and norms in the United States also perpetuates bias against poor and working-class white folks in rural communities.

We can't just pin institutional bias on the individuals working within those institutions. Certainly that's a factor, as when 18 percent of Latino registered voters report they have been told by officials at polling places that they can't vote. But systemic hate is also a product of the systems themselves—whether intentionally or inadvertently—because these systems reverberate and replicate the hate of the past. Racism, sexism, homophobia, Islamophobia, discrimination against physically impaired people, economic elitism, and other forms of hate shape our policies and practices and norms, which, in turn, then perpetuate hate even further. To combat systemic hate, we've got to get better at spotting it, which can be quite difficult, because systems are complex.

"Our analytical minds rarely tend toward a holistic view of complex systems," writes Valerie Hudson, a professor at the Bush School of Government and Public Service at Texas A&M University, and her coauthors in the book *Sex & World Peace*. "For example, take a moment and picture a tree. What do you see? Perhaps you envision a tall tree with many leaves and a big straight trunk with long branches. Do you think about the root system that is sometimes larger than the part of the tree aboveground—the roots that keep the tree alive?" The point of systemic thinking, the authors write, "is to see the entire tree."

According to the *Oxford English Dictionary*, a "system" is defined as "a set of things working together as parts of a mechanism or an interconnecting network" or "a complex whole." For example, the way that voting-rights laws, local elections-office practices, popular culture around voting, the history of violence against black voters, and the history of racism and white supremacy and black oppression in the United States all interact and interlock. This system not only shapes individual voting patterns but the entirety of our democracy. Which in turn means that when we see problems like low voter turnout, it's wise to widen our analysis to see not only individual behavior and factors but the systemic variables.

For another example of a problem caused by systemic hate, consider the opioid epidemic ravaging many small-town and rural white communities. In 1996, the drug OxyContin was first introduced to the market by Purdue Pharmaceuticals. Since then, drug overdoses in the United States have skyrocketed. In 2015, drug overdose was the leading cause of accidental death in the United States. And of the 52,404 Americans who died of drug overdoses in 2015, more than a third were from prescription pain relievers. In fact, the amount of prescription opioids sold has quadrupled, even though reports of pain have not gone up. So what's happening?

We could blame the addicts themselves. And like with black folks not turning out to vote, certainly individual responsibility is a factor. Drug abuse is an individual choice; no one is forcing addicts to swallow pills or put a needle in their arm. Yet there are also systemic dynamics at play. One is that opioid painkillers are being massively overprescribed by doctors. And bear in mind that if, because of racial bias, doctors are underprescribing painkillers to African Americans, that means overprescribing then disproportionately affects white communities. In Utah, a state that is almost 150 percent whiter than the country as a whole, pharmacists fill seventy-two hundred opioid prescriptions per day. That's more than 2.6 million prescriptions per year—in a state that only has three million residents. Another horrifying example? One pharmacy in Kermit, West Virginia—population 392—received almost nine million hydrocodone pills in just two years. Institutional players like pharmacies and pill distributers could have raised a red flag and intervened, but they didn't.

And that's still not the whole picture. Overprescription is also fueled by pharmaceutical companies aggressively promoting the wonders of opioids. They have even founded nonprofits, like the American Academy of Pain Management, which has used dubious research to create guidelines for doctors, encouraging more aggressive prescribing. Insurance companies also play a role. Because opioids are generally cheaper than other types of treatments for pain, such as physical therapy, acupuncture, and massage, insurers reimburse for painkiller prescriptions while limiting coverage for effective and healthy alternative treatments. This problem was so widespread in September 2016 that thirty-seven state attorneys general sent a letter to the head of the insurance-industry trade group, urging insurers to change this.

And the federal government contributes to the problem. Starting in 2014, Medicaid and Medicare inadvertently incentivized hospitals to prescribe opioids to poor and elderly patients. Patient satisfaction surveys, which the government uses to determine reimbursement rates for hospitals, included questions about whether patients felt their pain issues were addressed. Hospitals got paid more when patients reported that their pain was managed, so experts say these questions on the reimbursement survey contributed to increasing opioid prescriptions. In 2017, the government stopped including pain management questions in Medicaid and Medicare reimbursement calculations. But still, the US government has failed to regulate opioid pharmaceuticals aggressively—and has, in fact, looked the other way in cases of gross industry abuse—in part because of massive lobbying and campaign spending from these big businesses.

But that's not all. The economy also plays a role: opioid addiction and overdose rates are highest in white communities with high unemployment. A National Bureau of Economic Research study in 2017 found that when unemployment rises in a county, opioid overdoses and deaths rise, too. Federal Reserve chair Janet Yellen acknowledged the link during congressional testimony, saying of the epidemic, "I do think it is related to declining labor force participation among prime-age workers."

Specifically, the counties hardest hit by opioids are rural white communities that have seen their jobs hollowed out by what the *Atlantic* calls "this most recent, post-NAFTA era of deindustrialization." The result is that while life expectancy had generally been increasing for all racial and ethnic groups, recently white life expectancy has declined—driven by astronomical drug overdose rates.

Again, what does all this have to do with hate? It's not like the doctors and pharmacists in rural white communities hate their neighbors, right? But the fact that this crisis is centered in those communities has everything to do with systemic bias and hate. Arguably, it's because of a combination of racism and elitism that we as a country prioritize not only job creation for white people but job creation for educated middle-class and upper-class white people. Policies like the North American Free Trade Agreement lined the pockets of corporations—and their elite executives and investors—while by some accounts destroying over one million jobs and worsening economic inequity. If we truly valued the rural white working class, we wouldn't have passed policies that so disproportionately harm them. And even then, if we cared as much about rural white folks as we care about wealthy white coastal elites, we would have noticed sooner that they were dying of a drug epidemic and, instead of passing policies that made it worse, we would have done everything in our power to fix it.

Think about even those of us who try to be careful to not say anything antiblack or antigay but who casually and habitually demean rural white folks. That was certainly the mentality behind that Dumbfuckistan map I circulated so gleefully. And I'll also admit to having used phrases like "podunk" and "backwoods" more than I should have, to refer, condescendingly, to poor white communities.

In 2015, Chris Janson—the white southern country singer who wrote the pro-Trump theme song for the 2016 Republican National Convention—penned a song called "White Trash." One of the lines is, "Well if they'd had their way / They'd have thrown us away." Which, J. D. Vance recounts in his memoir, *Hillbilly Elegy*, is exactly what many rural white folks believe liberal elites think about them.

But it's not just liberals. In 2016, *National Review*'s Kevin Williamson, writing about the opioid crisis in rural white America, said, "The truth about these dysfunctional, downscale communities is that they deserve to die." It's arguable that this cultural disdain contributes to the systemic opioid crisis. The United States hates poor black folks *and* poor white folks, although in different degrees and different forms.

Systems that are shaped by hate produce hateful results. Unless we stop them. As Grace Bell Hardison exemplifies, we have levers with which we can buck the system. And the more of us who work together, the bigger the levers we can pull. But first we have to see them.

REMEMBER ROBBERS CAVE, psychologist Muzafer Sherif's experiment in which he separated boys into two groups at a summer camp and was able to quickly make them turn against each other and then later unite? It turns out that Sherif had conducted two experiments before Robbers Cave—with dramatically different outcomes. The first was in 1949, five years before Robbers Cave, and the second, in 1953, the year before Robbers Cave. Sherif considered both of those experiments failures, because despite the best attempts of his research teams to get the boys in the first two experiments to turn on each other, they ended up turning on a third group: the experimenters. In both studies, the boys became suspicious of the men who were supposedly counselors and camp staff, because the boys saw the "counselors" conspicuously observing them with recorders and notepads.

For instance, in the 1953 study at the phase where Sherif and his team intended to turn the groups of boys against each other—when researchers vandalized the camp of one group, expecting the boys to blame the other group—the boys figured out they were being manipulated by Sherif's team. They told the other group, and together, they complained. What's more, the boys started to suspect that the camp was some sort of experiment, asking questions of the researchers about why they were taking notes and why there were microphones hanging from the ceiling of the mess hall. Their suspicions were confirmed when one of the boys found a staff notebook of research observations. Sherif quickly disbanded the study.

In his analysis of all three of the studies, social psychologist Michael Billig makes an important point—Sherif's experiments didn't include just two groups, but rather three. The experimenters themselves were a group, and the most powerful one at that, in effect operating as and controlling the larger camp system with an express goal of stirring up conflict. In the final version of the study, Sherif successfully figured out how to more subtly conduct the research observations and at the same time generate conflict without the boys realizing they were being manipulated—in effect, making his systemic role invisible, within its context. Like the systems in a real society that stir hate and conflict without us even noticing.

There are two important takeaways from the totality of Sherif's studies. One is that, often, what we believe is natural conflict is the result of groups being intentionally pitted against one another by forces that have a vested interest in creating conflict. The other is that these manipulations, as well as the ways in which our systems are constructed to foster hate, can be so subtle that they're extremely difficult to detect. The kids in Sherif's first two studies were indignant that they were being manipulated and that the whole camp was a setup—which led them to stop fighting each other and instead fight the system. That's what we all need to do—become acutely aware of how our institutions and norms and otherwise-invisible social mechanisms are pitting us systemically against one another; feel deeply indignant about it; and attack *those systems* instead of each other. But first we have to unmask systemic hate so that we can help unite in opposing it.

I spent the first part of my career as a community organizer because as I looked at our economic, social, and political problems, it was clear they required the sort of large-scale change that is only possible when large groups of people together unmask and oppose hate. The disproportionate wealth gap between white families and black families; the way undocumented immigrants are lured into the country by US businesses and then denied basic rights; how women are paid less and given less opportunity for advancement than men—these are problems that individual initiative alone can't solve.

My first real project as a community organizer was helping LGBT employees in businesses and government agencies lobby their employers to create domestic partnership benefits plans—so that LGBT employees could include their partners on their health insurance and other workplace benefits. This wasn't something individuals could do alone—they couldn't just, one by one, create exceptions to corporate and government policies. But when they came together to press their case, employees were able to win change. Those victories were important, but even they were limited to one employer at a time. One of the many reasons to push for marriage equality was to achieve equal benefits not just company by company, or local government by local government, but all at once, for everyone. But that took even more people pushing.

Community organizing is premised on the belief that collective problems can be solved only through collective action that pushes for collective solutions. The solutions throughout this book—connection-speech, connection-spaces, and connection-thinking—get us part of the way toward the opposite of hate, but we also need big-picture solutions that broadly change policies, institutions, and cultural norms. That's where "connection-systems" come in. We need to enact laws and institutional practices—and promote social and cultural norms more broadly—that recognize we're all fundamentally equal and, at the same time, help us respect and relate to each other's differences. That looks like everything from overturning laws that have perpetuated inequity and injustice to passing policies that support inclusion and integration, to making sure people get equal pay and communities get equal resources, to reforming institutions that incentivize divisiveness and hate.

Consider the systemic problem of school segregation and inequity. Recall that when Scottie Nell Hughes and I went to the Moton Museum in Farmville, Virginia, we learned about the history of *Brown v. Board of Education* and how in the face of courts forcing racial integration of schools, white people desperately looked for ways to preserve segregation. That didn't just happen in the South. As more and more African Americans fled the South and moved north during the Great Migration throughout the early 1900s, white folks in the North also moved into all-white suburbs and exurbs because they didn't want to live next to black families and they didn't want their kids in school with black kids.

This "white flight"—encouraged by government and banking policy—reshaped public education for generations. So, just as the *Brown* decision was mandating formal integration, white folks were physically self-segregating to try to avoid *Brown*'s reach. Meanwhile, public schools in the South were at one point some of the most integrated in the United States, mainly because of federal court orders. "But since 2000, judges have released hundreds of school districts, from Mississippi to Virginia, from court-enforced integration," reports ProPublica, a public-interest journalism organization. And without oversight, many of those districts headed straight back toward segregation.

A result is that today in the United States, more than one out of every ten black and Latino students attend so-called "apartheid schools," in which whites make up less than 1 percent of enrollment. Incidentally, most of those schools are not in the South but in the Northeast and Midwest. And across the country, because so-called apartheid schools are in disproportionately poor communities and because school funding is apportioned mostly through local property taxes, apartheid schools receive less funding than wealthy white schools.

Bear in mind it's not just because of income inequality that black families are forced into poor neighborhoods but because property taxes are determined by home values, and those values have been affected by decades of redlining policies in the United States, through which banks and the government colluded to relegate black families to certain neighborhoods and then devalue the property in those neighborhoods. The result is that, for instance, the wealthy school district in Greenwich, Connecticut, spends $6,000 more per pupil per year than the poor district in Bridgeport, Connecticut, just a few miles away. Meanwhile, nationwide, "the achievement gap between black and white students, which greatly narrowed during the era in which schools grew more integrated, widened as they became less so."

Education scholar Jonathan Kozol reports that he's often asked about school inequity: "Can you really solve this kind of problem with money?" Yet the people who ask him this are often the ones spending tens of thousands of dollars a year to send their own kids to private schools, presumably because they actually do believe that more money makes for better schools. Certainly the problems in the education system have multiple dimensions, but there's no question that we can't expect kids to get equal educations if they don't benefit from equal resources.

When I raise this issue with my white friends, they often say, "Well, what am I supposed to do? Send my kids to crappy schools?" And I don't just hear this from white conservatives but also from white liberals. These are people who pride themselves on living in racially and economically diverse communities, but nonetheless they send their kids to private schools in which the vast majority of students are rich and white. As one white liberal friend once put it when I pressed her on this, "I will not sacrifice my children on the altar of my politics." But that sentiment not only overlooks the role white parents could play in working for change but the many great reasons they have for doing so. Also, in complex systems, just because the problems can't be fixed all at once doesn't mean we shouldn't fix the problems we can.

Racial and ethnic diversity is great for communities. One study found that ethnic diversity in a community increases home values and lowers crime. Another study found that as US cities have become more diverse, they have become safer. In the biggest cities in the US, crime "fell as the percentage of the population that is non-white and the percentage that is gay increased." The same has been found in the suburbs: "As suburbia diversified, crime rates fell," another scholar wrote. Plus nationwide polling data show that people who live in racially inclusive communities are happier, more optimistic, and less stressed—all of which corresponds to living healthier and more productive lives. It's sort of like the fleeing white folks are just shooting themselves in the foot, along with their children and the rest of us. It's by demanding integrated schools, both racially and socioeconomically, that parents can help to improve the system *for all kids.*

If that seems like just some hippie-dippie pipe dream, the school district in Omaha, Nebraska, Omaha Public Schools (OPS), offers some concrete evidence for hope. "When court-ordered busing began in 1976, 'white flight' began in earnest," writes investigative journalist Sharon Lerner. "Over the next four years, the number of students in OPS plummeted from 53,825 to 38,000."

Since then, other school districts were created, several of which technically fall within Omaha city limits but are controlled by suburbs or independent bodies. The Westside district, for instance, "sits, like Vatican City inside Rome, entirely within the bounds of Omaha and OPS," writes Lerner. Containing some of the most expensive homes in Omaha and boast-worthy SAT scores, Westside was created as an all-white independent school district just before the *Brown v. Board of Education* ruling. Meanwhile, although African Americans make up just under 5 percent of Nebraska's population statewide, they're now half of OPS students—or rather, *were*, before the district decided to do something about it.

Long fed up with the inequality between districts, in 2004 OPS administrators and community leaders noticed an obscure Nebraska state law that would make it possible for OPS to take over and control the other districts. In the face of that extreme threat, eleven districts hesitantly came together to create a "Learning Community." The joint program involves sharing tax revenue; in the 2010–2011 school year, OPS got $32 million more through the Learning Community's allocation than it would have gotten through its own property taxes, while eight districts received less than they would have.

Also the program makes it possible for students from one district to attend school in another district within the Learning Community if doing so increases that school's socioeconomic diversity. Which has allowed poor students from OPS to attend school in districts like Westside but has also allowed well-off students from suburban districts to attend OPS. One white girl decided to do so because she realized going to school with all white kids wouldn't prepare her for life in the twenty-first century. The OPS high school she chose had "students from over 40 different countries," she told Lerner. That student ended up winning a $10,000 college scholarship from Coca-Cola because of an essay she wrote "about tutoring her peers from Asia, Mexico, and the Sudan."

The Omaha experiment isn't without challenges, or controversy. Many people in the wealthier districts resent the program and continue to fight it. The lawyer representing OPS in ongoing legal battles told journalist Sharon Lerner a story of a white parent who, after a presentation defending the Learning Community, came up to the lawyer and said, "If I understood correctly, you're telling me that my child has 10 crayons and these kids have no crayons. And you want us to give some of our crayons to those kids. Now that's probably fair. But as a parent, I'm never going to get behind anything that takes away my child's crayons." We hear something of Arlie Russell Hochschild's "deep story" in her complaint, as though fixing the school funding imbalance is similar to people cutting the line, advancing themselves to the detriment of white people. That mom isn't thinking about why her kid has more crayons to begin with.

Still, despite such opposition, the community leaders and activists behind the Learning Community successfully put pressure on the better-off districts and got them to sign on. And now the schools are figuring out how to work together as their students also connect. The collective action in Omaha and the ultimate connection-system it achieved are powerful examples of how systemic challenges can be opportunities to bring people together rather than divide them.

Collective action by definition requires a group, but one person can definitely get the ball rolling. A great example of this is the work of Nahed Artoul Zehr, a Palestinian Christian who emigrated to the United States when she was six and now leads a Muslim rights organization in Nashville, Tennessee.

Nahed has a PhD in religious studies, and her academic career included teaching Islam and the Quran at the US Naval War College. But as she moved through the ranks of tenure-track academia, Nahed felt something was missing. She wanted to have more of an impact forging interfaith understanding among ordinary people, especially in the face of growing anti-Muslim sentiment in the United States. After running a four-week workshop on "understanding Islam" in her own Presbyterian congregation, Nahed quit academia and became executive director of the Faith and Culture Center, an organization that promotes understanding about Muslims and the Islamic faith.

Nahed quickly realized that most non-Muslims in Nashville simply didn't know any Muslims personally, which made it easier for their views to be shaped by negative stereotypes instead of fact. "What I've learned, and what I've seen," Nahed tells me when we talk over the phone, "is that paradigms change when you are in the same room with somebody who is not like you, and you have a conversation about things, which oftentimes don't really have anything to do with religion. They have to do with your shared experience as a human being."

To help more Muslims and non-Muslims share their experiences, Nahed created a series of dinner programs where people could literally break bread together and talk. It was that simple. But through just meeting one another and talking, as human beings, Nahed says, "People have had completely transformative experiences."

Then one day, a group of Evangelical Christian pastors from Nashville came to Nahed and asked for her help. They'd been hearing their congregants say some hateful things about Muslims, but the pastors didn't really know enough about Islam to respond effectively. And what they knew was often rumor, not fact. "We brought this group of folks together—Muslim leadership in Nashville and some folks who were associated with different evangelical churches in town," Nahed tells me. "We basically just conducted a relationship-building program." Which involved facilitated discussions about Islam and Christianity, such as about the status of women in Islam, and also in in Christianity.

But also, says Nahed, "We shared our meals together. We had some downtime together. And it was awesome."

Nahed recalls a funny moment during a conversation over breakfast. They were talking about the Hadiths, an important collection of stories about the life of Muhammad that shape how Muslims understand their faith. "I can't remember how this happened, but then we suddenly started talking about our favorite authors," Nahed says. "I don't know how we went from this to that," she continues, but suddenly, a Christian leader and a Muslim leader at the table were bonding over their shared love of William Faulkner. "Then we started talking about our favorite movies," she adds with a laugh. "We talked about what we have in common, what we all care about."

They came to understand that what we all have in common is more than—and more *important than*—any differences. And it's also how relationships are built. Now the pastors are expanding the program to include their congregants. Some members of evangelical churches are attending Friday prayers at a Nashville mosque, and they're having meals together, creating a wider, systematized practice and culture around connection.

Unfortunately, throughout the history of the world, some religious groups and institutions have contributed to and condoned hate, whether against other religions or other groups of people based on their race or gender or ethnicity. And sadly, that's still too often the case today. For instance, in Uganda, evangelical Christian churches pushed to criminalize the country's gay community—including proposing the death penalty for gay sex. In Myanmar, Buddhist monks have been the ones leading violent attacks against the country's Rohingya Muslim population.

Yet religious leaders and institutions have also played invaluable roles, past and present, in undermining the ideas and norms of hate and helping lead their congregants and the broader community in a better direction. Examples include the Southern Baptist

Convention, which played a leading role in the US civil rights movement; the Yeshivat Maharat, the first yeshiva to ordain Orthodox women as rabbis; the Episcopal Church, which became the first major Christian denomination to ordain openly gay bishops; the Al Fatah Pensantren, an all-transgender madrasa in Indonesia; and Pope Francis, who has put immigrant rights and environmental justice at the center of modern Catholic ministry.

Faith institutions have the capacity to either foster beliefs that fuel hate—or serve as spaces of cultural transformation that pursue hate's opposite. Just like businesses have an amazing capacity to foster connection—because the places we work are often more diverse than our neighborhoods and schools and congregations, and because the advertisements and products and services businesses create help define so much of our culture. All institutions have the opportunity to be part of the problem or part of the solution.

And as the Nashville example shows, systemic change always involves an interplay between individuals and institutions. Systemic change involves more than just individual leadership—even from powerful individuals. As a case in point, in September 2017, racial slurs were found scrawled on message boards at a preparatory school on the campus of the United States Air Force Academy. In response, the head of the Air Force Academy, Lieutenant General Jay Silveria, convened all four thousand cadets and fifteen hundred staff members and gave an impassioned speech in which he condemned hate in the starkest of terms. "If you're outraged by those words then you're in the right place," Silveria said. "You should be outraged not only as an airman, but as a human being." And then, after suggesting that it would be naive to think that everyone at the academy was immune from these sorts of biases, Silveria forcefully stated, "If you can't treat someone from another gender with dignity and respect, then you need to get out. If you demean someone in any way, you need to get out. If you can't treat someone from another race, or different color skin, with dignity and respect, then you need to get out."

It was a bold speech from a powerful individual in charge of a powerful institution—certainly one that could mark an important first step toward institutional and systemic change. But real institutional reform involves more than one single speech from one single leader. To begin with, while Silveria's speech rightfully signals intolerance for bias, it doesn't address the ways such bias is produced—including by the military itself. If Silveria and the United States Air Force by extension are serious about eradicating hate from the institution, they must interrogate the deep ways that the policies and practices of the Air Force perpetuate inequity and injustice. White airmen are promoted more frequently then airmen of color. Officers come disproportionately from more privileged economic backgrounds. Patriarchy is embedded in the very nature of military hierarchy. And Islamophobia has been weaponized through our military's widespread use of drones that cause mass civilian casualties—willful "collateral damage" that in turn fuels anti-American hate.

Certainly, the US military has made great strides in countering its legacy of misogyny and overt sexism by opening up service opportunities, including combat roles, to women. But in 2016, cases of sexual assault in the US military reached a record high—almost doubling from 2012. And statistics suggest that combat veterans are responsible for 21 percent of domestic violence nationwide. Addressing systemic hate in the military would mean not only addressing these problems but also addressing the fundamental reality that military action is necessarily premised on dehumanization of "the other."

In fact, much of military training is about helping soldiers overcome the natural disinclination we all have to not harm other human beings. The horror of killing others, especially in large numbers, seems to be involved in a rise in post-traumatic stress disorder (PTSD) in the US military. In his book about dehumanization, David Livingstone Smith tracks how the number of cases of PTSD has increased along with the accuracy and effectiveness of weapons technology. Certainly, there are those who would argue that instead of being an institution that combats hateful otherizing and dehumanization, the military encourages hate.

Lieutenant General Jay Silveria's speech is heroic. I personally wanted to get parts of it tattooed on my forearm. And certainly institutions, especially hierarchical ones like the military, can't change without leadership from the top. But many other individuals, both working within social systems and directly affected by them, and those surrounding the issue and the institution, must join the effort for change. Considerable social will is required for truly large-scale reform. And one key to building that will is unmasking not only the systemic problems, but addressing the systemic incentives that exacerbate hate. Unless we address the perverse incentives of hate, we will continue to be divided and we will never unite to advance change.

How can we work together to build momentum for legislative and regulatory change in the face of institutions that are dependent on whipping up hate between us? If we have any hope of systemically addressing the massive crisis of hate we face today worldwide, there's no question we need to address the ways in which our media and politics—by design—incentivize and exploit hate.

Take for exhibit A, Glenn Beck. When I first made the leap from community organizing to media, Fox News host Glenn Beck was at the top of the business; he had the number one show on cable television and was the number one thorn in the Obama administration's side. In 2010, Glenn Beck was listed as the fourth-most influential person in the world—ranked just after the pope. He'd built his massive following through unapologetic hate-mongering. In his heyday, he claimed, for example, that Barack Obama was more corrupt than Richard Nixon, and said Obama supported "killing 10 percent" of the American people with policies that amounted to "September 11th all over again."

Then suddenly, starting in 2014, he was sorry for all that. He still was in the midst of an apology tour of sorts when I visited him two years later at the media company he started after he left Fox, with offices just outside Houston.

"I didn't try to be divisive," Glenn tells me as we sit on a giant cream-colored leather couch in his office. "But you dress up in lederhosen, it's going to be divisive. I thought it was entertaining."

For the record, I own lederhosen. Half my family comes from Germany. And also, they're comfortable. But if you're a right-wing hate-monger who collects Nazi memorabilia, showing up on television in lederhosen as Glenn did is an unwise choice, unless you're trying to appeal to neo-Nazis. And let's not forget, this is also the man who said that "social justice" and "economic justice" are code words for Nazism.

Whether it was a conscious choice or not, the incentives to be divisive surrounded him. Once upon a time, Sarah Sobieraj and Jeffrey Berry explain in their book *The Outrage Industry*, broadcast media tried to be politically neutral and nonbiased, which federal regulations, to some extent, required and more generally incentivized. But in the 1980s, deregulation did away with government controls over content, such as the rule imposed for decades that broadcasters must present opposing viewpoints. Added to that, increased competition and new technology led to an environment where now "cable networks can produce content aimed at smaller, more homogeneous audiences"—which means networks have an excuse or even an incentive to play into those smaller audiences' particular biases to get their attention.

"I want you to know I'm not making excuses," Glenn adds as I try to stop myself from rolling my eyes. "I accept full responsibility for every word I said, okay?" He shrugs his shoulders. "I would ask for the benefit of the doubt that this was not my intent, but that intent doesn't change the end result." On this we agree.

"Decency is a fresh palette for Beck," the *New Yorker*'s Nicholas Schmidle sharply wrote, skewering Glenn's reversal as just another gimmick. But let's for a moment give Beck the benefit of the doubt he asks for. Heck, I like much of what he's been saying lately. Like: "We're not going to come together on politics. But we can come together on principles. It's just time for the hatred to end, or we're going to destroy ourselves." I could get that tattooed on my arm, too.

But the problem is that now hardly anyone is listening. His media company is going bankrupt. And the day after Donald Trump was inaugurated, when someone on Twitter accused Beck of creating Trump, Glenn Beck wrote, "The question is, what did we learn and how can we heal the divide and do no more damage." He got just thirty-eight retweets.

We can't lose sight of the fact that media hate-mongering is not the product of a few "bad apple" big mouths. As Sarah Sobieraj tells me when we talk on the phone, "I think it's really important people understand this isn't some reflection of the disintegration of modern society." The media is the way it is today, Sobieraj says, because "it's a reflection of the mandates and political economic underpinnings of the industry."

If the essential structures and economic incentives of the

industry could be altered, perhaps significant change would follow. After all, that tactic worked to get Glenn Beck off the air. Organizations like the racial justice group Color of Change went after the companies advertising on Beck's show, and later those advertising on Bill O'Reilly's show, with the idea that threatened embarrassment would get the brands to pull their ads. And the loss of ad revenue was a big reason Fox News pulled both shows.

Also, if you look at media with different mandates—Sobieraj points to NPR and PBS, nonprofit outlets that are funded by government and charitable donations—they're simply not bombastic. And while trust in the media was in decline well before Donald Trump's fake "fake news" assertions, PBS and NPR have continued to rank among the most trusted institutions by the American public.

Our society once supported regulations that required a degree of balance and a curbing of outright vitriol, because the idea that media figures should act with civility was a widely agreed-upon norm. We can revive that norm. Also, we can and must explore the potential of new technology platforms to make new business models viable and to defuse the power of hate-mongering, assuring that facts and well-reasoned arguments get more play in the news and on social media than smears and lies.

For instance, in light of the 2016 election being influenced by malicious fake news stories that spread recklessly throughout social media, scholars John Borthwick and Jeff Jarvis published a list of remedies the media could adopt. They include visibly branding posts and links from legitimate news sources so users know when they're sharing credible information. And certainly fact-checking needs to be expanded, perhaps under an independent bipartisan umbrella organization. I'm not saying any of this is easy. I am saying that we have good reason to believe it's possible.

And at the same time as dealing with the incentives of hate in the media, we have to rein in the nastiness of politicians who have also made hate not only systemic but successful within our election and political systems.

When the civil rights movement made it taboo to be explicitly racist in campaigning, white politicians in the United States became adept at using "racial dog whistles," turns of phrase that seem race-neutral but are encoded with biased messages that prey on and enflame white racial resentment. Just like only dogs can hear dog whistles, the idea is that only some voters can hear racial dog whistles—they get the point, while at the same time they can claim the messages *don't seem* overtly racist.

Ian Haney López, professor of law at the University of California, Berkeley, wrote *Dog Whistle Politics*, a history of the tactic. "The story of dog whistle politics begins with George Wallace," he says. Wallace has gone down in history as a notorious bigot, who bellowed, "Segregation now . . . segregation tomorrow . . . segregation forever!" from the steps of the state capital on the day of his inauguration as Alabama governor in 1963. But he first ran for governor, in 1958, as a racial moderate. He was even endorsed by the NAACP, while his opponent was endorsed by the KKK.

After Wallace lost that first governor's race, though, he reportedly told his campaign team, "Well, boys, no other son-of-a-bitch will ever out-nigger me again." Wallace made sure of that. As Haney López writes, "Four years later, Wallace ran as a racial reactionary, openly courting the support of the Klan and fiercely committing himself to the defense of segregation." He won. Wallace later recounted, "You know, I started off talking about schools and highways and prisons and taxes—and I couldn't make them listen. Then I began talking about niggers—and they stomped the floor."

In fact the Republican Party, which had been decimated in the South and thus in national elections for years, perked right up. The party realized that racist rabble-rousing could win southern white votes. In 1963, the conservative journalist Robert Novak reported after a Republican National Committee, "A good many, perhaps a majority of the party's leadership, envision substantial political gold to be mined in the racial crisis by becoming in fact, though not in name, the White Man's Party." The strategy to do so became known as the "Southern Strategy." But winning national elections required winning northern states, too, where overt race-baiting wouldn't fly, and so dog whistling was born.

Richard Nixon dog whistled his way to the White House. In the face of civil rights protests by the black community, Nixon used the language of "law and order" to promote, as Haney López writes, "a more 'quiet' form of violence in defense of the racial status quo, replacing lynchings with mass arrests for trespassing and delinquency."

Ronald Reagan took the dog-whistle cue from Nixon and blew it even harder. His first campaign stop as a presidential candidate in 1980 was at the Neshoba County Fair in Mississippi, the county in which the KKK infamously killed three civil rights workers, Andrew Goodman, Michael Schwerner and James Chaney, in 1964.

In his speech, Reagan proclaimed his support for "states rights"—dog-whistle code that the federal government should stay the hell out of the southern states' business and let them treat black people however they damn well pleased. Reagan also traded on the hateful stereotype of undeserving black people sucking up public assistance, in telling his fictional story of a "welfare queen" with "eighty names, thirty addresses [and] twelve Social Security cards." His racist pandering was deeply effective with white voters desperate to overlook the legacy of the country's racial inequities and believe in the deep story of the meritocratic line. In the 1980 election, 22 percent of Democrats voted for Ronald Reagan—driven, according to polling, by those who felt "civil rights leaders were pushing too fast" and that "the government should not make any special effort to help [black Americans] because they should help themselves."

Democrats have done it, too. Bill Clinton campaigned on "ending welfare as we know it," echoing Reagan. Clinton even borrowed some tricks from "Tricky Dick" Nixon. Clinton's version of Nixon's "law and order" was getting "tough on crime"—a dog whistle his wife, Hillary Clinton, blew even harder when, in 1996, she called black kids "super-predators," saying "we have to bring them to heel."

Of course, in the modern history of dog whistling, Donald Trump has blown everyone else away. He realized that there was enough fear, anger, and racial resentment harbored by enough white voters that he could trade in the whistle for a blowhorn. The fact that Trump's overtly hateful bombast—against Mexicans and Muslims and immigrants and women—appears to have not hurt him but actually helped him win is a deeply disturbing sign of just how pervasive bias is in the United States. Many Americans may wish to believe that Trump is an aberration. But he deftly stoked resentments that have long been systemically fueled by media figures and politicians, and which still, sadly, sell.

Trump has for years traded on white fear of losing cultural hegemony. In a 1989 interview, he said, "A well-educated black has a tremendous advantage over a well-educated white in terms of the job market." This, when in 1989 the median life expectancy for white men was 8.2 years more than for black men; median white household wealth was more than $100,000 while median black household wealth was under $10,000; and the average unemployment rate for white men was 4.1 percent while it was 8.55 percent for black men.

His ludicrous claim that Barack Obama wasn't born in the US, which so many thought was a bizarre stunt, was in fact another move from that same playbook. While Americans in general think that "blacks and Hispanics losing out because of preferences for whites" is the bigger problem in society today, most Trump supporters believe that "whites losing out because of preferences for blacks and Hispanics" is the bigger problem.

Trump didn't invent that idea. I remember a white male relative I barely knew insisting to me during lunch after my grandfather's funeral in 2001 that "white men are the most oppressed group in America today." Trump brazenly leveraged the anger and fear of those who hold that belief.

So what do we do? How do we not only unite for systemic solutions to hate but also overcome the incentives that keep the drumbeat of hate going? Because it's obviously easier to set groups against one another, to stoke competitive victimhood, to find scapegoats and pin blame on them. We certainly have a long tradition of that in the United States. And it's often easier to dehumanize and demonize than to understand, and to explain, the complex intertwining systemic factors that are the true causes of so many of the problems fueling anger and fear.

It's too easy to believe that the poverty and crime afflicting urban black communities is *their* fault, as Scottie Nell Hughes argues, not seeing it as the result of centuries of violence and oppression, economic discrimination, and white flight. Just as it's too easy to believe that poverty and crime afflicting rural white communities is *their* fault, not the product of discrimination and perverse health system incentives and the massive shift of manufacturing jobs from those rural towns to overseas. Because if it's *their* fault, then there's nothing for us to try and understand, let alone have to address. If it's hard enough to overcome our own individual prejudices and biases, overcoming systemic hate is an even steeper uphill battle.

And yet in the face of all these obstacles—with the status quo of injustice and hate not only so intransigent but simultaneously invisible—well-informed and well-organized groups of individuals have together moved mountains and changed hearts and minds in the history of the United States and around the world. Together, people ended chattel slavery in the United States and passed the Voting Rights and Civil Rights Acts. We banished child labor, stopped treating women as the legal property of their husbands, and adopted equal marriage rights for same-sex couples. In South Africa, collective action ended apartheid. Movements are advancing free speech rights in China, fighting industrial pollution in Thailand, and building democracy in Liberia. They're protecting food security and farmers' rights in India and winning land reform in Brazil.

In every moment in history in every corner of the globe, masses of people have fought together, and continue to fight, for major social change. Not because it is easy. Not because it is popular. Not even because it is clear we will win. But we fight for change because it is necessary and moral and just.

The more of us who band together to make the case for connection rather than division, to push and protest for systemic change, the more we can accomplish. As complicated as the systemic status quo is, the small and large formations of people who somehow find each other, find common interest, and capitalize on levers for change, against a deck of stacked odds, radically transform systems and the world around us.

Social movement practitioner and scholar Frances Kunreuther theorizes that the first step in achieving systemic change is "making visible the invisible"—helping to articulate the systemic injustices that are all around us but that we don't notice if we're not looking closely. Which is why it's so important not only that we understand systemic hate but that we help others do the same. Pointing out the way our criminal justice practices, immigration policies, economic arrangements, and social norms disadvantage some groups while unfairly helping others isn't senseless complaining. It's the strategic first step in eradicating systemic hate and creating a more fair and just world for all of us.

The good news is, systems and social norms aren't just abstract conglomerations of space dust—they are created by and controlled by human beings. Yes, they shape us, but we can also shape them, if we see ourselves as part of a larger and very much interconnected whole, capable of large-scale change. Something as simple as voting can seem like an individual act, like an individual leaf on the tree of civic participation, so inconsequential in the large scheme. But take it from Grace Bell Hardison, who still at age one hundred was fighting for her right to vote: the systemic levers we have as individuals for joining together and demanding change are an invaluable birthright of our democracy.

When you look at that picture of Grace as she cast her vote in 2016, you see a single elderly black woman sitting bolt upright in the passenger seat of a car with a smile on her face and her "I Voted" sticker on her blouse. You don't see all those obstacles she faced. But what you also don't see is all the other people, past and present, who persisted in fighting hate and reforming hateful systems so that Grace could hold that ballot in her hands.

When you're a part of a movement that fights against systemic hate and for systemic justice, you not only get to see the roots of change—you get to be part of them. Speaking from experience, there's no greater feeling of honor or hope.

CONCLUSION

The Journey Forward

How do we hold people accountable for wrongdoing and yet at the same time remain in touch with their humanity enough to believe in their capacity to be transformed?

—bell hooks

IN 1949, JUST after the atrocities of World War II and the Holocaust, George Orwell published *1984*. This dystopian novel imagines Orwell's native Britain as the fictional Oceania, taken over by a tyrannical political regime that governs with emotional manipulation. Individual thinking is outlawed, but citizens are under constant surveillance, just in case. Most go along with the regime willingly—in large part because of propaganda of misinformation, fear-mongering, and hate against a mysterious "other."

Every day in Oceania, all citizens are required to take part in the Two Minutes Hate, when they would watch a film that demeans and demonizes Oceania's enemies. The Two Minutes Hate is dramatically produced with "hideous, grinding speech, as of some monstrous machine running without oil," and shows "row after row of solid-looking men with expressionless Asiatic faces, who swam up to the surface of the screen and vanished, to be replaced by others exactly similar." It's propaganda of hate, and even Orwell's even-keeled protagonist, who harbors doubts about the

Oceania regime, can't help but be swept in. Everyone is. Orwell writes, "Before the Hate had proceeded for thirty seconds, uncontrollable exclamations of rage were breaking out from half the people in the room . . . A hideous ecstasy of fear and vindictiveness, a desire to kill, to torture, to smash faces in with a sledge hammer, seemed to flow through the whole group of people like an electric current, turning one even against one's will into a grimacing, screaming lunatic. And yet the rage that one felt was an abstract, undirected emotion which could be switched from one object to another like the flame of a blowlamp."

In 2013, Cass Sunstein, an academic and former member of the Obama administration, described Glenn Beck's show on Fox News as comparable to Orwell's Two Minutes Hate. In 2016, the alt-right publication *Breitbart* said that journalists and celebrities attacking Donald Trump amounted to a daily Two Minutes Hate. Meanwhile, President Trump's Twitter feed has also been equated to a regular Two Minutes Hate.

The point of Two Minutes Hate in *1984* was to distract people from the real problems that were affecting them—their own government and its oppressive actions—by directing their attention and anger elsewhere. Reflecting on the lessons of Orwell's book, a student in Georgia told her teacher, "We do need a public enemy, but not like that. Crime or poverty should be more of the public enemy that the world works to fight against." What if our hate is not only causing violence and pain and division but getting in the way of us solving the real problems that hurt us all?

I began writing this book in the days after the 2016 mass shooting at a nightclub in Orlando, Florida, and found myself finishing it in the days after the 2017 mass shooting at an outdoor festival in Las Vegas, Nevada. The shooting in Orlando, which was at the time considered the deadliest mass shooting in US history, involved a

Muslim American man opening fire inside a LGBT nightclub on "Latin Night"—thus most of the victims were queer Latinos. The shooting in Las Vegas involved a white man using military-grade weapons to fire from a hotel room window a quarter of a mile away on a crowd attending a country music show.

In some ways, these two crimes couldn't have been more different—in terms of the people who committed them and the communities they targeted. The left and right argue about how to mitigate these sorts of crimes. The right wants to place restrictions on Muslims entering the US. The left wants to ban the sale of assault weapons. But we all seem to assume that whatever motivates these particular acts, the hate and violence at their root are fundamentally inevitable and unavoidable.

After the Orlando shooting, President Obama called it "an evil, hateful act." President Trump called the Las Vegas shooting "an act of pure evil." We tend to label as evil that which we can't figure out how to otherwise explain. But probably the purest representation of evil, at least in Western culture, is the devil, and in the Bible, the devil isn't born evil but rather is the fallen angel Lucifer, who according to John 8:44 "abode not in the truth." In fact, the Gnostics believed that the devil was actually created when Christ "cast off his shadow from himself."

One of the many things I've always appreciated about Christianity is the notion that we are all sinners. It's admonishing and encouraging at the same time, reminding us that we all contain darkness and light, and have to strive to be our own better angels. Buddhism also emphasizes this dualism of good and evil—as the Japanese Buddhist priest Nichiren wrote, "Opposing good is called evil, opposing evil is called good."

And yet our highest spiritual or philosophical aspirations aside, the fact is that we tend to think of good and evil in very black-and-white terms—and we like to think that *we're good* and *they're evil.* Which is why the stories of people like Arno Michaelis and Bassam Aramin are so upsetting, because we find within them ordinary people, just like ourselves, who did profoundly heinous things. It's why Hannah Arendt's and Elizabeth Minnich's scholarship around evil and its supposed banality is so unsettling, because we don't want to face the fact that the potential complicity with evil—let alone the capacity for evil—lies within us. And it's why the horrors of Rwanda are so unimaginable, because we don't want to believe that we could do what, in actuality, most any human being is capable of. Recognizing the evil within ourselves and the good in others can deeply rupture our own sense of security. On the other hand, it's the first step to making ourselves and the world around us better.

What I've learned is that all hate is premised on a mind-set of otherizing. The sanctimonious pedestal of superiority on which we all put ourselves while we systematically dehumanize others is the essential root of hate. In big and small ways, consciously and unconsciously, we constantly filter the world around us through the lens of our explicit and implicit biases. This abets rationalization and looking the other way about widespread injustices, such as dismissing entire communities that don't have access to health care, or entire nations locked in civil war because they fall outside the sphere of our moral concern.

We think we're good people, but we don't see how that sphere of moral concern is constricted by hate, by the history and habits and culture of who matters and who doesn't in our society, which we have all bought into, whether we mean to or not. So we shake our heads about excessive corporate greed and we shake our fists against neo-Nazis marching in the streets, but not enough of us admit that they're reflections of the society we've all created, let alone acknowledge that they're reflections of ourselves.

We have a crisis of hate in the United States and around the world, and we can't begin to address it if we don't first learn to see it—making the invisible visible—uncovering the inadvertent, implicit, deliberate, and conscious forms of hate all around us *and in ourselves.* "Real change is systemic and self-implicating, urging us to see our role in vast, complex problems," writer Anand Giridharadas said in a speech at the first Obama Foundation Summit in October 2017. Leo Tolstoy wrote, "Everyone thinks of changing the world, but no one thinks of changing himself." We have to do both. Before it's too late.

As I wrote this book, well-meaning friends kept checking up on me. They figured the longer I spent studying hate, the more depressed I would get. But for me, the biggest surprise of this journey has been how optimistic and uplifted I feel. Yes, hate is profound—complicated and vexing as well as ugly and sad. But it is not inevitable, in any given individual or community or institution or system. Alongside the hateful history of the world are stories of transcending that hate: finding peace after genocide, granting liberty after oppression, even just inching toward equality in the wake of horrific injustice. Hate is no more hardwired into our world than it is into our brains. Change is possible.

I know this now not only because I read the psychology and biology and neuroscience research, but because I met people like Arno and Bassam and John and Marie-Jeanne and so many others—people who plumbed the greatest depths of hatred in our world and nonetheless managed to find a way out. If they can stop hating, there's certainly hope for the rest of us.

So what is the opposite of hate? Just as Holocaust survivor and writer Elie Wiesel said, "The opposite of love is not hate, it's indifference," the opposite of hate is also not love. You don't have to love people to stop hating them. You don't even have to like them. You also don't have to concede the validity of their views. Bassam was very clear that he still sees the Israelis in general as his enemies, but at the same time he no longer hates them.

The opposite of hate also isn't some mushy middle zone of dispassionate centrism. You can still have strongly held beliefs, beliefs that are in strong opposition to the beliefs of other people, and still treat those others with civility and respect. Ultimately, the opposite of hate is the beautiful and powerful reality of how we are all fundamentally linked and equal as human beings. The opposite of hate is *connection*.

When I was about nine years old, I went on a field trip during summer camp. We were in the woods somewhere, going on a hike; I don't remember where exactly. But in the wisps of sunlight that fell through the gaps in the leaves above, every couple steps I would catch a thin strand of something, suspended along the path, glistening. I asked my counselor what these strands were, and she told me they were parts of the interconnected web of the universe, the thin strands that connect us all together with every other living thing. I'll admit here that I was a fairly sheltered kid and, then as now, pretty gullible, but still, for whatever reason, I believed her. Completely and totally. To the point where, even today when I glimpse a single spider's strand glinting in the sunlight, I still imagine it's a thin but mighty cord from our interconnected humanity, an ethereal manifestation of our philosophical and spiritual truth. Also, if a tiny little spider can weave that long thread and swing six feet from one tree to another, shouldn't we advanced human beings with our big brains and smartphones be able to connect?

These aren't just the peace-and-love platitudes of a person

who sort of still believes that spiderweb strands are the existential threads of the universe. Understanding—and expressing—our equal interconnectedness is the practical path to ending hate. It's what Martin Luther King Jr. meant when he spoke about the "interrelated structure of reality" and what john powell means when he talks about "claiming a shared, mutual humanity." And it's what every major and minor world religion teaches, though, sadly, it's not something all followers seem to fully grasp. This sense of connection is not just some heady abstraction, nor some bland platitude, but a transformative tool for finding our way out of hate and toward a positive, constructive alternative. We can relate to each other and to society in general in ways that perpetuate hate. Or we can spread inclusion and equality and justice—by choosing to connect.

That doesn't mean connection is an easy choice. In fact, the world seems rigged against it. While I promise that none of us are hardwired to hate transgender people or black people or poor people or Republicans or Democrats, our tendency toward tribalism does make us quick to latch on to society's existing prejudices and to further burrow into historical habits of hate. On top of that, our current systems and institutions incentivize hate, whether propagating resentment through media and electoral fear-mongering or promulgating stereotypes through brazen hate-mongering, or through the less overt mechanisms of biased policing and segregating communities. We have to change not only our own hearts and minds but the institutions, practices, systems, and culture all around us.

The first step is challenging the hate inside ourselves. We need to become more conscious of our own hate—in all its forms, *in all of us*—and work to catch and challenge our ideas and assumptions. At the same time, if we want to stop the hate in our societies, we must support policies and institutions that bring us together, rather than divide us. And when we make that decision to connect, when we come together in connection-spaces facilitated by connection-systems, we also need to talk to each other differently. With the generosity and open-mindedness and kindness and compassion of connection-speech, instead of hate.

That's it. That's all we have to do. Which doesn't mean it's that simple.

It's popular these days to talk about being "woke," but really, with the possible exception of bell hooks, I'm not sure any of us is ever fully woke—we're at best in a constant state of awakening. I, for one, felt more "awake" when Barack Obama was in the White House. Basking in the surety of power along with a sense of inevitable victory in the overall march toward progress, I could gaze down upon the running-out-of-power, running-out-of-time dinosaurs of the old culture-war right wing, like Sean Hannity, and offer a benevolent olive branch. I was fully committed to winning gracefully. Until we lost.

When Donald Trump was elected, it felt like the world was suddenly slammed by an asteroid of hate. It's not that I was so naive as to think all hate had disappeared from our history and hearts, but there was more of it lying dormant than I'd realized, and I didn't expect hate to make such a comeback. And yet amidst my indignation about the overt hate—against immigrants and Muslims and transgender people and women—surging all around me, there I was hating the haters for being hateful. It turns out that "self-work" isn't a noun you arrive at but a verb you have to keep on doing. Just like the opposite of hate isn't a destination but a journey.

Personally, I haven't figured out how to stop hating, let alone how to consistently pursue meaningful, mutually respectful connections. I'm constantly catching myself hating someone or something, and not at the casual broccoli-hating level but in more significant and consequential ways. From being pissed at a slow driver and thinking he's Asian. To saying that maybe most Trump voters are deplorable racists. To wondering if the trans person I just met is a "real woman." My own hate constantly oozes out in small and big ways. In other words, I haven't arrived at some place of enlightenment. I've simply realized I need to *turn on the light*—and start noticing things differently and trying to be different.

This opposite-of-hate thing is an ongoing upstream struggle against the current of society's accumulated history and habits of hate. We have to keep working at it. Over and over again. At the rate I'm going, I'll be lucky if I'm woke by the time I'm dead. But at least I'm trying, and I think that's the point. As the comedian John Fugelsang says, "Remember, if you're gonna fight hate, don't whine if a little gets on you—just wash it off before it sticks." Ooze, wash, rinse, repeat—and hopefully, over time, get better. But at least be part of the solution instead of willfully or naively perpetuating the problem.

In one of my favorite speeches of all time, the writer David Foster Wallace told a parable about two young fish who were swimming along when they came across an older fish swimming in the opposite direction. As he swam past, the older fish said to the younger fish, "Morning, boys. How's the water?" The two young fish keep swimming along for some time until finally one fish turns to the other fish and asks, "What the hell is water?"

Hate has always been elemental to our existence, always bubbling at the surface of our culture and politics and lurking deep within. But we don't always notice it. And if we don't even notice it in ourselves, we can't notice it in the fishbowl of society around us. Deciding to turn away from hate and pursue its opposite is a daily decision and a daily act, one we must constantly recommit to as vigorously as possible, in spite of all the obstacles. But the good news is, it's possible. Just look at the terrorist who became a peace activist. Or the white supremacist who became a Buddhist. Or the bully who learned to apologize to her victim.

ONE SPRING EVENING, I found myself near the city where the private investigator I'd hired believed that Vicky Rarsch was living. I'd just finished giving a speech and was heading toward my hotel when I realized that the town the PI had emailed me was just thirty minutes away. I plugged the address into my GPS and started driving.

All along, I'd tried to convince myself that my search for Vicky was purely selfless, but it never was. I wanted to know that she was okay, that she'd had an okay life, that I hadn't contributed to its ruin. And while I definitely wanted to apologize, because it was the right thing to do, and I told myself I didn't really care if she forgave me, that wasn't entirely true. I wanted to be forgiven. I wanted a clean conscience.

The private investigator had managed to find out a few details about Vicky. She had a brother and a sister, and, from what we could tell, her mom was a highly educated and respected professional. We could never figure out why Vicky had moved around so much nor why she had changed her legal name—first and last—at least two times. But what we did figure out was that she was now married to a woman and working in technology. And supposedly living in an outer-ring city suburb at the address to which I was now heading.

I drove in silence, with the radio off, wiping my increasingly sweating palms on my pants every few miles or so. Outside, a light rain started falling as I turned the corner onto the street where Vicky supposedly lived. Toward the end of the block, on the right, was a nice two-family house with a small yard. My plan all along was to pull up and park, march right up to the door, ring the doorbell, and confess all my crimes. But I drove right by, too petrified to stop. All those years ago, I wasn't afraid to torment Vicky, but now I was afraid to apologize?

I chickened out. I circled the block a half dozen times, slowing down and trying to peer in whatever windows were visible, hoping to catch a glimpse of someone who looked like a happy, healthy grown-up Vicky. But I didn't see a thing. And suddenly I realized it was like I was back in fifth grade, stalking Vicky outside the bathroom. I felt gross and creepy—and more than a little pathetic—and I drove away.

A day later, back at home, I sent Vicky a letter. When I finally found her on Facebook, I messaged the letter to her there, too. And I apologized. I ended my letter by writing, "I have no expectation that you'll accept this apology or respond to this letter. I simply wanted you to know that my thoughts are with you and I hope you have had a beautiful life that transcends all the ugliness I inflicted on you." And that was that. That was all I could do, right?

Then I decided to do one thing more. My daughter had been telling me how the kids at school were calling her Medusa and how bad it made her feel, but also angry, because they all thought she was mean, which just made her want to be meaner. So I sat Willa down and told her that I used to be a bully. I told Willa what I had done to Vicky, how much I regretted it, how bad I felt even now. And I told her that I still struggled to not think and say mean things, but that I was trying hard not to be mean and she could try hard, too. We could try together. Willa put her head on my shoulder and hugged me tightly as my eyes welled up with tears.

A few days after our heart-to-heart, I found a drawing that Willa had made in her second-grade class. It had a big, beautiful tree with maybe a hundred leaves, each individually drawn in a dozen shades of green. Underneath the branches stood a couple, a man and a woman. He was wearing a tuxedo. She was wearing a long red dress, and pearls around her neck. And they were kissing. The man had dark-brown skin and the woman's skin was light peach.

On the back of the drawing, Willa had written, "I think most people draw people with their own skin color. For an example, let's say I have white skin and today I drew one of my first black people. I think people with black skin or white skin should draw black and white people. Remember we are all a force for good and together and united and all have love inside of us even if we can't see it we just have to help those people pull it out."

I'm not saying that if my kid had drawn just white characters, that would make her a racist. But on some level, she seemed to understand that her choices in her drawings were related to larger issues of injustice—and she was making a conscious decision to do something about it. As an eight-year-old. I'll be honest with you, every time Willa has a temper tantrum instead of going to bed or gets in trouble for saying mean things on the school bus, I feel utterly hopeless. But in that one moment, Willa gave me hope, not only for her but for all of us.

And then I heard back from Vicky. Her message to me through Facebook was tense, even strained. She said she didn't remember me and wasn't sure if she was the person I was seeking—though of course I had no doubt it was her. Then she wrote, "I've debated if I should respond to this, and I think I should, if only to keep you from hurting others.

"Messages such as this cannot absolve you of your past actions," Vicky continued. "The only way to do that is to improve the world, prevent others from behaving in similar ways, and foster compassion." Which isn't forgiveness but is exactly the connection I needed.

And, for the record, Vicky, I really am sorry. And I really am trying to do my part to help others do better, too.

ACKNOWLEDGMENTS

I WOULD LIKE to start by saying that, contrary to what I might have said or thought during particularly frustrating moments, I do not hate everyone who encouraged me to write this book. My only fear now is that whoever I forget to thank here will still think I'm a jerk. But here goes.

The list of supportive friends and mentors who have encouraged my voice in general, and this book in particular, could fill its own volume, but a nonexhaustive list has to include Kelly Stoetzel, Chris Anderson, Joshua Prager, Pat Mitchell, Sarah Ellison, Katy Perry, Puja Dhawan, Cindy Hwang Chiang, Chely Wright, Stacy London, Marissa Graciosa, Sean Hannity, Jean Hardisty, Anjali Kumar, Kate Gardiner, Alyssa Mastromonaco, Lindsey Taylor Wood, Susan McPherson, Claudia Schulman, adrienne maree brown, Emily May, Jessica Bennett, Sarah Sophie Flicker, Nell Scovell, Michael Skolnik, Rachel Griffiths, Sheryl Sandberg, Monica Lewinsky, Heather McGhee, Cleo Wade, Van Jones, Sunny Hostin, Valerie Kaur, Vanita Gupta, Ilyse Hogue, and Michelle Ringuette. In addition, I wouldn't have the career and platform I have now were it not for the constant championing of people like Megyn Kelly, Alisyn Camerota, Jeff Zucker, Amy Entelis, Rebecca Kutler, Julie Burton, John Neffinger, Seth Pendleton, Lauren Fritts, Emma Sprague, Tara Setmayer, Matt White, Chris Hayes, Jehmu Greene, and Kit Laybourne. A deep and special thanks to Urvashi Vaid and Geraldine Laybourne, who are the reasons I am the person I am today and have the voice I have. I wouldn't be here without you.

A number of people read a very imperfect first draft of this text and gave invaluable advice, including Puja Dhawan, Gabe Gonzalez, Meg Harkins, Frank Harkins, Urvashi Vaid, Cleo Wade, Matt Kohut, dream hampton, Melinda Kohn, Don Kohn, Jeff Welcker, Gloria Welcker, and Paul Hansen. Mina Cikara, Amy Cuddy, Andrea Varadi, Maytha Alhassen, Nicholas Carlisle, and Gloria Steinem helped me sort through important dimensions of what ended up herein. I'm grateful to all those who lent the words in this book their own words of support, including Elizabeth Gilbert, Van Jones, Sunny Hostin, Adam Grant, DeRay Mckesson, Anand Giridharadas, Sean Hannity, Donna Brazile, Wendy Davis, and Sarah Silverman. And, of course, I'm deeply thankful to everyone I interviewed, whose words and wisdom improved me and this book immeasurably. A special thanks to Bassam Aramin, Dareen Jubeh, John Giraneza, Marie-Jeanne Uwimana, Francoise Uzamukunda, Solange Uwera, Scottie Nell Hughes, Arno Michaelis, Pete Simi, Jennifer Kubota, Nahed Artoul Zehr, Robert Sternberg, and, believe it or not, all of my trolls. I wish you only the best in life. And I wish Vicky every happiness today that I played a part in denying her in the past.

I literally could not have written this book without the financial and in-kind support of Lauren Embrey, Pat West, Suzanne Lerner, Mary Ford, Ana Navarro, Susan Danziger, Laine Romero-Alston, Richard Healey, Cynthia Renfro, Sharon Alpert and the Nathan Cummings Foundation, Luz Vega-Marquis and the Marguerite Casey Foundation, and especially Cathy Raphael, who has supported me from the very beginning of the beginning. My friends Frank Harkins, Diana Kane, and Paul Takeuchi provided invaluable artistic help in the creation of this final product and more.

Amy Gash and the entire team at Algonquin are deeply wonderful and supportive and patient human beings, for which I am profoundly grateful. The lifesaving Emily Lavelle has done yeowoman's work to help spread this book and its vision throughout the universe. Emily Loose is like Xanax in human form. Her brilliant structural mind and judicious editing is evident in every line of this book, and I'm grateful to have found her. Emma Parry, my literary agent, is the only one in a long line of literary agents who managed to get a completed book out of me, so hats off to her. Her soothing British accent definitely helped. And I should thank the rest of my representation team, including Kimberly Carver at 3 Arts and Andrew Lear at UTA, if only so they'll read this and remember to call me back.

I am blessed to have the best parents on the planet. Even though I was furious when they moved me to the middle of nowhere after fifth grade, I discovered writing as a way to address my isolation. And I think that's worked out pretty well. Also, every day since my birth, my parents have remained my biggest cheerleaders, and everything I've ever done is because they taught me I could do anything. I'm also fortunate to have a large coterie of fantastic in-laws, who have more recently cheered me on and put up with me frantically writing during family vacations. I'm so grateful for all of you.

Last, but certainly not least, as they say, my partner, Sarah Hansen, and our daughter, Willa Hansen-Kohn, are what truly made this book possible—not only through their daily sacrifices during the stress of book writing but in showing me the deepest kindness, compassion, and love that I hope this book points us all toward.

NOTES

INTRODUCTION

1 "No one is born hating another person" Nelson Mandela, *Long Walk to Freedom* (Boston: Back Bay, 1995), 622.

2 "rub raw the sores of discontent," Alisky said As cited by Mark Leibovich in "In Turmoil of '68, Clinton Found a New Voice," *New York Times*, September 5, 2007, http://www.nytimes.com/2007/09/05/us/politics/05clinton.html.

7 "We are all potential dehumanizers" David Livingstone Smith, *Less Than Human* (New York: St. Martin's, 2011), 25.

8 In the twenty-five years the Pew Research Center has surveyed Republicans "Partisanship and Political Animosity in 2016," Pew Research Center, June 22, 2016, http://www.people-press.org/2016/06/22/partisanship-and-political-animosity-in-2016/.

8 Hate crimes in the US increased by 20 percent Grant Smith and Daniel Trotta, "U.S. Hate Crimes Up 20 percent in 2016 Fueled by Election Campaign-Report," Reuters, March 13, 2017, https://www.reuters.com/article/us-usa-crime-hate/u-s-hate-crimes-up-20-percent-in-2016-fueled-by-election-campaign-report-idUSKBN16L0BO.

8 anti-Semitic incidents rose by 86 percent Doug Criss and Carma Hassan, "Anti-Semitic Incidents Rose a Whopping 86% in the First 3 months of 2017," CNN.com, April 24, 2017, http://www.cnn.com/2017/04/24/us/antisemitic-incidents-reports-trnd/index.html.

9 one Trump opponent tweeted David Horsey, "Do Americans Hate Each Other Too Much to Find Common Ground?" *Los Angeles Times*, January 3, 2017, http://www.latimes.com/opinion/topoftheticket/la-na-tt-americans-hate-20170102-story.html.

CHAPTER 1

Tweets without a corresponding note could not be cited here because they have since been deleted from Twitter, in most cases when the user's account was suspended or otherwise deactivated.

19 "Sally Kohn is a mental midget" Linda Likes Bacon (@LindaLikesBacon), "Sally Kohn is a mental midget," Twitter, November 11, 2016, 11:59 a.m., https://twitter.com/lindalikesbacon/status/797166955937615873.

19 "GO JUMP OFF A BRIDGE" Linda Likes Bacon (@LindaLikesBacon), "GO JUMP OFF A BRIDGE," December 26, 2015, 3:38 p.m., https://twitter.com/lindalikesbacon/status/680895520542449664.

19 "Your dog is cute" Linda Likes Bacon (@LindaLikesBacon), "Your dog is cute. But you are freaking hideous," October 3, 2016, 3:24 p.m., https://twitter.com/lindalikesbacon/status/783070301521317888.

22 a study in 1967 on political attitudes Edward E. Jones and Victor A. Haar, "The Attribution of Attitudes," *Journal of Experimental Social Psychology* 3 (1967): 1–24.

22 a study in which Stanford University students Lee Ross, "The Intuitive Psychologist and His Shortcomings: Distortions in the Attribution Process," *Advances in Experimental Social Psychology* 10. 173–220 (New York: Academic Press. 1977).

23 Thomas Pettigrew took things one step further Thomas F. Pettigrew, "The Ultimate Attribution Error: Extending Allport's Cognitive Analysis of Prejudice," *Personality and Social Psychology Bulletin* 5, no. 4 (October 1979): 461–76.

24 According to a 2016 poll "On Views of Race and Inequality, Blacks and Whites Are Worlds Apart," Pew Research Center, June 27, 2016, http://www.pewsocialtrends.org/2016/06/27/on-views-of-race-and-inequality-blacks-and-whites-are-worlds-apart/.

24 in a 2015 poll, 20 percent of African Americans Wayne Drash, "Poll: 1 in 5 Blacks Report 'Unfair' Dealings with Police in Last Month," CNN, November 30, 2015, http://www.cnn.com/2015/11/29/us/criminal-justice-racism-cnn-kff-poll/index.html.

24 black people in general commit a smaller share of crimes David A. Harris, *Driving While Black: Racial Profiling on Our Nation's Highways*, an American Civil Liberties Union special report, June 1999, https://www.aclu.org/report/driving-while-black-racial-profiling-our-nations-highways.

24 Rebecca Hetey and Jennifer Eberhardt presented a group Rebecca C. Hetey and Jennifer L. Eberhardt, "Racial Disparities in Incarceration Increase Acceptance of Punitive Policies," *Psychological Science* 25, no. 10 (2014): 1949–54, http://journals.sagepub.com/doi/abs/10.1177/0956797614540307.

25 "the extent to which 'blackness' retains its racial stigma" Jamelle Bouie, "White People Are Fine with Laws That Harm Blacks," *Slate*, August 7, 2014, http://www.slate.com/articles/health_and_science/science/2014/08/racial_bias_in_criminal_justice_whites_don_t_want_to_reform_laws_that_harm.html.

25 two out of five white Republicans Aaron Blake, "Republicans' Views of Blacks' Intelligence, Work Ethic Lag Behind Democrats at a Record Clip," *Washington Post*, March 31, 2017, https://www.washingtonpost.com/news/the-fix/wp/2017/03/31/the-gap-between-republicans-and-democrats-views-of-african-americans-just-hit-a-new-high/?utm_term=.eaa57241bfc5.

25 26 percent of Republicans and 18 percent of Democrats Blake, "Republicans' Views."

26 *correctly* believe that most welfare recipients are white Martin Gilens, *Why Americans Hate Welfare: Race, Media, and the Politics of Antipoverty Policy* (Chicago: University of Chicago Press, 1999).

26 As philosopher David Livingstone Smith puts it Smith, *Less Than Human*, 275.

27 "The mujahideen will give America" Jason Burke and Rory Carroll, "Poor Bedouin Who Became a Butcher," *Guardian*, June 8, 2006, https://www.theguardian.com/world/2006/jun/09/iraq.rorycarroll.

28 "Essences are imagined to be shared by members" Smith, *Less Than Human*, 275.

29 Consider during the 2008 presidential campaign when Barack Obama decried Katherine Q. Seelye and Jeff Zeleny, "On the Defensive, Obama Calls His Words Ill-Chosen," *New York Times*, April 13, 2008, http://www.nytimes.com/2008/04/13/us/politics/13campaign.html.

29 Hillary Clinton referred to Trump voters Dan Merica and Sophie Tatum, "Clinton Expresses Regret for Saying 'Half' of Trump Supporters Are 'Deplorables,'" CNN, September 12, 2016, http://www.cnn.com/2016/09/09/politics/hillary-clinton-donald-trump-basket-of-deplorables/index.html.

30 "our very different pains rhyme" Anand Giridharadas, "Democracy is Not a Supermarket," *Medium*, October 31, 2017, https://medium.com/@AnandWrites/why-real-change-escapes-many-change-makers-and-why-it-doesnt-have-to-8e4833204 2a8.

30 "an avertive or hostile attitude" Gordon W. Allport, *The Nature of Prejudice* (New York: Addison-Wesley, 1979), 14–15.

30 "unusually resistant to rational influence" Ralph L. Rosnow, "Poultry and Prejudice," *Psychology Today* 5, no. 10 (March 1972): 53–56.

31 Consider the phenomenon of "affinity fraud" "Fleecing the flock," *Economist*, January 28, 2012, http://www.economist.com/node/21543526.

31 among the five stages of social conditioning terrorists use "Social Psychological Conditioning," ChangingMinds.org, http://changingminds.org/techniques/conversion/social_psychological_conditioning.htm.

31 "Haha I see what you did there" Sally Kohn (@sallykohn), "Haha I see what you did there you so clever but if I were a dude I'd be straight bro but anyway," August 22, 2016, 5:08 p.m., https://twitter.com/sallykohn/status/767876138026856448.

33 "Hate is neither the opposite of love" Robert J. Sternberg, *The Psychology of Hate* (American Psychological Association, 2004), 38.

38 Later, he sort of boasts Steven (@ArlingtonSteve), "Bitch," Twitter, July 8, 2016, 10:09 a.m., https://twitter.com/ArlingtonSteve/status/751463290052763648.

40 over half of Americans who expect incivility to worsen "Civility in America VII: The State of Civility," Weber Shandwick, http://www.webershandwick.com/news/article/civility-in-america-vii-the-state-of-civility.

40 In a 2016 study, Justin Cheng Taylor Kubota, "Stanford Research Shows That Anyone Can Become an Internet Troll," Stanford News Service, February 6, 2017, https://news.stanford.edu/2017/02/06/stanford-research-shows-anyone-can-become-internet-troll/.

41 researchers found that men who had played and lost an interactive video game Caitlin Dewey, "Men Who Harass Women Online Are Quite Literally Losers, New Study Finds," *Washington Post*, July 20, 2015, https://www.washingtonpost.com/news/the-intersect/wp/2015/07/20/men-who-harass-women-online-are-quite-literally-losers-new-study-finds/?utm_term=.0d57ba3b9318

41 individuals who have low self-esteem Annerieke Oosterwegel, "Collective Self-Esteem, Personal Self-Esteem, and Collective Efficacy in In-Group and Outgroup Evaluations," *Current Psychology* 18, no. 4 (December 1999): 326–39, https://www.researchgate.net/profile/Annerieke_Oosterwegel/publication/225677411_Collective_Self-Esteem_Personal_Self-Esteem_and_Collective_Efficacy_in_In-group_and_Outgroup_Evaluations/links/0deec523b301bf3832000000.pdf.

41 perpetrators actually experience a temporary boost Kelli Craig-Henderson, "Examining Hate-Motivated Aggression," *Aggression and Violent Behavior* 7 (February 2002): 85–101, https://www.researchgate.net/publication/222022936_Examining_hate-motivated_aggression_A_review_of_the_social_psychological_literature_on_hate_crimes_as_a_distinct_form_of_aggression.

41 people more inclined to "self-disclose" John Suler, "The Online Disinhibition Effect," *Cyberpsychology & Behavior* 7, no. 3 (June 2004): 321–26, https://www.ncbi.nlm.nih.gov/pubmed/15257832.

45 In 2008, Megan created a Twitter account Adrian Chen, "Unfollow," *New Yorker*, November 23, 2015, https://www.newyorker.com/magazine/2015/11/23/conversion-via-twitter-westboro-baptist-church-megan-phelps-roper.

47 Susan Benesch offers a great set of guidelines Dangerous Speech Project, https://dangerousspeech.org/.

47 It dovetails with the civil libertarian position Susan Benesch et al., "Counterspeech on Twitter: A Field Study," a report for Public Safety Canada under the Kanishka Project, October 14, 2016, https://dangerousspeech.org/counterspeech-on-twitter-a-field-study/.

47 Benesch provides a moving example Susan Benesch et al., "Counterspeech on Twitter."

49 "viewed as powerful or intimidating" Susan Benesch et al., "Considerations for Successful Counterspeech," October 14, 2016, https://dangerousspeech.org/considerations-for-successful-counterspeech/.

50 most Americans say they don't like mudslinging "Putting a Positive Spin on Negative Campaigning," *All Things Considered*, National Public Radio, June 23, 2012, http://www.npr.org/2012/06/23/155636624/putting-a-positive-spin-on-negative-campaigning.

50 about two-thirds of Hillary Clinton's campaign ads Denise-Marie Ordway and John Wihbey, "Negative Political Ads and Their Effect on Voters," Journalists Resource, September 25, 2016, https://journalistsresource.org/studies/politics/ads-public-opinion/negative-political-ads-effects-voters-research-roundup.

CHAPTER 2

53 "I imagine one of the reasons people cling" James Baldwin, *Notes of a Native Son* (Boston: Beacon Press: 1984), 101.

59 "Very often both sides believe" Daniel Bar-Tal, Lily Chernyak-Hai, Noa Schori, and Ayelet Gundar, "A Sense of Self-Perceived Collective Victimhood in Intractable Conflicts," *International Review of the Red Cross* 91, no. 874 (June 2009), https://www.icrc.org/eng/assets/files/other/irrc-874-bartal-chernyakhai-schori-gundar.pdf.

59 "The struggle over the status of the sole victim" Daniel Bar-Tal and Phillip L. Hammack, "Conflict, Delegitimization, and Violence," in *The Oxford Handbook of Intergroup Violence*, ed. Linda R. Tropp (New York: Oxford University Press, 2012), 29–52.

66 psychopaths are estimated to make up just 1 percent Wynne Parry, "How to Spot Psychopaths," Live Science, October 20, 2011, https://www.livescience.com/16585-psychopaths-speech-language.html.

66 "you're four times more likely to find a psychopath" "A Psychopath Walks into a Room. Can You Tell?" *All Things Considered*, National Public Radio, May 21, 2011, http://www.npr.org/2011/05/21/136462824/a-psychopath-walks-into-a-room-can-you-tell.

67 many terrorists feel justified in their terrorism Paul Heroux, "Are Terrorists

Insane?" *Huffington Post*, https://www.huffingtonpost.com/paul-heroux/are-terrorists-insane_b_976755.html.

67 Bruce Hoffman writes of terrorists Bruce Hoffman, *Inside Terrorism*, revised ed. (New York: Columbia University Press, 2006), xv.

67 "neither irrational nor desperate" Hoffman, 154.

67 "the only way to convince Israeli decision makers" Hoffman, 155.

67 "In the Middle East, perceived contexts in which suicide bombers" Scott Atran, "Genesis of Suicide Terrorism," *Science* 299, no. 5612 (March 7, 2003): 1534–39, http://science.sciencemag.org/content/299/5612/1534.full.

67 "If we can fulfill our goals without violence" Hoffman, 152–53.

69 The *Times of Israel* newspaper has called Dov Lieber and Luke Tress, "At Israel's Most Infamous Crossing, Even a Good Day Can Be Bad," *Times of Israel*, May 17, 2016, http://www.timesofisrael.com/at-israels-most-infamous-crossing-even-a-good-day-can-be-bad/.

70 "The quintessential Palestinian experience" Rashid Khalidi, *Palestinian Identity* (New York: Columbia University Press, 1997), 1.

71 The influential psychologist Erich Fromm Erich Fromm, *Man for Himself: An Inquiry into the Psychology of Ethics* (New York: Holt, 1990), 216.

71 As Robert Sternberg writes, "According to Fromm" Robert J. Sternberg and Karin Sternberg, *The Nature of Hate* (New York: Cambridge University Press, 2008), 46.

75 "person who is actively opposed or hostile to someone or something" *Oxford English Dictionary*, https://en.oxforddictionaries.com/definition/enemy.

76 The *New York Times* reported that Abir Greg Myre, "Father of Dead West Bank Girl Seeks Peace With Israelis," *New York Times*, January 23, 2007, http://www.nytimes.com/2007/01/23/world/middleeast/23mideast.html.

76 The Israeli government denied Dan Izenberg, "'Compensate Killed Girl's Family,'" *Jerusalem Post*, August 16, 2010, http://www.jpost.com/Israel/Compensate-killed-girls-family.

76 "that the bullet that struck Abir was fired recklessly" Izenberg, "Compensate."

76 Israeli security forces killed 373 Palestinians "B'Tselem: 373 Palestinians Killed by Israeli Forces in 2007," The Electronic Intifada, December 30, 2007, https://electronicintifada.net/content/btselem-373-palestinians-killed-israeli-forces-2007/3302.

76 As of 2014, for the almost 14 years "This Chart Shows Every Person Killed in the Israel-Palestine Conflict since 2000," updated by Max Fisher, July 14, 2014, https://www.vox.com/2014/7/14/5898581/chart-israel-palestine-conflict-deaths.

80 Chen was patrolling one of the checkpoints "Chen Alon: Tel Aviv," Combatants for Peace, http://cfpeace.org/personal-stories/chen-alon/.

81 "I think it's a form of knowledge" ". . . About Radical Intimacy and Missing Visions," Nachbarschafts und Gemeinschaftstheater, https://www.theater-rote-ruebe.de/lesenswertes/chen-alon/.

82 Masi Noor found that the answer to competitive victimhood Nurit Shnabel, Samer Halabi, and Masi Noor, "Overcoming Competitive Victimhood and Facilitating Forgiveness through Re-categorization into a Common Victim or Perpetrator Identity,"

Journal of Experimental Social Psychology 49 (April 2003): 867–77, https://www.researchgate.net/publication/260133236_Overcoming_competitive_victimhood_and_facilitating_forgiveness_through_re-categorization_into_a_common_victim_or_perpetrator_identity.

CHAPTER 3

85 "The essential dilemma of my life is" Somak Ghoshal, "Jhumpa Lahiri: The Lives of Others," Livemint, January 25, 2014, http://www.livemint.com/Leisure/zWhN5FKCyq3Mci96bD7nWO/Jhumpa-Lahiri--The-lives-of-others.html.

85 "A deep sense of love and belonging" Brené Brown, "Want to Be Happy? Stop Trying to Be Perfect," CNN, November 1, 2010, http://www.cnn.com/2010/LIVING/11/01/give.up.perfection/index.html.

85 "The tendency to form groups" E. O. Wilson, "Biologist E. O. Wilson on Why Humans, Like Ants, Needs a Tribe, *Newsweek*, April 2, 2012, http://www.newsweek.com/biologist-eo-wilson-why-humans-ants-need-tribe-64005.

86 "Our bloody nature" Wilson, "Biologist E. O. Wilson," *Newsweek*.

86 "Not only have wars shaped geopolitical boundaries" James Waller, *Becoming Evil* (New York: Oxford University Press, 2002), xiv.

86 "Humans may be hardwired to get edgy" Robert Sapolsky, "Peace among Primates," in *The Compassionate Instinct*, eds. Dacher Keltner, Jason Marsh, Jeremy Adam Smith (New York: Norton, 2010), 34.

87 "just some dumb shit that people made up" Michael Harriot, "When the Irish Weren't White," *The Root*, March 17, 2017, http://www.theroot.com/when-the-irish-weren-t-white-1793358754.

87 owned more than six hundred black men, women, and children Karen Grigsby Bates, "Life at Jefferson's Monticello, as His Slaves Saw It," *Weekend Edition Sunday*, National Public Radio, March 11, 2012, http://www.npr.org/2012/03/11/148305319/life-at-jeffersons-monticello-as-his-slaves-saw-it.

87 Jefferson also once said that free blacks were "pests" Paul Finkelman, "The Monster of Monticello," editorial, *New York Times*, November 30, 2012. http://www.nytimes.com/2012/12/01/opinion/the-real-thomas-jefferson.html.

88 Jelani Cobb says, "If you look at the history of black" *13th*, directed by Ava DuVernay (Sherman Oaks, CA: Kandoo Films, 2016), Netflix.

88 counted 917 white supremacist groups in the United States in 2016 "Hate Groups Increase for Second Consecutive Year as Trump Electrifies Radical Right," Southern Poverty Law Center, February 15, 2017, https://www.splcenter.org/news/2017/02/15/hate-groups-increase-second-consecutive-year-trump-electrifies-radical-right.

88 the number of anti-Muslim hate groups almost tripled "Hate Map," Southern Poverty Law Center, accessed November 9, 2017, https://www.splcenter.org/hate-map.

88 "white supremacist groups had already carried out" Jana Winter, "FBI and DHS Warned of Growing Threat from White Supremacists Months Ago," *Foreign Policy*, August 14, 2017, http://foreignpolicy.com/2017/08/14/fbi-and-dhs-warned-of-growing-threat-from-white-supremacists-months-ago/.

88 Other research suggests that between 2008 and 2006 Winter, "FBI and DHS Warned."

90 "We must secure the existence of our people" "14 Words," Anti-Defamation League, https://www.adl.org/education/references/hate-symbols/14-words.

91 some of the lyrics from the song "Centurion—14 Words," on YouTube, https://www.youtube.com/watch?v=DH3CFrpOeAY.

93 in the 2010 Census, 92 percent of Mequon's QuickFacts: Mequon, Wisconsin, United States Census Bureau, accessed November 9, 2017, https://www.census.gov/quickfacts/fact/table/mequoncitywisconsin/PST045216.

93 In 2016, Donald Trump won 57 percent "Wisconsin Presidential Race Results: Donald J. Trump Wins," *New York Times*, August 1, 2017, https://www.nytimes.com/elections/results/wisconsin-president-clinton-trump.

93 In 2012, Mitt Romney fared even better "Wisconsin Presidential Race Results."

94 journalist Dan Korem published a study showing Dan Korem, *Suburban Gangs: The Affluent Rebels* (Richardson, TX: International Focus Press, 1994), http://www.ifpinc.com/books/suburban-gangs/.

94 Pete Simi . . . found that the members of right-wing hate groups come from "Why They Join," *Intelligence Report*, February 25, 2014, https://www.splcenter.org/fighting-hate/intelligence-report/2014/why-they-join.

95 another study found that expressions of overt racism by whites Jack Glaser et al., "Studying Hate Crime with the Internet," *Journal of Social Issues* 58, no. 1 (2002): 177–93. https://gspp.berkeley.edu/assets/uploads/research/pdf/GlaserDixitGreen2002.pdf.

97 Robert Christgau suggests, "It was also a subculture" Robert Christgau, "All the Young Punks," review of *Please Kill Me* by Legs McNeil and Gillian McCain, *New York Times*, July 28, 1996, http://www.nytimes.com/1996/07/28/books/all-the-young-punks.html.

97 Leee Black Childers once described punk as Christgau, "All the Young Punks."

98 Though not all skinheads are racist Jennifer Abbots, "True 'Skinheads' Are Not the Racist Thugs of Media Fame," letter to the editor, *New York Times*, April 19, 1994, http://www.nytimes.com/1994/04/19/opinion/l-true-skinheads-are-not-the-racist-thugs-of-media-fame-829412.html?mcubz=1.

98 But I looked it up on Wikipedia "Skrewdriver," Wikipedia, accessed November 9, 2017, https://en.wikipedia.org/wiki/Skrewdriver.

98 a Skrewdriver song called "White Power" on YouTube Skrewdriver, "White Power," video posted to YouTube on August 17, 2014, https://www.youtube.com/watch?v=z6Tyv2PqzlI.

99 Pete Simi . . . explains that most white supremacists "Why They Join," *Intelligence Report*.

99 In fact, there's research suggesting that it's mostly through first choosing Rebecca Littman and Elizabeth Levy Paluck, "The Cycle of Violence: Understanding Individual Participation in Collective Violence," *Advances in Political Psychology* 36, suppl. 1 (2015), https://static1.squarespace.com/static/5186d08fe4b065e39b45b91e/t/54f12c27e4b05fe3d5dd183c/1425091623300/Littman_Paluck_PP.pdf.

99 French sociologist Gustave Le Bon Robert Zaretsky, "Donald Trump and the Myth of Mobocracy," *Atlantic*, July 27, 2016, https://www.theatlantic.com/international/archive/2016/07/trump-le-bon-mob/493118/.

99 In 2002, sociologist Ziad Munson published a study Ziad W. Munson, *The Making of Pro-Life Activists* (Chicago: University of Chicago Press, 2009), 6.

100 Former federal prosecutor and Congressional investigator Ken Ballen Ken Ballen, *Terrorists in Love* (New York: Free Press, 2011).

101 "Group processes, like individual processes, are dynamic" Waller, *Becoming Evil*, 39.

101 In 1954, social psychologist Muzafer Sherif invited Muzafer Sherif, *The Robbers Cave Experiment: Intergroup Conflict and Cooperation* (Middletown, CT: Wesleyan University Press, 1988).

103 In a completely different study, conducted in 2007, Katherine Kinzler Katherine D. Kinzler and Elizabeth S. Spelke, "Do Infants Show Social Preferences for People Differing in Race?," *Cognition*. 119, no. 1 (April 2011):1–9, https://www.ncbi.nlm.nih.gov/pmc/articles/PMC3081609/.

104 "Human beings are consistent in their codes of honor" E. O. Wilson, *On Human Nature* (Cambridge: Harvard University Press, 2004), 163.

104 Jay Van Bavel conducted a study Jay J. Van Bavel and William A. Cunningham, "Self-Categorization with a Novel Mixed-Race Group Moderates Automatic Social and Racial Biases," *Personality and Social Psychology Bulletin* 35, no. 3 (March 2009): 321–35, http://journals.sagepub.com/doi/abs/10.1177/0146167208327743.

104 In 2001, psychologist Rebecca Bigler and her colleagues Brian Mattmiller, "Professor Finds That in Shirts, as well as Skin, Color Matters," November 23, 1998, University of Wisconsin, Madison News, http://news.wisc.edu/professor-finds-that-in-shirts-as-well-as-skin-color-matters/.

105 In 1973, social psychologist Henri Tajfel conducted a "minimal group" study Michael Billig and Henri Tajfel, "Social Categorization and Similarity in Intergroup Behaviour," *European Journal of Social Psychology* 3, no. 1 (January/March 1973), http://onlinelibrary.wiley.com/doi/10.1002/ejsp.2420030103/full.

106 Bryan Stevenson . . . "Slavery didn't end in 1865, it evolved" Stav Ziv, "What It Means to Be Black in America: 'Slavery Didn't End in 1865. It Evolved,'" *Newsweek*, July 29, 2017, http://www.newsweek.com/racism-america-slavery-lynching-brooklyn-museum-eji-643474.

106 Bryan Stevenson . . . "While we passed civil rights laws" Matthew Green, "Bryan Stevenson: On Teaching America's Long History of Racial Injustice," KQED News, March 9, 2017, https://ww2.kqed.org/lowdown/2017/03/09/bryan-stevenson-on-why-we-cant-forget-americas-troubled-racial-history/.

106 "We might have natural biases to favor some groups" Paul Bloom, *Just Babies: The Origins of Good and Evil*, (New York: Crown, 2013), 114.

107 Angela tells me over the phone Angela King and Tony McAleer, phone conversation with author, August 19, 2006.

108 "If you look at ISIS recruiting techniques for kids" Annie Armstrong, "Ex-Neo Nazis Explain What's Driving the Alt-Right," *Vice*, February 17, 2017, https://www.vice.com/en_uk/article/bmpn7q/ex-neo-nazis-explain-whats-driving-the-alt-right.

109 "Modern groups are psychologically equivalent" Wilson, "Biologist E. O. Wilson," *Newsweek*.

109 Human nature may embrace motives that lead to aggression Gareth Cook, "History

and the Decline of Human Violence," *Scientific American*, October 4, 2011, https://www.scientificamerican.com/article/history-and-the-decline-of-human-violence/.

109 "Humans have a capacity for warfare" Brandon Keim, "Human Nature May Not Be So Warlike After All," *Wired*, July 18, 2013, https://www.wired.com/2013/07/to-war-is-human-perhaps-not/.

110 Psychologists Martin Schmelz and Sebastian Grüneisen . . . trained Michael Price, "True Altruism Seen in Chimpanzees, Giving Clues to Evolution of Human Cooperation," *Science*, June 19, 2017, http://www.sciencemag.org/news/2017/06/true-altruism-seen-chimpanzees-giving-clues-evolution-human-cooperation.

111 "The only species difference found" Felix Warneken et al., "Spontaneous Altruism by Chimpanzees and Young Children," *PLoS Biology* 5, no. 7: e184, https://doi.org/10.1371/journal.pbio.0050184, http://journals.plos.org/plosbiology/article?id=10.1371/journal.pbio.0050184.

111 Psychologist Frans de Waal . . . "probably as old as mammals and birds" Frans de Waal, "Putting the Altruism Back into Altruism: The Evolution of Empathy," *Annual Review of Psychology* 59 (2008): 279–300, https://www.ncbi.nlm.nih.gov/pubmed/17550343.

113 "White people, it is time for us to have" Michael Skolnik, "White People, We Know Those Angry, White Men Carrying Tiki-Torches. We Must Not Be Silent!" *Medium*, August 13, 2017, https://medium.com/@OfficialMichaelSkolnik/white-people-we-know-those-angry-white-men-carrying-tiki-torches-5ff218cc663b.

114 Christian Picciolini . . . "I couldn't deny the fact that I" Christina Couch, "Recovering from Hate," *Nova*, PBS, Jul 29, 2015, http://www.pbs.org/wgbh/nova/next/body/hatred/.

114 Angela King . . . "I was shown kindness" King and McAleer, phone conversation with author.

114 Tony recalls "feeling safe" King and McAleer, phone conversation with author.

115 Yet sociologists like Eduardo Bonilla-Silva . . . argue Adia Harvey Wingfield, "Color-Blindness Is Counterproductive," *Atlantic*, September 13, 2015, https://www.theatlantic.com/politics/archive/2015/09/color-blindness-is-counterproductive/405037/.

115 As Justice Harry Blackmun wrote in a 1978 Supreme Court "Blackmun's Opinions Reflect His Evolution Over the 24 Court Years," *New York Times*, March 5, 1999, http://www.nytimes.com/1999/03/05/us/blackmun-s-opinions-reflect-his-evolution-over-the-24-court-years.html.

116 Sherif changed the terms of their situation yet again Sherif, *The Robbers Cave Experiment*.

CHAPTER 4

119 "If you love peace, then hate injustice" John Michael Talbot and Steve Rabey, *The Lessons of Saint Francis: How to Bring Simplicity and Spirituality into Your Daily Life* (New York: Plume, 1998), 220.

120 "The main problem nowadays is not the folks" John Blake, "The New Threat: 'Racism without Racists,'" CNN, November 27, 2014, http://www.cnn.com/2014/11/26/us/ferguson-racism-or-racial-bias/index.html.

121 "racism is systemic or institutionalized" Eduardo Bonilla-Silva, *Racism without Racists: Color-Blind Racism and the Persistence of Racial Inequality in America* (New York: Rowman & Littlefield, 2013), 8.

123 as Hillary Clinton told CNN's Fareed Zakaria William Saletan, "Implicit Bias Is Real. Don't Be So Defensive," *Slate*, October 5, 2016, http://www.slate.com/articles/news_and_politics/politics/2016/10/implicit_bias_is_real_don_t_be_so_defensive_mike_pence.html.

123 NBC's Lester Holt asked her Saletan, "Implicit Bias Is Real," *Slate*.

124 "suggesting that everyone, including our police, are basically racist" Saletan, "Implicit Bias Is Real," *Slate*.

124 "Enough of this seeking every opportunity to demean law enforcement" Saletan, "Implicit Bias Is Real," *Slate*.

124 "There's way too much research on implicit bias" Saletan, "Implicit Bias Is Real" *Slate*.

124 "Blacks and whites receive the same narratives" Theodore R. Johnson, "Black-on-Black Racism: The Hazards of Implicit Bias," *Atlantic*, December 26, 2014, https://www.theatlantic.com/politics/archive/2014/12/black-on-black-racism-the-hazards-of-implicit-bias/384028/.

126 A 1942 poll confirms this Mildred A. Schwartz, *Trends in While Attitudes Toward Negroes*, report no. 119 (Chicago: National Opinion Research Center, 1967), http://www.norc.org/PDFs/publications/NORCRpt_119.pdf.

128 Kubota explains to me how stereotypes Jennifer Kubota, interview with author, September 20, 2016.

129 The unconscious "makes associations based on frequency" "Opening the Question of Race to the Question of Belonging," *On Being with Krista Tippett*, June 25, 2015, https://onbeing.org/programs/john-a-powell-opening-the-question-of-race-to-the-question-of-belonging/7695/.

129 Elizabeth Phelps and her research team conducted Elizabeth Phelps et al., "Performance on Indirect Measures of Race Evaluation Predicts Amygdala Activation," *Journal of Cognitive Neuroscience* 12, no. 5 (September 2000), 729–38, http://www.mitpressjournals.org/doi/abs/10.1162/089892900562552.

131 As john a. powell…titled *The Science of Equality* Rachel D. Godsil et al., "Addressing Implicit Bias, Racial Anxiety, and Stereotype Threat in Education and Health Care, *Science of Equality* 1 (November 2014), Perception Institute, https://perception.org/wp-content/uploads/2014/11/Science-of-Equality.pdf.

131 black patients who report chest pain were 40 percent less likely Brian D. Smedley, Adrienne Y. Stith, and Alan R. Nelson, *Unequal Treatment: Confronting Racial and Ethnic Disparities in Health Care* (Washington, DC: National Academies Press, 2003), https://www.nap.edu/read/12875/chapter/1.

131 studies have revealed that white doctors spend less time Fariss Samarrai, "Study Links Disparities in Pain Management to Racial Bias," UVA Today, April 04, 2016, https://news.virginia.edu/content/study-links-disparities-pain-management-racial-bias.

131 black patients are "systemically undertreated" Kelly M. Hoffman et al., "Racial Bias in Pain Assessment and Treatment Recommendations, and False Beliefs about

Biological Differences between Blacks and Whites," *Proceedings of the National Academy of Sciences* 113, no. 16 (2016), 4296–4301, http://www.pnas.org/content/113/16/4296.abstract.

131 examined an extraordinary 60 million cases of pain medication Astha Singhal, Yu-Yu Tien, Renee Y. Hsia, "Racial-Ethnic Disparities in Opioid Prescriptions at Emergency Department Visits for Conditions Commonly Associated with Prescription Drug Abuse," *PLoS One* 11, no. 8, https://doi.org/10.1371/journal.pone.0159224.

132 "defendants whose appearance was more stereotypically black" Jennifer L. Eberhardt et al., "Looking Deathworthy: Perceived Stereotypicality of Black Defendants Predicts Capital-Sentencing Outcomes," Cornell Law Faculty Publications, paper 41 (2006), http://scholarship.law.cornell.edu/cgi/viewcontent.cgi?article=1040&context=lsrp_papers.

132 "officers on average spoke less respectfully to black" Rob Voigt et al., "Language from Police Body Camera Footage Shows Racial Disparities in Officer Respect," *Proceedings of the National Academy of Sciences* 114, no. 25 (2017), 6521–26, http://www.pnas.org/content/114/25/6521.

132 researchers have found that teachers tend to devote Rachel D. Godsil et al., *The Science of Equality*.

132 "In college, professors are less responsive to inquiries" Lisette Partelow, "The Ubiquitous Nature of Implicit Bias," *U.S. News & World Report*, October 19, 2016, https://www.usnews.com/opinion/knowledge-bank/articles/2016-10-19/dangerous-to-deny-implicit-bias-and-its-consequences-for-people-of-color.

133 In one of these studies, researchers sent in resumes Marianne Bertrand and Sendhil Mullainathan, "Are Emily and Greg More Employable Than Lakisha and Jamal? A Field Experiment on Labor Market Discrimination," *American Economic Review* 94, no. 4 (September 2004), http://www.uh.edu/~adkugler/Bertrand&Mullainathan.pdf.

133 In 2016, when African American high school student Adia Brown Cindy Long, "The Far-Reaching Effects of Implicit Bias in the Classroom," *NEA Today*, January 26, 2016, http://neatoday.org/2016/01/26/implicit-bias-in-the-classroom/?_ga=2.252136265.1788395455.1508250573-797414129.1508250573.

133 African American ob-gyn Tamika Cross Kristina Rodulfo, "Black Women Fight Stereotypes With #WhatADoctorLooksLike," *Elle*, October 17, 2016, http://www.elle.com/culture/news/a40064/black-women-doctors-whatadoctorlookslike-hashtag/.

134 they are "replicated in everyday micro-behaviors" Rachel D. Godsil et al., *The Science of Equality*, 26.

134 The American Psychological Society's magazine Jill D. Kester, "A Revolution in Social Psychology," *APS Observer Online* 14, no. 6 (July/August 2001), http://www.psychologicalscience.org/observer/0701/family.html.

134 "The IAT is more than just an abstract measure" Malcolm Gladwell, *Blink: The Power of Thinking Without Thinking* (Boston: Back Bay, 2007), 85.

134 "researchers are comfortable with the idea implicit bias is a problem" Issie Lapowsky, "In the VP Debate, Mike Pence Got Implicit Bias Pretty Wrong," *Wired*, October 7, 2016, https://www.wired.com/2016/10/vp-debate-mike-pence-got-implicit-bias-pretty-wrong/.

136 a "prejudice habit-breaking intervention" Patricia G. Devine et al., "Long-Term

Reduction in Implicit Race Bias: A prejudice Habit-Breaking Intervention," *Journal of Experimental Social Psychology*, 48, no. 6 (November 2012): 1267–78, https://www.ncbi.nlm.nih.gov/pmc/articles/PMC3603687/.

137 According to US Census Bureau data, New York City Jed Kolko, "America's Most Diverse Neighborhoods and Metros," *Forbes*, November 13, 2012, https://www.forbes.com/sites/trulia/2012/11/13/finding-diversity-in-america/#ab843734b89e.

137 my zip code is in the top quartile "Brooklyn, NY 11217 ZIP Code Profile," NY HomeTownLocator, accessed November 9, 2017, http://newyork.hometownlocator.com/zip-codes/data,zipcode,11217.cfm.

140 net worth of white households was on average $100,700 higher Thomas Shapiro, "Commentary: Close the Racial Wealth Gap," CNN, June 10, 2009, http://www.cnn.com/2009/LIVING/06/10/shapiro.wealth/index.html?iref=nextin.

140 Arlie Russell Hochschild published *Strangers in Their Own Land* Arlie Russell Hochschild, *Strangers in Their Own Land: Anger and Mourning on the American Right* (New York: New Press, 2016), 135–37.

142 as writer Ta-Nehisi Coates observes Ta-Nehisi Coates, "The First White President," *Atlantic*, October 2017, https://www.theatlantic.com/magazine/archive/2017/10/the-first-white-president-ta-nehisi-coates/537909/.

145 Ta-Nehisi Coates nails this central hypocrisy Coates, "The First White President."

146 "I don't think we're free in America" Bryan Stevenson, interview by Judy Woodruff, *PBS NewsHour*, PBS, April 13, 2017, https://www.pbs.org/newshour/brief/212727/bryan-stevenson.

146 "People can have implicit racial bias" john a. powell, email to author, July 6, 2017.

147 "It would be disingenuous, if not in flagrant" Mahzarin R. Banaji, Brian A. Nosek, and Anthony G. Greenwald, "No Place for Nostalgia in Science: A response to Arkes and Tetlock," commentary, August 9, 2004, http://www.fas.harvard.edu/~mrbworks/articles/2004_Banaji_PI.pdf.

147 "the thumbprint of the culture" "The 'Thumbprint of the Culture': Implicit Bias and Police Shootings," transcript of interview by Shankar Vedantam, *Hidden Brain*, National Public Radio, June 5, 2017, http://www.npr.org/templates/transcript/transcript.php?storyId=531578107.

147 "We behave in ways that are not known to our own" "The 'Thumbprint of the Culture,'" National Public Radio.

148 psychologists Daniel Yudkin and Jay Van Bavel Daniel A. Yudkin, Tobias Rothmund, Mathias Twardawski, Natasha Thalla, and Jay J. Van Bavel, "Reflexive Intergroup Bias in Third-Party Punishment," *Journal of Experimental Psychology* 145, no. 11 (2016): 1448–59, https://www.researchgate.net/publication/303401393_Reflexive_Intergroup_Bias_in_Third-Party_Punishment.

149 In another experiment, Princeton University psychologist Susan Fiske Mary E. Wheeler and Susan Fiske, "Controlling Racial Prejudice: Social-Cognitive Goals Affect Amygdala and Stereotype Activation," *Psychological Science* 16, no. 1 (January 2005):56-63, https://www.ncbi.nlm.nih.gov/pubmed/15660852.

149 And remember the study in which Elizabeth Phelps Phelps et al., "Performance on Indirect Measures of Race Evaluation," *Journal of Cognitive Neuroscience*.

149 But one more study I'll cite shows promising signs Jackob N. Keynan et al., "Limbic

Activity Modulation Guided by Functional Magnetic Resonance Imaging–Inspired Electroencephalography Improves Implicit Emotion Regulation," *Biological Psychiatry* 80, no. 6 (September 15, 2016): 490–96, http://www.biologicalpsychiatry journal.com/article/S0006-3223(16)00003-2/fulltext.

150 therapist Athena Staik calls "soft-wired" Athena Staik, "The Neuroscience of Changing Toxic Thinking Patterns (1 of 2)," *Neuroscience & Relationships with Dr. Athena Staik*, Psych Central, https://blogs.psychcentral.com/relationships/2011/08 /the-neuroscience-of-changing-toxic-thinking-or-behavior-patterns/.

150 According to Yudkin and Van Bavel Yudkin et al., "Reflexive Intergroup Bias," *Journal of Experimental Psychology*.

152 statistically, white high school dropouts have higher Matt Bruenig, "White High School Dropouts Have More Wealth Than Black and Hispanic College Graduates," Policyshop, Demos, September 23, 2014, http://www.demos.org/blog/9/23/14/white -high-school-dropouts-have-more-wealth-black-and-hispanic-college-graduates.

153 Subjects who thought they'd read rap lyrics rated Carrie B. Fried, "Who's Afraid of Rap: Differential Reactions to Music Lyrics," *Journal of Applied Social Psychology* 24, no. 4 (1999): 705–21, http://endrapontrial.org/wp-content/uploads/2015/08/Fried -1999.pdf.

153 "Race is an idea, not a fact" Nell Irvin Painter, *The History of White People* (New York: Norton, 2011), ix.

CHAPTER 5

155 "Forgiveness is not forgetting" "On Revolutionary Love" "Quotes from Valarie," ValarieKaur.com, http://valariekaur.com/about/quotes-from-valarie/.

155 During a period of one hundred days in 1994 Samantha Power, "Bystanders to Genocide," *Atlantic*, September 2001, https://www.theatlantic.com/magazine /archive/2001/09/bystanders-to-genocide/304571/.

155 genocide scholar Daniel Goldhagen, "willing executioners." Daniel Jonah Goldhagen, *Hitler's Willing Executioners: Ordinary Germans and the Holocaust* (New York: Vintage, 1997).

157 "Rwandan obsession to cattle rates back to history" Lillian Nakayima, "Rwandans and Their Attachment to Cows," *New Times*, June 20, 2009, http://www.newtimes .co.rw/section/read/78971.

160 "If, by misfortune I caught sight" Donald G. Dutton, *The Psychology of Genocide, Massacres, and Extreme Violence: Why "Normal" People Come to Commit Atrocities* (Westport, CT: Praeger Security International, 2007): 102, http://www.al-edu.com /wp-content/uploads/2014/05/Dutton-The-Psychology-of-Genocide-Massacres -and-Extreme-Violence.pdf.

160 "Hell is other people" Jean-Paul Sartre, *No Exit* (New York: Samuel French, 1958).

160 "Hell is yourself" George Seldes, *The Great Thoughts, Revised and Updated: From Abelard to Zola, from Ancient Greece to Contemporary America, the Ideas That Have Shaped the History of the World* (New York: Random House, 2011).

160 American ethicist Nel Noddings warns, "Evil" Mark Larrimore, ed., "Nel Noddings, *Women and Evil*," *The Problem of Evil: A Reader* (Malden, MA: Blackwell, 2001), 383–84.

161 less than fifty confirmed examples . . . constituted a tiny fraction "Rwanda: A Brief History of the Country," Outreach Programme on the Rwanda Genocide and the United Nations, http://www.un.org/en/preventgenocide/rwanda/education/rwandagenocide.shtml.

161 active resisters of Nazi atrocities against Jews Daniel Rothbart and Jessica Cooley, "Hutus Aiding Tutsis during the Rwandan Genocide: Motives, Meanings and Morals," *Genocide Studies and Prevention* 10, no. 2 (2016), http://scholarcommons.usf.edu/cgi/viewcontent.cgi?article=1398&context=gsp.

163 "Hutus and Tutsis cannot properly be called distinct" Philip Gourevitch "After the Genocide," *New Yorker*, December 18, 1995, http://www.newyorker.com/magazine/1995/12/18/after-the-genocide.

163 A UN report on the genocide described "Rwanda: A Brief History of the Country," Outreach Programme on the Rwanda Genocide and the United Nations.

164 "Hutus in Rwanda had been massacring Tutsis" Gourevitch, "After the Genocide," *New Yorker*.

165 "Every Hutu should know that every Tutsi" Anna M. Wittmann, *Talking Conflict: The Loaded Language of Genocide, Political Violence, Terrorism, and Warfare* (Santa Barbara, CA: ABC-CLIO, 2016), 185.

166 "stand near this place and encircle them" William A. Donohue, "The Identity Trap: The Language of Genocide," *Journal of Language and Social Psychology* 31, no. 13 (2012), https://dokumen.tips/documents/the-identity-trap-the-language-of-genocide.html.

171 About Eichmann's banality, Arendt wrote Hannah Arendt, *Eichmann in Jerusalem: A Report on the Banality of Evil* (New York: Penguin, 2006).

171 "a curious, quite authentic inability to think" Hannah Arendt, "Thinking and Moral Considerations," *Social Research* 38, no. 3 (Autumn 1971), 417.

171 "Since my first encounters with dramatic injustices" Elizabeth Minnich, *The Evil of Banality: On The Life and Death Importance of Thinking* (New York: Rowman & Littlefield, 2016), 10.

172 "Behavior towards the victims that would previously" Dutton, *The Psychology of Genocide*, 109

172 As genocide scholar James Waller puts it Waller, *Becoming Evil*, 20.

172 Croatian writer Slavenka Drakulic observed Slavenka Drakulic, *They Would Never Hurt a Fly: War Criminals on Trial in The Hague* (London: Abacus, 2004), 168.

173 "Large crowds of white people" *Lynching in America: Confronting the Legacy of Racial Terror*, 3rd ed., Equal Justice Initiative, https://lynchinginamerica.eji.org/report/.

1743 sociologists Stewart Tolnay and E. M. Beck reported Mark Berman "Even More Black People Were Lynched in the U.S. Than Previously Thought, Study Finds," *Washington Post*, February 10, 2015, https://www.washingtonpost.com/news/post-nation/wp/2015/02/10/even-more-black-people-were-lynched-in-the-u-s-than-previously-thought-study-finds/?utm_term=.02c7e84061cb.

174 "marked from 15 volts (Slight Shock) to" Saul McLeod, "The Milgram Experiment," SimplyPsychology, 2007, https://www.simplypsychology.org/milgram.html.

175 in 2017, a group of researchers basically replicated "Conducting the Milgram

Experiment in Poland, Psychologists Show People Still Obey," *Science Daily*, March 14, 2017, https://www.sciencedaily.com/releases/2017/03/170314081558.htm.

175 In the 1950s, Asch conducted a groundbreaking experiment Solomon Asch, *Social Psychology* (New York: Prentice Hall, 1952).

176 Gregory Berns and a team at Emory University replicated Asch's study Gregory S. Berns et al., "Neurobiological Correlates of Social Conformity and Independence during Mental Rotation," *Biological Psychiatry* 58 (2005):245–53, http://www.ccnl.emory.edu/greg/Berns%20Conformity%20final%20printed.pdf.

177 Christian Crandall and Amy Eshelman studied 105 C. S. Crandall, A. Eshleman, and L. O'Brien, "Social Norms and the Expression and Suppression of Prejudice: The Struggle for Internalization," *Journal of Personality and Social Psychology* 82, no. 3 (March 2002):359–78, https://www.ncbi.nlm.nih.gov/pubmed/11902622.

177 Hutu and Tutsi students refused to follow a militia's orders Geoffrey Macnab, "Back to Hell," *Guardian*, March 15, 2005, https://www.theguardian.com/film/2005/mar/15/rwanda.

177 Josephine Dusaminama, a Hutu woman, hid thirteen Tutsis Achille Tenkiang, "Rwandan Stories of Resistance: Josephine Dusaminama," Goldin Institute, https://www.goldininstitute.org/news/24-goldin-news/616-rwandan-stories-of-resistance-josephine-dusaminama.

177 "I was ready to die with them" Gregory Warner, "Remembering Rwandans Who Followed Their Conscience," NPR, April 8, 2014, https://www.npr.org/sections/parallels/2014/04/08/300508669/remembering-rwandans-who-followed-their-conscience.

178 Aurelia Mok and Michael Morris have produced strong research evidence Aurelia Mok and Michael W. Morris, "Asian-Americans' Creative Styles in Asian and American Situations: Assimilative and Contrastive Responses as a Function of Bicultural Identity Integration," *Management and Organization Review* 6 (2010): 371–90.

178 Research by anthropologist Jennifer Burnet Elizabeth Svoboda, "In a Genocide, Who Are the Morally Upright?" *Sapiens*, February 23, 2017, https://www.sapiens.org/culture/rwandan-genocide-rescuers/.

179 "Dehumanization isn't a way of talking" Smith, *Less Than Human*, 13.

180 there were ninety-five thousand orphans in Rwanda "Rwanda: Ten Years after the Genocide," UNICEF, September 4, 2012, https://www.unicef.org/infobycountry/rwanda_genocide.html.

183 "Black and Third World people are expected" Audre Lorde, "Our Difference Is Our Strength," in *Identity Politics in the Women's Movement*, ed. Barbara Ryan (New York: NYU Press, 2001), 315.

185 "Hate generalizes, love specifies" Robin Morgan, *The Word of a Woman: Feminist Dispatches* (New York: Norton, 1994).

186 "Nothing is easier than to denounce the evildoer" Louise Richardson, *What Terrorists Want: Understanding the Enemy, Containing the Threat* (London: John Murray, 2006), 1.

188 the government-created *ingando* Hilary Matfess and Foreign Policy In Focus, "Are Rwanda's Post-Genocide Youth Programs Paving the Way for Future Unrest?"

Nation, January 24, 2014, https://www.thenation.com/article/are-rwandas-post-genocide-youth-programs-paving-way-future-unrest/.

188 As Hutu prisoners have been released Chi Mgbako, "Ingando Solidarity Camps: Reconciliation and Political Indoctrination in Post-Genocide Rwanda," *Harvard Human Rights Journal* 18 (2005), http://www.leitnercenter.org/files/Publications/Mgbako.pdf.

188 "to share from a common dish" Mgbako, "Ingando Solidarity Camps."

188 "a dangerous undertaking in a country" Mgbako, "Ingando Solidarity Camps."

189 as the *New York Times* reported, a university professor Josh Kron, "For Rwandan Students, Ethnic Tensions Lurk," *New York Times*, May 16, 2010, http://www.nytimes.com/2010/05/17/world/africa/17rwanda.html.

CHAPTER 6

191 "The chain reaction of evil" Martin Luther King, *Strength to Love* (New York: Fortress, 2010), 47.

191 and states adopted poll taxes "The Struggle for Voting Rights," from *Free at Last: The U.S. Civil Rights Movement*, Learn NC, UNC School of Education, http://www.learnnc.org/lp/editions/nchist-postwar/6031.

192 If your father or grandfather could vote "1899 North Carolina Literacy Test Requirement," The Object of History, National Museum of American History, http://objectofhistory.org/objects/extendedtour/votingmachine/?order=5.

192 in 1922, members of the KKK reportedly flew over Topeka Philip Bump, "The Long History of Black Voter Suppression in American Politics," *Washington Post*, November 2, 2016.

192 in the 1980s, the Republican National Committee created Mariah Blake, "The Ballot Cops," *Atlantic*, October 2012, https://www.theatlantic.com/magazine/archive/2012/10/the-ballot-cops/309085/.

193 The party was sued in 1982 "GOP Memo Admits Plan Could 'Keep Black Vote Down,'" *Los Angeles Times*, October 25, 1986, http://articles.latimes.com/1986-10-25/news/mn-7435_1_republican-national-committee.

193 In 2013, Shelby County, Alabama, sued to overturn Dana Liebelson, "The Supreme Court Gutted the Voting Rights Act. What Happened Next in These 8 States Will Not Shock You," *Mother Jones*, April 8, 2014, http://www.motherjones.com/politics/2014/04/republican-voting-rights-supreme-court-id/.

193 Alabama passed a strict requirement that all voters show ID Ari Berman, "Alabama, Birthplace of the Voting Rights Act, Is Once Again Gutting Voting Rights," *Nation*, October 1, 2015, https://www.thenation.com/article/alabama-birthplace-of-voting-rights-act-once-again-gutting-voting-rights/.

194 tried to disenfranchise Grace Bell Hardison Ari Berman, "North Carolina Republicans Tried to Disenfranchise a 100-Year-Old African-American Woman," *Nation*, October 27, 2016, https://www.thenation.com/article/north-carolina-republicans-tried-to-disenfranchise-a-100-year-old-african-american-woman/.

194 "It is a shame that I had" Sarah Larimer, "100-Year-Old Grace Bell Hardison Collects Her 'I Voted' Sticker," *Washington Post*, November 8, 2016, https://www.washingtonpost.com/politics/2016/live-updates/general-election/real-time-updates

-on-the-2016-election-voting-and-race-results/100-year-old-grace-bell-hardison-collects-her-i-voted-sticker/?utm_term=.18c0938da9ae.

195 when 18 percent of Latino registered voters report Adrian D. Pantoja, "Latino Voters Continue to Face Barriers at Polling Places," *Huffington Post*, October 25, 2016, https://www.huffingtonpost.com/latino-decisions/latino-voters-continue-to_b_12638110.html.

195 "Our analytical minds rarely tend toward a holistic" Valerie Hudson, Bonnie Ballif-Spanvill, Mary Caprioli, and Chad Emmett, *Sex & World Peace* (New York: Columbia University Press, 2014), 1.

196 In 1996, the drug OxyContin was first Christopher Bowe "Fixing Pharma's Incentives Problem in the Wake of the U.S. Opioid Crisis," *Harvard Business Review*, June 13, 2016, https://hbr.org/2016/06/fixing-pharmas-incentives-problem-in-the-wake-of-the-u-s-opioid-crisis.

196 In 2015, drug overdose was the leading cause of accidental death "Opioid Addiction: 2016 Facts & Figures," American Society of Addiction Medicine, https://www.asam.org/docs/default-source/advocacy/opioid-addiction-disease-facts-figures.pdf.

197 In Utah, a state that is almost 150 percent whiter "Quick Facts: Utah," United States Census Bureau, July 1, 2016, accessed November 9, 2017, https://www.census.gov/quickfacts/UT.

197 pharmacists fill seventy-two hundred opioid prescriptions per day Julie Turkewitz, "'The Pills Are Everywhere': How the Opioid Crisis Claims Its Youngest Victims," *New York Times*, September 20, 2017, https://www.nytimes.com/2017/09/20/us/opioid-deaths-children.html.

197 One pharmacy in Kermit, West Virginia "How the DEA's Efforts to Crack Down on the Opioid Epidemic Were Derailed," *60 Minutes*, October 13, 2017, https://www.cbsnews.com/news/how-the-dea-efforts-to-crack-down-on-the-opioid-epidemic-were-derailed/.

197 Overprescription is also fueled by pharmaceutical Celine Gounder, "Who Is Responsible for the Pain-Pill Epidemic?" *New Yorker*, November 8, 2013, https://www.newyorker.com/business/currency/who-is-responsible-for-the-pain-pill-epidemic.

197 Because opioids are generally cheaper Katie Thomas and Charles Ornstein, "Amid Opioid Crisis, Insurers Restrict Pricey, Less Addictive Painkillers," *New York Times*, September 17, 2017, https://www.nytimes.com/2017/09/17/health/opioid-painkillers-insurance-companies.html?_r=0.

197 thirty-seven state attorneys general Dennis Hoey, "Maine's Janet Mills, 36 Other Attorneys General Urge Incentives for Opioid Alternatives," *Portland Press Herald*, September 18, 2017, http://www.pressherald.com/2017/09/18/mills-36-other-attorneys-general-urge-incentives-for-opioid-alternatives/.

197 Medicaid and Medicare inadvertently incentivized Karen Dandurant, "Removing the Incentive for Doctors to Prescribe Opioids," Fosters.com, November 13, 2016, http://www.fosters.com/news/20161113/removing-incentive-for-doctors-to-prescribe-opioids.

198 the US government has failed to regulate opioid pharmaceuticals "How the DEA's Efforts," *60 Minutes*.

198 A National Bureau of Economic Research study Olga Khazan, "How Job Loss Can Lead to Drug Use," *Atlantic*, July 19, 2017, https://www.theatlantic.com/health/archive/2017/07/how-job-loss-can-lead-to-drug-use/534087/.

198 "I do think it is related to declining" Jeanna Smialek, "Yellen Says Opioid Use Is Tied to Declining Labor Participation," Bloomberg, July 13, 2017, https://www.bloomberg.com/news/articles/2017-07-13/yellen-says-opioid-use-is-tied-to-declining-labor-participation.

198 Specifically, the counties hardest hit Victor Tan Chen, "All Hollowed Out," *Atlantic*, January 16, 2016, https://www.theatlantic.com/business/archive/2016/01/white-working-class-poverty/424341/.

198 while life expectancy had generally been increasing Sabrina Tavernise, "White Americans Are Dying Younger as Drug and Alcohol Abuse Rises," *New York Times*, April 20, 2016, https://www.nytimes.com/2016/04/20/health/life-expectancy-decline-mortality.html?_r=0188.

198 Policies like the North American Free Trade Agreement Lori Wallach, "NAFTA at 20: One Million U.S. Jobs Lost, Higher Income Inequality," *Huffington Post*, [not dated], accessed November 9, 2017, https://www.huffingtonpost.com/lori-wallach/nafta-at-20-one-million-u_b_4550207.html.

199 "Well if they'd had their way" Chris Janson, "White Trash," https://www.lyrics.com/lyric/32221386.

199 *National Review's* Kevin Williamson Kevin D. Williamson, "Chaos in the Family, Chaos in the State," *National Review*, March 28, 2016, http://www.nationalreview.com/article/432876/donald-trump-white-working-class-dysfunction-real-opportunity-needed-not-trump.

200 It turns out that Sherif had conducted previous experiments before that Gina Perry, "The View from the Boys," *Psychologist* 27 (November 2014), 834–37, https://thepsychologist.bps.org.uk/volume-27/edition-11/view-boys.

203 "But since 2000, judges have released hundreds" Nikole Hannah-Jones, "Segregation Now," ProPublica, April 16, 2014, https://www.propublica.org/article/segregation-now-full-text.

203 more than one out of every ten black and Latino Valerie Strauss, "School Segregation Sharply Increasing, Studies Show," *Washington Post*, September 22, 2012, https://www.washingtonpost.com/blogs/answer-sheet/post/school-segregation-sharply-increasing-studies-show/2012/09/22/5b34111a-04c6-11e2-91e7-2962c74e7738_blog.html?utm_term=.cda16f89b09.

203 most of those schools are not in the South Hannah-Jones, "Segregation Now," ProPublica.

204 the wealthy school district in Greenwich, Connecticut Alana Semuels, "Good School, Rich School; Bad School, Poor School," *Atlantic*, August 25, 2016, https://www.theatlantic.com/business/archive/2016/08/property-taxes-and-unequal-schools/497333/.

204 nationwide, "the achievement gap" Hannah-Jones, "Segregation Now," ProPublica.

204 Education scholar Jonathan Kozol reports Marge Scherer, "On Savage Inequalities: A Conversation with Jonathan Kozol," *Educational Leadership* 50, no. 4 (December 1992/January 1993), http://www.ascd.org/publications/educational-leadership/dec92/vol50/num04/On-Savage-Inequalities@-A-Conversation-with-Jonathan-Kozol.aspx.

205 One study found that ethnic diversity Kathleen Miles, "Ethnic Diversity Increases Home Value and Lowers Crime in Southern California, Study Says," *Huffington Post*, June 7, 2012, updated June 08, 2012, https://www.huffingtonpost.com/2012/06/07/ethnic-diversity-home-value_n_1579123.html.

205 In the biggest cities in the US, crime "fell . . ." The same has been found in the suburbs Richard Florida, "Why Crime Is Down in America's Cities," *Atlantic*, July 2, 2011, https://www.theatlantic.com/national/archive/2011/07/why-crime-is-down-in-americas-cities/240781/.

205 Plus nationwide polling data show Carol Graham and Sergio Pinto, "Unhappiness in America: Desperation in White Towns, Resilience and Diversity in the Cities," Brookings, September 29, 2016, https://www.brookings.edu/research/unhappiness-in-america-desperation-in-white-towns-resilience-and-diversity-in-the-cities/.

205 "When court-ordered busing began in 1976" Sharon Lerner, "Segregation Nation," *American Prospect*, June 9, 2011, http://prospect.org/article/segregation-nation.

205 Containing some of the most expensive homes in Omaha Rhea R. Borja, "NAACP Suit Challenges Breakup of Omaha Schools," *Education Week*, May 23, 2006, http://www.edweek.org/ew/articles/2006/05/24/38omaha.h25.html.

207 "If I understood correctly, you're telling me" Lerner, "Segregation Nation," *American Prospect*.

207 A great example of this is the work of Dr. Nahed Artoul Zehr Nahed Artoul Zehr, interview with author, June 29, 2017.

210 "If you're outraged by those words" Jonah Engel Bromwich, "Air Force General Addresses Racial Slurs on Campus: 'You Should Be Outraged,'" *New York Times*, September 29, 2017, https://www.nytimes.com/2017/09/29/us/air-force-academy-racial-slurs.html?_r=0.

211 White airmen are promoted more frequently Stephen Losey, "Race and the Air Force: The Truth about How Minorities Get Promoted," *Air Force Times*, March 1, 2016, https://www.airforcetimes.com/news/your-air-force/2016/03/01/race-and-the-air-force-the-truth-about-how-minorities-get-promoted/.

211 Patriarchy is embedded in the very nature Michael Ortiz, "Whether or Not Women Are Allowed in Combat, the Military Serves the Patriarchy," Truthout, February 25, 2013, http://www.truth-out.org/opinion/item/14519-whether-or-not-women-are-allowed-in-combat-the-military-serves-the-patriarchy.

211 But in 2016, cases of sexual assault in the US military Reuters, "Sexual Assault Reports in U.S. Military Reach Record High: Pentagon," NBC News, May 1, 2017, https://www.nbcnews.com/news/us-news/sexual-assault-reports-u-s-military-reach-record-high-pentagon-n753566.

211 And statistics suggest that combat veterans are responsible Stacy Bannerman, "High Risk of Military Domestic Violence on the Home Front," editorial, SFGate, updated April 7, 2014, http://www.sfgate.com/opinion/article/High-risk-of-military-domestic-violence-on-the-5377562.php.

212 the number of cases of PTSD has increased Smith, *Less Than Human*, 233.

213 "killing 10 percent" Linda Feldmann, "Glenn Beck Leaving Fox: His 10 Most Controversial Statements (So Far)," *Christian Science Monitor*, April 7, 2011, https://www.csmonitor.com/USA/Elections/2011/0407/Glenn-Beck-leaving-Fox-his-10-most

-controversial-statements-so-far/Beck-Suggests-Obama-Admin.-Might-Kill-10-Percent-Of-Population-Is-More-Corrupt-Than-Nixon.

213 "September 11th all over again" Travis M. Andrews, "Glenn Beck—Yes, That Glenn Beck—Tells New Yorker, 'Obama Made Me a Better Man,'" *Washington Post*, November 8, 2016, https://www.washingtonpost.com/news/morning-mix/wp/2016/11/08/in-shocking-reversal-glenn-beck-tells-new-yorker-obama-made-me-a-better-man/?utm_term=.09ee805c152c.

214 "cable networks can produce content aimed at" Jeffrey M. Berry and Sarah Sobieraj, *The Outrage Industry: Political Opinion Media and the New Incivility* (New York: Oxford, 2014), 17.

214 "Decency is a fresh palette for Beck" Nicholas Schmidle, "Glenn Beck Tries Out Decency," *New Yorker*, November 14, 2016, https://www.newyorker.com/magazine/2016/11/14/glenn-beck-tries-out-decency.

214 "We're not going to come together on politics" Marc Fisher, "Glenn Beck Wants to Heal the America He Divided—One Hug at a Time," *Washington Post*, March 14, 2017,https://www.washingtonpost.com/lifestyle/style/glenn-beck-wants-to-heal-the-america-he-divided--one-hug-at-a-time/2017/03/14/70067648-f970-11e6-be05-1a3817ac21a5_story.html?utm_term=.2605c95900ee.

214 "The question is, what did we learn" Glenn Beck (@glennbeck), "The question is, what did we learn and how can we heal the divide and do no more damage," January 22, 2017, 5:55 p.m., https://twitter.com/glennbeck/status/823348323402862592?ref_src=twsrc%5Etfw.

215 PBS and NPR have continued to rank among Amy Mitchell, Jeffrey Gottfried, Jocelyn Kiley, and Katerina Eva Matsa, "Political Polarization & Media Habits," Pew Research Center, October 21, 2014, http://www.journalism.org/2014/10/21/about-the-study-2/.

215 They include visibly branding posts and links from Jeff Jarvis, "A Call for Cooperation Against Fake News," *Medium*, November 18, 2016, https://medium.com/whither-news/a-call-for-cooperation-against-fake-news-d7d94bb6e0d4.

216 "The story of dog whistle politics begins with" Ian Haney López, *Dog Whistle Politics: How Coded Racial Appeals Have Reinvented Racism and Wrecked the Middle Class* (New York: Oxford, 2014), 13–14.

217 "A good many, perhaps a majority of" Haney López, 18.

217 Haney López writes, "a more 'quiet' form of violence" Haney López, 24.

217 "welfare queen" with "eighty names, thirty addresses" Haney López, 58.

218 "civil rights leaders were pushing too fast" Haney López, 59.

218 "super-predators," saying "we have to bring them to heel" Anne Gearan and Abby Phillip, "Clinton Regrets 1996 Remark on 'Super-Predators' after Encounter with Activist," *Washington Post*, February 25, 2016, https://www.washingtonpost.com/news/post-politics/wp/2016/02/25/clinton-heckled-by-black-lives-matter-activist/?utm_term=.01173ad4a9da.

218 In a 1989 interview, he said "a well-educated" AJ Vicens and Natalie Schreyer, "The Trump Files: Watch Donald Say He Would Have Done Better as a Black Man," *Mother Jones*, June 20, 2016, http://www.motherjones.com/politics/2016/06/donald-trump-black-man-advantage/.

218 the median life expectancy for white men was 8.2 years Janell Ross, "Trump Once Had a Dream: He Would Start Over Again as 'an Educated Black.' About That . . . ," *Washington Post*, June 21, 2016, https://www.washingtonpost.com/news/the-fix/wp/2016/06/21/trump-once-had-a-dream-he-would-start-over-again-as-an-educated-black-about-that/?utm_term=.ff246d9eb407.

219 "blacks and Hispanics losing out because" Scott Clement, "Discrimination against Whites Was a Core Concern of Trump's Base," *Washington Post*, August 2, 2017, https://www.washingtonpost.com/news/the-fix/wp/2017/08/02/discrimination-against-whites-was-a-core-concern-of-trumps-base/?utm_term=.c8a67ef60cce.

221 "making visible the invisible" "Theory and Definition of Terms," Building Movement Project, accessed November 9, 2017, http://www.buildingmovement.org/our_tools/detail/theory_and_definition_of_terms.

CONCLUSION

223 "How do we hold people accountable" Melvin McLeod, "There's No Place to Go but Up," *Shambhala Sun*, January 1998, https://www.lionsroar.com/theres-no-place-to-go-but-up/.

223 "hideous, grinding speech" George Orwell, *1984* (New York: Signet, 1961).

224 In 2013, Cass Sunstein, an academic Tim Murphy, "Former Obama Official Compares Glenn Beck's Attacks to Orwell's 'Two Minutes Hate,'" *Mother Jones*, March 21, 2013, http://www.motherjones.com/politics/2013/03/cass-sunstein-glenn-beck-two-minutes-hates/.

224 In 2016, the alt-right publication *Breitbart* Daniel J. Flynn, "2016 Gave Us 262,800 'Two Minutes Hates.' Some Lasted Longer Than Others," *Breitbart*, December 30, 2016, http://www.breitbart.com/big-government/2016/12/30/5837287/.

224 Meanwhile, President Trump's Twitter feed Natelegé Whaley, "'1984' Book: Here Are 4 Eerie Similarities to Trump's America," Mic, January 25, 2017 https://mic.com/articles/166589/1984-book-here-are-4-eerie-similarities-to-trump-s-america#.VdU1Guo6m.

224 Reflecting on the lessons of Orwell's book, a student in Georgia Sarah Sansbury, "Ending Our Own 'Two Minutes' Hate,'" *Teaching Tolerance*, September 8, 2011, https://www.tolerance.org/magazine/ending-our-own-two-minutes-hate.

225 After the Orlando shooting, President Obama Halimah Abdullah and Erik Ortiz, "President Obama: Nation and Orlando 'Shaken by an Evil, Hateful Act,'" NBC News, June 16, 2016, https://www.nbcnews.com/storyline/orlando-nightclub-massacre/president-obama-traveling-orlando-stand-solidarity-after-shooting-n593551.

225 President Trump called the Las Vegas Kevin Liptak, "Trump on Las Vegas Massacre: 'An Act of Pure Evil,'" CNN, updated October 2, 2017, http://www.cnn.com/2017/10/02/politics/donald-trump-las-vegas-shooting-remarks/index.html.

225 "abode not in the truth" John 8:44, *The Holy Bible: King James Version* (Dallas: Brown Books, 2004).

225 "cast off his shadow from himself" Stephen A. Hoeller, *The Gnostic Jung and the Seven Sermons to the Dead* (Wheaton, IL: Quest Books, 1982), 108.

225 as the Japanese Buddhist priest Nichiren wrote "Good and Evil," Soka Gakkai International, http://www.sgi.org/about-us/buddhism-in-daily-life/good-and-evil.html.

227 "Real change is systemic and self-implicating" Anand Giridharadas, "Democracy Is Not a Supermarket," *Medium*, October 31, 2017, https://medium.com/@AnandWrites/why-real-change-escapes-many-change-makers-and-why-it-doesnt-have-to-8e48332042a8.

227 "Everyone thinks of changing the world" Wendy Toliver, *Little Giant Encyclopedia of Inspirational Quotes* (New York: Sterling, 2004), 60.

228 "The opposite of love is not hate" Elie Wiesel, interview with *U.S. News & World Report*, October 27, 1986.

231 "Remember, if you're gonna fight hate" John Fugelsang (@JohnFugelsang), "Remember, if you're gonna fight hate, don't whine if a little gets on you - just wash it off before it sticks," Twitter, September 28, 2017, 10:21 a.m., https://twitter.com/JohnFugelsang/status/913408338259570690.

231 "Morning, boys. How's the water?" Jenna Krajeski, "This Is Water," *New Yorker*, September 19, 2008, https://www.newyorker.com/books/page-turner/this-is-water.

THE OPPOSITE OF HATE

Cracks in the Wall
A Conversation with Sally Kohn

Questions for Discussion

Cracks in the Wall
A Conversation with Sally Kohn

You started writing this book just after Donald Trump was elected, when you felt hate was threatening to overwhelm you and the country. How are you feeling these days?

I'm working on this paperback edition in the wake of the mass shooting at the Tree of Life synagogue in Pittsburgh in the fall of 2018. When the world is this dark, it sometimes feels impossible that the sun could ever rise. But I've also had the great good fortune of talking about all of this with readers across the country this past year. I've shared the stories and tools in this book, and they've shared with me how they are pushing back, how they are making changes in their lives. During my book tour, I met a woman who works on religious tolerance issues who told me how she's trying to come to terms with her own classism and bias against poor people, and I met a seventy-something white man who told me about the extension classes he's taking at his community center on how to dismantle racism and misogyny. These are just some of the innumerable beacons of hope.

So you've been able to stay focused on hope instead of fuming at the other side?

I don't mean to suggest I'm not angry. But hate is different from anger. Anger can be constructive. We *should* be angry about the extreme injustice and inequality all around us, and that righteous anger is what makes us want to fight for change. Anger is active in that sense. Whereas hate is complacent. Sometimes we use one word when we mean the other, but in essence, if I'm angry at you, I'm probably going to talk to you and share how I'm feeling and try to work it out. But if I hate you, I never want to talk to you again—let alone try to change things.

Sometimes it's really hard not to scream at someone whose beliefs offend every fiber of your being. Is that anger or hate?

Only you can know what you really feel. But hating is a toothless, ineffective means of changing anyone else's views. Of all the people I've met and all the research I've read of people leaving even the most extreme lives of hate behind, not a single person changed because they were hated into it. Or because someone screamed at them enough. We need to engage people in respectful, humane, emotionally correct ways. All the research and the collected wisdom, including the examples in this book, show that's what really leads to change.

But isn't engaging people who hate also giving them a platform for their hate and in a sense validating them?

I don't have to agree with your beliefs to try to understand those beliefs and even validate your feelings. By treating others with dignity, you're not giving them a platform to hate; instead you are creating a possibility for transformation. There's a saying in community organizing that you "meet people where they're at." Plus, we have to remember that no one is born racist, or Republican, or an elitist East Coast liberal. We develop our views through our environment and our experiences. Now, if you're afraid of Muslims committing acts of terrorism, I can respond with all the facts about how white right-wing extremists have actually committed more mass violence in the United States since September 11, and I can talk about how the media nonetheless devotes three times more coverage to violence committed by Muslim extremists, but still there you are with your feelings. And whether you *should* feel afraid or not, you do. I have to meet you there. But that doesn't mean I should leave you there!

But if someone is being attacked for his or her beliefs or very existence, is not attacking back just being weak and letting the haters win?

That depends on how you define "winning." I think sticking to your values in the face of unprecedented attacks is a moral victory and the bravest thing any of us can do. I believe everybody deserves respect, even those I vehemently disagree with, not because they earn it, not because of how they behave, but by virtue of just existing. And it seems to me that if I abandon those values and say that now I'm gonna hate because the other side did it first or does it more, then I'm letting them define not only their values but also *mine*. I've given them even more power—power *over* me!

But too often lately, we act as though standing up for what we believe in necessitates stomping on others—not just their beliefs but their entire existence. Sometimes it seems that hate has become something we do, especially on the left, to signal what kind of people we are—that we're the kind of person who is against hate and wants to fight it. We rant on Twitter or declare ourselves haters of hate. It's easier to posture about others' lack of compassion than it is to practice compassion ourselves. Easier, but ultimately not constructive for them—or us!

So letting go of hate and working for positive change is good not just for "them," but also for us?

There are so many studies suggesting that hate is bad for the health of the hater, yes. And it simply doesn't feel good, let's be honest. You know that. But also, I've been so inspired by the radiant joy I've experienced from people who are working to confront hate in themselves and others. I met a woman with a childhood friend on the opposite end of the political spectrum who set up monthly conversations where they read articles from opposing sides about different issues and talk about what they've learned. I talked to a man who reached out to the person he had bullied as a child to apologize and try to make amends. An elderly Jewish woman told me that reading this book was the first time in her life she'd ever felt compassion for a Palestinian. A young woman confessed that she had stopped going to family holidays because she was sickened by her family's politics and sick of arguing with them, but now she's decided that reconnecting with her relatives was the only chance she had at ultimately changing their views. And when they tell me these stories, the overwhelming emotion I sense from them is relief. Hate was a burden they're grateful not to carry anymore.

One of the most eye-opening rewards of reading your book is helping us acknowledge and confront the hate in ourselves.

Everything we know from psychology and neuroscience suggests that awareness is the first step. Obviously, practically, you can't fix a problem until you know you have a problem. But also cognitively, when we learn to see or "catch" our unconscious habits, then we can try to change them. Specifically, in my speaking events with corporate audiences or congregations or college students, I try to encourage everyone to find three concrete things they can do to foster connection in their own lives and to fight hate. These can be big or small steps. Like following four or five commentators from the opposite side of the political divide and making a point of reading their columns, or getting your book group that has read only white authors for the last year to read and discuss a book by a woman of color. Or calling up the mosque or the synagogue or the evangelical church in your community, a place you've never set foot in, and asking whether you can attend services or maybe a social event. And then bringing others with you.

Maybe you have a job you're hiring for at work and of course you're going to hire the best person for the job, but how inclusive is your recruiting? You could try reaching out to the local LGBT community group or local veterans' organization and encouraging their members to apply. Maybe it even means thinking about the neighborhood you live in, whether all your neighbors look like you and think like you, or whether your kids go to school with kids who only look like them and live like them. At all levels of our lives and work and communities and businesses and government, we can encourage policies and practices of inclusion and connection—not just because it's the right thing to do morally (it is!), but also because it's a key way to combat hate.

How do you stay positive?

I'm not always. I spend a lot of time feeling sad about the extreme atrocities we human beings are capable of. But I try to look for cracks in the wall of hate. The songwriter Leonard Cohen wrote, "There's a crack in everything. That's how the light gets in." I think about that white man in his seventies taking extension classes to learn about systemic oppression and inequality. I asked him why he was even bothering. He's retired; he could be out there golfing or something. He told me he wants to grow and learn and change and "be part of the solution." Good lord, if that doesn't give you hope, then you best get your pulse checked. All around us are these cracks, big and small, and if you look for them, you can find the light. And then choose to be the light yourself.

Questions for Discussion

1. In *The Opposite of Hate*, Sally Kohn confronts her social media trolls and is surprised to discover some of them are not the people she expected. She is able to find some common ground. What do her experiences tell us about online encounters versus real-life encounters?

2. If you agree that we are in a period of heightened nastiness, what factors do you think are responsible? Social media? Politics? The media? The economy?

3. Using the example of her own relatives at family gatherings, Kohn considers how to handle conversations with people whose political beliefs are very different from her own. Are there places in your life where you interact with the "other" side? Do you talk about hot-button issues or avoid them? What have you learned from this book about how you might better approach these conversations?

4. After talking with neuroscientists, Kohn learns that our brains are hardwired to create in-groups and out-groups, but who falls into these categories is not set in stone at all. Our tendency toward tribalism does make us quick to latch on to society's existing prejudices. Do you agree that systemic change is possible? Where do we start?

5. What in-groups do you belong to? Are there people you otherize?

6. Kohn talks to researcher Elizabeth Minnich, who distinguishes between intensive evil, committed by small groups and individuals, and extensive evil, committed by whole societies and sometimes the norm for a time. How do you think societies should deal with

perpetrators of extensive evils? Are there limits to what you could ever forgive? Why do you think John from Rwanda was able to transcend hate and marry the daughter of the man who killed his family?

7. One topic covered in *The Opposite of Hate* is unconscious hate or implicit bias. Would you ever take the implicit bias test that Kohn took? Does knowing we all have unconscious prejudices make you feel kinder to those who exhibit the biases more openly? Did this book cause you to reevaluate any of your own assumptions or beliefs? Which ones?

8. Kohn also discusses the phenomenon of "competitive victimhood," in which two parties at odds each think their suffering is worse than the other's. They are convinced that their own side's actions are merely defense or acceptable retaliation. Have you seen this? Is it present in your workplace? Your relationships? Our society?

9. In chapter three, Kohn discusses how the innate human desire to belong to a group has brought people into—and out of—hateful organizations. Have you ever been swept up by the desire to belong and done something you later regretted?

10. Do you agree that there is a difference between anger and hatred? Between compromise and concession?

11. Kohn seeks forgiveness of the schoolmate she bullied in fifth grade. How do you think the fact that she is not forgiven will influence her future actions? Was her asking to be forgiven putting the burden on the victim, as Audre Lorde suggests on page 181? Whom is forgiveness for—the victim or the victimizer?

12. Do you agree with Kohn that the opposite of hate is connection? What do you plan to do to counteract hate?

PAUL TAKEUCHI

Sally Kohn is one of the leading progressive voices in America today. A CNN political commentator and columnist, she was previously a Fox News contributor, and before that worked for over fifteen years as a community organizer. Kohn's writing has appeared in the *Washington Post*, the *New York Times*, RollingStone.com, Elle.com, *USA Today*, *Time*, and many other outlets. She is also a popular keynote speaker and frequently leads media and speaking-skills workshops for grassroots activists and corporate leaders. Kohn lives in Brooklyn with her partner, Sarah Hansen, and their daughter, Willa.